THE ORGANIZATION OF THE ENERGY INDUSTRY

Also by Lynn F. Pearson

WORKING LIFE AND LEISURE

The Organization of the Energy Industry

Lynn F. Pearson

First published 1981 by
THE MACMILLAN PRESS LTD
London and Basingstoke
Companies and representatives
throughout the world

ISBN 0 333 27084 3

Printed in Hong Kong

Contents

List of Figures

Preface

The number of organizations involved in the energy industry is ever increasing, and although there is something of a lull in activity between the Windscale and projected fast reactor inquiries, changes continue to occur. The details of personnel and organizations in the text are correct to my knowledge until November 1978.

I would like to thank Robert Harrison and Alan Jones for their invaluable advice and encouragement during the preparation of this book, which was written while I was a Research Officer at the Sunderland Polytechnic Energy Workshop, and which formed part of a programme of research into energy policy funded by Sunderland Polytechnic Research Committee. The staff of the Sunderland Polytechnic Library, particularly Ian Whittington, and the staff of Sunderland Central Library have also been of great assistance. Finally I would like to thank Mrs Noreen Gray for typing the manuscript and its endless revisions.

November 1978   LYNN F. PEARSON

List of Abbreviations

ABRC	Advisory Board for the Research Councils
ACEC	Advisory Council on Energy Conservation
ACORD	Advisory Council on Research and Development for Fuel and Power
AERE	Atomic Energy Research Establishment
AGR	Advanced Gas Cooled Reactor
APC	Atomic Power Construction
APG	A Power for Good
ARC	Agricultural Research Council
AUEW	Amalgamated Union of Engineering Workers
AUEW−TASS	Amalgamated Union of Engineering Workers− Technical, Administrative and Supervisory Section
BACM	British Association of Colliery Management
BGC	British Gas Corporation
BNA	British Nuclear Associates
BNDC	British Nuclear Design and Construction
BNES	British Nuclear Energy Society
BNF	British Nuclear Forum
BNFL	British Nuclear Fuels Limited
BNOC	British National Oil Corporation
BP	British Petroleum
BRE	Building Research Establishment
BSSRS	British Society for Social Responsibility in Science
CBI	Confederation of British Industry
CCMS	Committee on the Challenges of Modern Society
CEB	Central Electricity Board
CEEP	European Centre of Public Enterprises
CEGB	Central Electricity Generating Board
CEI	Council of Engineering Institutions

CENE	Commission on Energy and the Environment
CEPCEO	Association of the Coal Producers of the European Community
CHP	Combined Heat and Power
CHPG	Combined Heat and Power Group
CIE	Coal Industry Examination
CIE/R & DWG	Coal Industry Examination/Research and Development Working Group
CIGRE	International Conference on Large High-Voltage Electric Systems
CINCC	Coal Industry National Consultative Council
CITG	Coal Industry Tripartite Group
CITG/R & DWP	Coal Industry Tripartite Group/Research and Development Working Party
CoEnCo	Committee for Environmental Conservation
COND	Campaign Opposing Nuclear Dumping
CPAG	Child Poverty Action Group
CPRE	Council for the Protection of Rural England
CPRS	Central Policy Review Staff
CRE	Coal Research Establishment
CSD	Civil Service Department
CSO	Central Statistical Office
CSS	Council for Science and Society
DEA	Department of Economic Affairs
D.En.	Department of Energy
DHSS	Department of Health and Social Security
DI	Department of Industry
DOE	Department of the Environment
DT	Department of Trade
DTI	Department of Trade and Industry
EAS	Energy Audit Scheme
EAW	Electrical Association for Women
EC	Electricity Corporation
ECE	Economic Commission for Europe
ECO	European Coal Organization
ECRC	Electricity Council Research Centre
ECSC	European Coal and Steel Community
EEA	European Energy Association
EEB	European Environmental Bureau
EEC	European Economic Community

EETPU	Electrical, Electronic, Telecommunications and Plumbing Union
ENCORD	Interdepartmental Committee on Energy Conservation R & D
ENT	Energy Technology Division
EQAS	Energy Quick Advice Service
ERA	Electrical Research Association
ERG	Energy Research Group
ERR	Earth Resources Research
ERSU	Energy Research Support Unit
ESS	Energy Survey Scheme
ETSU	Energy Technology Support Unit
EURATOM	European Atomic Energy Community
FO	Foreign Office
FOE	Friends of the Earth
GEC	General Electric Company Limited
GGP	Gas Gathering Pipelines (North Sea) Limited
GMWU	National Union of General and Municipal Workers
HSE	Health and Safety Executive
IAEA	International Atomic Energy Agency
ICCR	International Committee for Coal Research
ICI	Imperial Chemical Industries
ICRP	International Commission for Radiological Protection
IEA	International Energy Agency
IEE	Institution of Electrical Engineers
IETS	Industrial Energy Thrift Scheme
I.Gas.E.	Institution of Gas Engineers
IGS	Institute of Geological Sciences
IIED	International Institute for Environment and Development
IMF	International Monetary Fund
I.Min.E.	Institute of Mining Engineers
INE	Institution of Nuclear Engineers
INFCEP	International Fuel Cycle Evaluation Programme
Inst.F.	Institute of Fuel
IOS	Institute of Oceanographic Sciences
ISES	International Solar Energy Society

JET	Joint European Torus
JPAC	Joint Policy Advisory Committee
JRC	Joint Research Centre
MAFF	Ministry of Agriculture, Fisheries and Food
MATSU	Marine Technology Support Unit
MEC	Committee of Ministers on Energy Conservation
MISER	Methodology of Industrial Sector Energy Requirements
MOD	Ministry of Defence
MOS	Ministry of Supply
MRC	Medical Research Council
MRDE	Mining Research and Development Establishment
NACODS	National Association of Colliery Overmen, Deputies and Shotfirers
NALGO	National Association of Local Government Officers
NATO	North Atlantic Treaty Organization
NCAT	National Centre for Alternative Technology
NCB	National Coal Board
NCCL	National Council for Civil Liberties
NEA	Nuclear Energy Agency
NEB	National Enterprise Board
NEC	National Executive Committee
NEDC	National Economic Development Council
NEDO	National Economic Development Office
NEL	National Engineering Laboratory
NERC	Natural Environment Research Council
NIES	Northern Ireland Electricity Service
NII	Nuclear Installations Inspectorate
NJCC(GB)	National Joint Co-ordinating Council for Great Britain
NMI	National Maritime Institute
NNC	National Nuclear Corporation
NNC	Network for Nuclear Concern
NOA	National Oil Account
NoSHEB	North of Scotland Hydro-Electric Board
NPAB	Nuclear Power Advisory Board
NPC	Nuclear Power Company Limited

NPL	National Physical Laboratory
NPT	Non-Proliferation Treaty
NRDC	National Research Development Council
NRPB	National Radiological Protection Board
NUM	National Union of Mineworkers
OECD	Organization for Economic Cooperation and Development
OEEC	Organization for European Economic Cooperation
OETB	Offshore Energy Technology Board
OPEC	Organization of Petroleum Exporting Countries
OSFLAG	Offshore Structures Fluid Loading Advisory Group
OSO	Offshore Supplies Office
PAR	Programme Analysis and Review
PARLIAGE	Parliamentary Liaison Group for Alternative Energy
PERG	Political Economy Research Group
PESC	Public Expenditure Survey Committee
PFO	Principal Finance Officer
PIAC	Petroleum Industry Advisory Committee
PIC	Planning Inquiry Commission
PLP	Parliamentary Labour Party
PWR	Pressurized Water Reactor
RCEP	Royal Commission on Environmental Pollution
RRR	Required Rate of Return
RSPB	Royal Society for the Protection of Birds
RTPI	Royal Town Planning Institute
RWMAC	Radioactive Waste Management Advisory Committee
SCNI	Select Committee on Nationalized Industries
SCRAM	Scottish Campaign to Resist the Atomic Menace
SCST	Select Committee on Science and Technology
SEI	Society for Environmental Improvement
SERA	Socialist Environment and Resources Association
SGHWR	Steam Generating Heavy Water Reactor
SLICE	Committee for Studies Leading to Industrial Conservation of Energy

SMD	Simultaneous Maximum Demand
SNG	Substitute Natural Gas
SNP	Scottish National Party
SPRU	Science Policy Research Unit
SRC	Science Research Council
SSEB	South of Scotland Electricity Board
SSRC	Social Science Research Council
STA	Solar Trade Association
TCPA	Town and Country Planning Association
TDR	Test Discount Rate
TGWU	Transport and General Workers' Union
TNPG	The Nuclear Power Group
TRC	The Radiochemical Centre Limited
TRRL	Transport and Road Research Laboratory
TUC	Trades Union Congress
UNIPEDE	International Union of Producers and Distributors of Electrical Energy
UNLOSC	United Nations Law of the Sea Conference
UKAEA	United Kingdom Atomic Energy Authority
UKOOA	United Kingdom Offshore Operators' Association
UKOSRP	United Kingdom Offshore Steels Research Project
WEC	World Energy Conference
WESC	Wave Energy Steering Committee
WGES	Working Group on Energy Strategy

1 Introduction

Energy policy is more than a search for an illusion; it is a prescription for frustration.   (Powell, 1976)

Nevertheless, an increasing number of workers in government, nationalized and private industry and the academic worlds are involved with the evolution of a British energy policy. Over the last quarter-century first the Suez crisis, then the growing world environmental movement and finally the emergence of OPEC has provoked a British response in the form of an increasing awareness of the importance of reliable energy supplies and the need for a considered energy policy. The British energy situation is still in a state of flux where decisions with long term implications need to be taken on the basis of inadequate and controversial information; decisions which will have an effect on or possibly even determine the life-style of future generations. The government is being supplied with more data and statistics than ever before on the various forms of energy source and is, in turn, being increasingly open by producing papers on the latest research and forecasts. This new concern for public participation has grown along with the wide-ranging discussion on energy policy, in spite of the fact that energy policy as an issue has not yet become an everyday concern for most of the electorate.

The number of institutions, committees and groups concerned with energy has also increased, and this examination of the energy industry and energy policy will attempt to pin down the exact function of all the energy related organizations and their relationships between each other and with the government. Government, of course, cannot be treated as an entity, because the differing functions and objectives of such bodies as the Treasury, the Department of Energy, the political parties, the Cabinet, and select committees. The nationalized industries, too, are unlikely to have the same view of the major issues in energy policy as either the government or the various pressure groups. It is hoped to identify the important actors and interest groups within the area of energy policy, and to define their roles and responsibilities. Each actor or group may have a different view of the objectives of energy policy and of their own functions, and may thus produce a range of policy options. A framework of policy analysis may help to clarify the workings of the policy-making process. Another important question is the definition of policy and policy-making; as a working definition, policy-making may be said to be the process of adjustment to future uncertainties. Policy itself can be regarded as a set of decisions taken with a distinctive perception of the environment.

Studies of policy-making may result in the definition of a circular system where each actor and institution has some influence on the next in line, and feedback from previous actions sets guidelines of new policy decisions. A reasonable point of entry into this system in order to study energy policy-making is to look at the official source of policy, Parliament, and the policy administrators, the Civil Service. The government is the overt source of energy policy in this country, and although institutions such as the nationalized industries have a certain amount of independence with regard to financial aims and their own policy, overall responsibility for making and enforcing energy policy lies with the government. Thus this survey begins with a study of the parts of the Civil Service and government related to energy policy. The Treasury is considered first as it is the ultimate source of finance for most energy projects and thus sets constraints on their outcomes. The internal structure of the Treasury and the main decision-makers within the department are then related to the Department of Energy (D.En.) both ministerial and departmental sections, and placed in the context of the Civil Service as a whole. On the parliamentary side, bodies such as the Cabinet Energy Committee and the relevant select committees are described and shown to be part of the government – Civil Service relationship. Other bodies such as the Central Policy Review Staff (CPRS) which have an occasional connection with energy policy-making are also noted.

The D.En. is then considered in some detail, beginning with its present-day structure and workings, to show the complexity of the institutional relationships and to clarify the roles of various committees and groups. The evolution of the department, with its beginnings in the Department of Mines, is shown to illustrate the changing ideas of fuel and energy policy over the last quarter century. Finally some consideration is given to the civil servants who actually staff the department now, the politicians whose responsibility it is and the policy of open government being pursued by D.En. To understand one of the most important constraints on policy-making – finance – it is necessary to come to grips with government procedures concerning public spending; that is the yearly spending application cycle with the use of PESC (Public Expenditure Survey Committee) and PAR (Programme Analysis and Review) by D.En. and the Treasury. These methods result in the annual White Paper on government expenditure plans.

Unfortunately, the simplistic study of institutionalized policy-making may not reveal a great deal about the actual workings of government; the relationships between the various departments of the Civil Service, between politicians in Parliament, select committee and Cabinet are not to be found in official papers. Here other sources, such as political diaries and interview studies, give a good background to the official conduct of government. There is a fine balance to be drawn between too great a reliance on the obvious official channels of communication and overemphasis of the behind the scenes influences within a body of people who have worked together for many years. The official structure outlines the basis of the system but merges with the network of relationships between civil servants and politicians to form a policy-making body. It is within this body, below the surface of the official titles and the publicized information, that policy is evolved; individual influence at this level may be important but is difficult to pin down, and investigation of decision-making can be reduced to a guessing game played with limited data. Even details of membership of a body such as the Cabinet Energy Committee are secret, so that the inevitably biased accounts of political diaries are one of the few sources available to the researcher.

The position outside government is not necessarily any better as considerations of commercial secrecy intrude, but at least yearly reports and balance sheets of the nationalized industries are published. The nationalized industries (British Gas Corporation, National Coal Board, Central Electricity Generating Board, Electricity Council, South of Scotland Electricity Board and North of Scotland Hydro-Electric Board) theoretically follow the overall policy objectives given to them by the government, but their relationship with the various shades of government varies, and they have a high degree of influence over decisions affecting the future of their industries. At present, each nationalized industry is treated individually within the context of the energy requirements of the country, and this can lead to recriminations between, for example, the electricity and gas industries when gas prices were thought to be too low with respect to the real costs of gas. The structure of each of these industries and their interaction with government and other nationalized industries is considered in this section, along with their financial position and aims. It is useful to be able to define the objectives of each industry and to compare these with the issues as seen by its competitors and by the D.En. The D.En. may perceive the role of the NCB, say, in a different light to the NCB's definition of its own role and responsibilities.

To follow on from the completely nationalized industries, the history of the nuclear industry with its proliferation of companies is explained and the present structure examined. The remaining nationalized industry, oil (British National Oil Corporation), and the multinational oil companies with interests in British oil and gas are then looked at in the context of British energy policy. There are many more institutions with an energy connection, for example the research bodies and the various interest groups, and these all act in relation to central government to form the particular atmosphere in which energy policy decisions are made. One factor which is beginning to have more effect on British decisions is the increasing number of EEC regulations concerning energy policy.

Britain's relationship with the EEC over energy matters has not always been happy, due to the imbalance between the general European lack of energy resources and Britain's sudden and short term abundance. The EEC energy policy is still in its formative stages, but its influence on British energy policy and the international effects of the new US initiative on conservation cannot be ignored. Other strictly non-governmental influences on energy policy-makers include the political parties as a whole, with their Energy Committees and conference discussions. The trade unions also are beginning to discuss energy policy as such, rather than simply its relationship with their particular interests.

All these groups, from nationalized industries, through multi-national companies and local pressure groups, to political parties and trade unions, exert some influence on each other and with those in government who theoretically decide upon policy. Clearly all policy-making does not take place at high levels in Civil Service or Cabinet; it can be an accumulation of small decisions to extend a previous policy, or a new initiative taken by the nationalized industries, which are not entirely controlled by their ministers. It is vital to understand the channels of communication, both official and informal. An official body, such as the Working Group on Energy Strategy, with its members drawn from the higher Civil Service and the boards of nationalized energy industries, exists to coordinate the views of the policy-makers within government and the industries. This and other formal committees do not preclude the existence of influence by means of the quiet chat or the trade-off in Cabinet. The choice of reactor system for the next round of nuclear power station construction in early 1978 was preceded by a series of private talks between the Secretary of State for Energy, Tony Benn, and all manner of representatives of the nuclear industry, ranging from the CEGB to nuclear engineers from American companies. Even if it may be impossible to determine exactly which decisions were influenced by the various bodies of opinion, at least it can be useful to know the relationships which exist between policy-makers and the rest of the world.

Having covered the main actors, both individual and institutional, the survey goes on to detail the main policy issues as seen by D.En. and by other interested bodies. The main source of information concerning D.En.'s view of energy policy is its own publications, and in this section comparisons are made between policy statements produced over the years in order to understand how D.En.'s views have changed with time. The options available for each issue are considered, as defined by D.En. and by groups with alternative ideas, such as Friends of the Earth. The subject of issue definition is of considerable interest, for if a subject is seen to be a problem area by one group and not by another, certain options are never allowed to become viable in practice, even if they are technical or theoretical possibilities. The reasoning behind the selection of issues for discussion is hardly ever raised in the apparently open technically based debates, which often assume a continuation of present-day life-style, values and institutions. Government planners tend to forecast on the basis of a limited view of future possibilities, and with the aim of catering for future needs as perceived according to their value systems. Their goals tend to be narrowly defined in terms of energy supply and demand, whereas the aims of interest groups, who may also produce forecasts, may be more widely based and involve different life-styles. Thus the debate is conducted on technicalities but with a background of totally different assumptions about the future, resulting in a certain amount of unnecessary hostility which obscures the technical issues. Unfortunately there are few arenas in which energy issues can be openly debated, and even fewer where alternative ideas of future life-styles can be aired. Change in the definition of issues is equally important, and this part of the survey seeks to identify the areas of energy policy in which change is taking or has taken place, and the reasons for the changes. The question of suitability of policy and policy outcomes is considered as far as is possible when the time-scale of cause and effect is more often decades than a year or months.

Finally, the actual production of energy policy is investigated; one D.En. decision is taken and considered in detail, using all available sources such as press reports and official D.En. notices. The final decision on policy change and initiation is always the outcome of a process which originates with an idea, and ideas come from a variety of sources including party researchers, D.En. workers, the media, and all the relevant groups and institutions. Once the idea has surfaced and has a foothold in D.En., it becomes part of the bargaining within D.En. itself and between the Treasury and D.En. Changes in the structure of D.En., ministerial reshuffles and changes of government can all enhance or reduce the chances of an idea becoming part of future policy. Policy does change with time, but the alterations in attitude may be so small individually as to seem insignificant; slight differences of emphasis in the wording of statements, or a small numerical change in a forecast can be enough to show some sort of policy movement. At this stage it may be useful to introduce the idea of policy-making models, which can help to identify large scale processes which work through an apparent maze of small effects. Various models are considered for their relevance to energy policy-making, their explanatory powers and ability to include known processes and facts. To be useful, a policy-making model should be capable of increasing the intelligibility of the policy-making process.

Decisions taken in the name of energy policy may or may not amount to a policy either coherent within itself or with respect to outside influences such as market forces or political pressures. The political clout of the various interested parties changes from time to time, as government, public opinion and international affairs come up with new priorities. Some aspects of policy stay in fashion longer than others. This review of energy policy tries to define the most general and lasting influences on energy policy, and indeed if energy policy can be said to exist at all in its own right rather than as a result of decisions in allied and politically more important fields such as economic and industrial policy. The future of energy policy may depend on the quality and breadth of advice received by the policy-makers, and their ability to comprehend an increasingly wide range of options. There is also a clash of time-scales; for a government with the short term aim of remaining in power, energy policy is unlikely to be a popular issue, combining present-day abundance with the possible need to enforce strict conservation measures. There is no immediate and apparent need to change the old habits of energy use, thus the task of pursuing policies which demand change is made more difficult. The time-scale relevant to many aspects of energy policy makes it a difficult area to even comprehend; ordering a nuclear power station must be done ten years ahead of when it will be needed to produce electricity, decisions have to be made now concerning the depletion rate of North Sea oil, and the consequences will only to be felt twenty to thirty years from today, and the rundown of the coal industry instituted in the late 1950s is presently being reversed. Other power production systems have even longer lead times, to the extent where some are totally unproven as yet. Technical complexity, differing expert advice and commercial concerns have to be added to the difficulties of taking any energy related decision. This is not a problem unique to the energy field; arguments concerning Concorde, the Channel Tunnel and the third London airport have many of the same characteristics. However, the coordination of long term decisions involving several energy sources intensifies the problem in the energy field.

The difficulties involved in producing a clear-cut energy policy are immense, but so are the future benefits; the life-style of the entire population will be affected, probably forever, by decisions taken within the next decade. Possible futures range between the plutonium economy and freezing in the dark, with 'save it' and a few as yet unimagined options in the middle. Most options (except perhaps freezing in the dark!) have their proponents, their vested interests, their advantages and disadvantages for one or another section of the population. The fact that people are highly adaptable to change (witness the lack of upheaval caused by the seemingly annual winter power cuts) should be no incentive to let things ride and wait for change to happen suddenly. Although the great British energy debate has not yet taken off, at least an effort has been made to provide the basis of public debate, information on the choices. The small flow of energy related publications is rapidly turning into a flood, and all sections of the media are taking the subject to heart with everything from plays to face-to-face discussion. The intractable side of the debate is the time-scale; it is very hard to visualize the future thirty years from now, and even harder to think about choosing an optimum life-style for that time. The difficulty is increased because of the lack of opportunity for decision-making available to most people in their own lives at present. Of course, even if the public debate happens and concurs on an idea of one possible future, it is unlikely that decisions taken will have exactly the predicted results. All sorts of outside influences can combine to nullify the best forecasts — even the amount of recoverable oil and gas in the North Sea is still a subject for intense argument — so without agreed figures upon which to base forecasts, the likelihood of accurate prediction is low.

However, this is no reason to avoid public debate and decision-making. Decisions are often forced upon governments, and it is surely better that they are made with the benefit of wide discussion beforehand. It is to be hoped that this review of the current energy policy situation helps towards a clearer understanding of how the policy-making mechanisms work and how and where they can be influenced. Objectivity is always a problem in any study involving politics and policy-making, the mere selection of certain points in the process or the use of a model implying certain views about the structure and workings of the overall system.

A totally objective study is an impossibility, but at least this review attempts to avoid errors of omission and selectivity. It is also helpful to look for internal changes or inconsistencies when considering particular organizations. The difficulty of producing objective accounts should be no barrier to revealing the complex official structure of the government and energy industry, which in turn should quicken the flow of information and criticism within the policy-making system as a whole and help to remove the veil of expert opinion which tends to obscure the issues of energy policy.

2 The Machinery of Government

The object of this chapter is to explain the basic workings of government and administration, placing some emphasis on the bodies concerned with energy policy and expenditure. The Department of Energy will be considered at greater length in the following chapter, so only the machinery for controlling expenditure of government departments and the overall policy-making context will be described here. Expenditure and policy-making are two sides of the same coin, and the Treasury, though small in actual numbers of staff, exerts a great degree of control over departmental spending and policies. Several detailed accounts of the Treasury have been published, as befits its place at the centre of British government, thus it is not necessary to go into its history and development here. For greater background information see Heclo and Wildavsky (1974), Bridges (1964), or Brittan (1969).

According to the *Civil Service Year Book* (Civil Service Department, 1977, vol. 671), 'The Treasury is responsible for the overall management of the economy.' The Treasury staff, for this mammoth task of controlling over £56 billion expenditure per year (*Guardian*, 13 January 1978, p. 4), numbers approximately 1000 (Brittan, 1969, p. 4), with only 150 of those actually involved in policy-making. The total size of the Home Civil Service in October 1977 was 485,900 (CSO *Monthly Digest of Statistics*, No. 383, p. 20) and spending departments – such as Environment with 59,200 staff or Health and Social Security with 99,100 – outnumber the tiny Departmental Treasury. The size of the Treasury in comparison to its responsibility is one of the factors defining its method of working; clearly, with such a small staff it cannot literally direct every penny of public spending; it must concentrate on general policies and forms of expenditure, preferring, for example, programmes with inbuilt cash limits to those which might begin at a low level but eventually cost a department a great deal. Its role is to negotiate continually constraints on departmental spending.

The Departmental Treasury is headed by its Permanent Secretary, Sir Douglas Wass, a career civil servant who has worked his way up through the Treasury, having entered as an assistant principal in 1946. Apart from the occasional year abroad at the Brookings Institute or with the International Monetary Fund, Sir Douglas progressed steadily through the Treasury, finally being promoted to Permanent Secretary in 1974. The Treasury has undergone some structural reorganization recently, in common with the rest of the Civil Service, as a result of the Fulton Committee report of 1968. The Treasury lost its responsibility for the general supervision of the Civil Service, which went to the newly created Civil Service Department, and was slightly reorganized internally. The current structure consists of four main sectors, three with their own second permanent secretary – overseas finance, domestic economy, public services – and the chief economic adviser's sector, which takes care of short and medium term forecasting and gives specialist advice to the other three sectors.

The domestic economy sector is the one which has responsibility for the nationalized energy industries. The overseas finance sector is also involved through its interest in overseas aspects of oil policy, but the domestic economy sector under its second permanent secretary, Lawrence Airey, is the one most directly involved with energy policy. Airey has been in the Civil Service since 1949, and had two years in the Cabinet Office before moving to the Treasury in 1958, where his promotion has been quite rapid. He was an ex-officio member of the board of the British National Oil Corporation in 1976–7, by virtue of his position as Deputy Secretary for Industry. The domestic economy sector is divided into two parts, Counter Inflation and Public Finance, and Industry, each with its own deputy secretary. Fred Jones, an economist who originally worked for the TUC and was a tutor at Ruskin College before joining the Civil Service, is the deputy secretary concerned with Industry. He represents the Treasury on the BNOC board. He oversees three groups; Industrial Policy (IP), Industry and Agriculture (IA), and Public Enterprises (PE). PE is the group which takes care of administration of the energy industries, and its under-secretary is N. J. Monck. He was previously principal private secretary to the Chancellor of the Exchequer, Denis Healey, until his promotion to under-secretary in 1977. Sheriff (1976) found that career success for higher civil servants was associated with service in the private office of a senior minister, so it is quite probable that Monck will stay in this post no longer than the previous incumbent, who held the post approximately two years. Even in the short existence of the Department of Energy, it has already had two under-secretaries in the Treasury with responsibility for its expenditure.

The Public Enterprises Group is split into three divisions, the Energy Division (PE1), the Transport and Industries Division (PE2) and the Nationalized Industries Policy Division (PE3). PE3 has responsibility for the general policy of the nationalized industries, but the nationalized energy industries in particular, along with North Sea Oil and energy policy, are dealt with by PE1, with its assistant secretary E. P. Kemp. Kemp has been the assistant secretary since mid 1977, and had worked under Fred Jones as an assistant secretary in the Accounts and Purchasing Group before they both moved to the Domestic Economy Sector. Thus within the first six months of 1977 the assistant, under- and deputy-secretaries concerned most directly with energy in the Treasury had all been replaced. The second permanent secretary had also moved, but this involved a simple step up for Airey, from deputy secretary in Economic Management; however, his direct knowledge of energy-related matters would not necessarily be very high. Most promotions at a high level in the Treasury are movements within the department, so there are presumably few problems with learning new methods of working relevant to specific groups or divisions. The general ability to criticize estimates and ask the right questions is more important than specific subject knowledge.

Figure 1 shows an outline of the basic Treasury structure relevant to energy matters. Overseas Finance B, in the Overseas Finance Sector, has responsibility for certain aspects of oil policy specifically in the Aid and Export Group (AEF). This is the same level as the Public Enterprises Group (PE). The Oil and Overseas Services Division (AEF2 of AEF) has a principal responsible for overseas aspects of oil policy. Each assistant secretary is in charge of about five principals, so that negotiations between D.En. and the Treasury are conducted by half a dozen higher civil servants on the Treasury side and the Principal Finance Officer (PFO), an under-secretary, in the D.En. The PFO heads the Finance and Nationalized Industry Division of D.En., which is split into two branches with an assistant secretary for each one. PFOs have a difficult position in any department, as they must establish confidential relationships with the Treasury whilst not appearing to have sold out their departments. PFOs of all depart-ments now have regular meetings together, which help them to be more of a collective force against the Treasury when cuts in

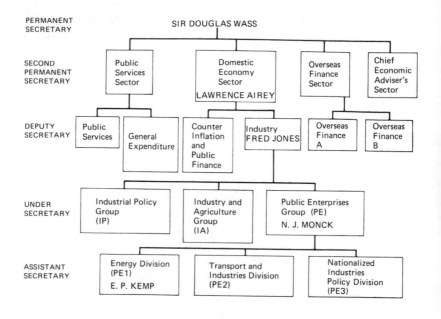

FIGURE 1   The Treasury structure

expenditure programmes are demanded. The formal pattern to which the Treasury and the PFOs work is governed by the yearly round of the spending process. Departments develop new expenditure plans and change policies as a result of the previous year's experience while the Treasury begins its task of forecasting the following year's economic performance. Department meets Treasury when the spending plans are submitted to the small group of Treasury officials who are responsible for that department's expenditure, and then follows the long process of argument and negotiation. Disagreements may be sent up to the next, ministerial level, and may even reach the Chancellor of the Exchequer as the last resort. Most problems are only taken as far as the Chief Secretary to the Treasury, the second minister in the Treasury who also holds Cabinet rank. The Chief Secretary deals with individual spending ministers and Cabinet committees, and is allowed to take decisions on the principle that there is no appeal from the Chief Secretary to the Chancellor, but only to the entire Cabinet itself. Thus the Chief Secretary is a powerful figure in the Treasury, although during the main expenditure review the Chancellor takes a more direct interest in the departmental bids. Eventually all the bids go to the Cabinet for discussion, alteration and approval, probably after further discussion by Cabinet committees for particular subjects. The agreed sum is then paid into the Exchequer account at the Bank of England from which the Treasury alone draws funds to release to the departments. Throughout the following year the Treasury will monitor the spending of each department, and as soon as one spending cycle finishes, the next one begins.

The Department of Energy, a small department with only 1300 staff, is one of the spending departments and part of a highly complex system of committees, departments and boards which form the administrative centre of British government. Each department has at its head a permanent secretary — a civil servant who is also the Accounting Officer for the department and therefore responsible to Parliament for the legality and efficiency of expenditure. On the ministerial side, each department has either a Secretary of State, as in D.En., or other similar minister, with several junior ministers who deal with particular facets of the department's work. They each have a private secretary who is a civil servant, and a parliamentary private secretary who is an MP. Ministers carry the responsibility for departmental affairs both in Parliament and in Cabinet. Not all ministers are of Cabinet rank, although all Secretaries of State are in the Cabinet. It is unusual to find more than one representative of each department in the Cabinet, the Treasury being the exception to this rule with the Chancellor and the Chief Secretary. The Cabinet normally meets once a week, with extra meetings when necessary, and any matter may be put on the agenda as long as the required 48 hours' notice can be given to members. (This is so that any relevant papers may be read.) Needless to say, this rule appears to be broken quite often. The Prime Minister is in charge of the agenda of each meeting, and apart from the usual review of Parliamentary business, any major policy decisions come through Cabinet. Before they reach Cabinet, they will probably be discussed within the appropriate Cabinet Committee. Cabinet Committees are standing and *ad hoc* committees set up by the Prime Minister to ensure that policies are considered in a broad context before they reach Cabinet, where time may be limited. Apart from specific departmental representation, they consist of ministers from allied and interested fields, but the membership of committees is not revealed to the public. A Cabinet Energy Committee exists and is known as ENM; some of its membership may be inferred from statements such as that of

Secretary of State for Energy, Tony Benn, to the Select Committee on Science and Technology (HC534-ii, Session 1976/77, Q. 280) in answer to a question concerning coordination between government departments:

> I have no complaints about this but it is a fact that a matter as important as energy touches a dozen or more departments and they are legitimately interested. I will describe them very simply. The Home Office has responsibility for security, the Ministry of Defence for protection of the North Sea oil rigs, the Treasury has responsibility for investment programmes, the Foreign Office for international matters, the Scottish Office sponsors the SSEB and has a special interest in energy matters there, the Welsh Office in development of the Celtic Sea, the Department of Industry for supplying industries and the Department of Trade for the balance of payments. No re-organisation of the Government could conceivably draw under one Ministry executive responsibility over such a wide area. That is why the Cabinet has an energy committee in which many of these interests are reflected and I have a duty in all these matters of reporting back to the energy committee and seeking approval for major policy initiatives.

With one minister from each of the above departments and one D.En. representative, this would give a maximum of nine members. As no minutes of Cabinet committee meetings are available, and no political diaries have shown an interest in energy matters, newspaper reports are the only available source of information on the proceedings of this committee. Page (1978) discovered that the Energy Committee included Joel Barnett (Chief Secretary to the Treasury), Roy Hattersley (Secretary of State for Prices and Consumer Protection), Shirley Williams (Secretary of State for Education and Science), David Owen (Foreign Secretary) and Bruce Millan (Secretary of State at the Scottish Office). Tony Benn is naturally a member, but not the chairman; this post is filled by Eric Varley, Secretary of State for Industry. As the Prime Minister is able to select members of Cabinet committees, he can balance right wing, left wing and moderate members as he pleases, and in the case of the Energy Committee he has decreased Tony Benn's personal influence by giving the chairmanship to the moderate Eric Varley. Without Varley, the committee does not meet, as there is no vice-chairman.

Tony Benn is also a member of the major economic committee, EY, which meets at least fortnightly and occasionally considers energy matters.

There are no further governmental policy-making bodies concerned directly with energy, apart from Parliament itself which has the final decision on any legislation. There are several other institutions, both Civil Service and Parliament-based, which have a bearing on energy; there are a large number of interdepartmental committees devoted to liaison in particular areas, such as the 'interdepartmental group of officials . . . established . . . to examine the scope for energy saving in buildings, industry, transport and other sectors . . .' (D.En., Press Notice Ref. No. 427, 12 December 1977, notes). The work of these committees is not made public except by means of policy changes resulting from their deliberations. The bases of their work remain unknown to a great extent; the Select Committee on Overseas Development has been told that 'disclosure of information about interdepartmental committees was against Whitehall convention and could not be supplied' (Whale, 1978) during their investigation of the Overseas Development Ministry. Even the existence of interdepartmental committees is poorly publicized.

One body which does meet in public session is the Select Committee on Science and Technology. Select committees have been in existence for many years, but the new generation of committees on specific subjects have been set up since 1956, when the Nationalized Industries Committee was given the task of securing information from ministers which was often commercially confidential and could not be obtained through normal parliamentary channels. The Select Committee on Science and Technology (SCST) was set up by Richard Crossman as a part of the reforms he originated while Lord President of the Council and Leader of the House of Commons in 1966. Select committees have a membership consisting of MPs chosen as far as possible in the same ratio as House of Commons membership in the current session. Members are officially picked by a Select Committee on Selection, but in fact the party whips have a strong position in offering advice on which members are anxious, willing or available to serve (Butler and Sloman, 1975, p. 160). When the government has a small majority the overall committee membership is given a government majority of one. Select committees are reappointed at the beginning of each session, and given powers to 'send for persons, papers and records, to sit

notwithstanding any Adjournment of the House, to adjourn from
place to place and to report from time to time . . .' (HC534-i, Session
1976/77, p. ii). These powers are wide, and any subject may be
selected for investigation whether or not the relevant minister agrees.
However, the committees have no real power, as their reports are
often ignored by Parliament or debated months after publication, in
the small hours of the morning. Their power of enforcement lies with
Parliament, and it is only rarely that a refusal to give information to a
committee is challenged. The SCST investigation of nuclear power
policy (HC117, Session 1972/73, Q. 1) was refused access to the
Department of Trade and Industry Vinter Report on nuclear reactor
policy, which has never been published. The use of the powers of the
House of Commons by the Select Committee on Nationalized
Industries in early 1978 (they forced the British Steel Corporation to
reveal certain estimates of production which had been confidential)
may mark a step towards more powerful select committees.
However, select committees are not seen to be important by those
MPs interested in promotion to ministerial levels. John Mackintosh,
the late Labour MP, quoted in the *Sunday Times* (Whale, 1978) talked
about the selection of committee members: 'I've been in the whip's
office when they've been discussing the appointment of committee
members, and they're perfectly open about it. "How about so-and-
so?" "Knows too much about it." "What about Bloggs?" "Trouble-
maker"'. In spite of this lack of determination when faced with Civil
Service or ministerial obstruction, the select committees do a useful
job in that nearly all evidence taken is published, and this includes
many nationalized energy industry papers in the case of SCST. There
is a move towards more open government, and in fact Sir Douglas
Allen, the recently retired head of the Home Civil Service, circulated
a letter to heads of department in July 1977 changing the policy on
publishing background material relating to policy studies and reports.
He wrote 'Henceforth the working assumption should be that such
material will be published unless they (the responsible Minister or
Ministers) decide that it should not be' (Norton-Taylor, 1978). The
Department of Energy has a very good record for publishing
material, mainly in its Energy Papers series, but there are still energy
related matters which are not fully revealed to the public. The
discussion on choice of nuclear reactor type which took place in early
1978 was only partially open, perhaps because of the nuclear
industry's argument that '. . . information is so subject to distortion
and misrepresentation in the media that open access would result in

emotional and political pressures' (Tucker, 1978). Nevertheless Tony Benn seems to have a real commitment to open government, even in the technically complex and sensitive area of energy policy.

The complexity of the issues involved in modern policy-making and the lack of advisory bodies not dominated by established interests encouraged the 1970 Conservative government under Edward Heath to set up the Central Policy Review Staff (CPRS) under Lord Rothschild. The CPRS was to act as a 'think tank' for the Cabinet, providing independent advice on policy matters, able to work quickly when necessary and to look at the political realities of alternative choices. It was composed of both civil servants and outsiders, of various academic backgrounds but with a bias towards administrative analysts (these were civil servants) and economists; of the fifteen staff, seven were civil servants and only two appointments were political – Lord Rothschild himself and Brian Reading, the Prime Minister's personal economic adviser. The CPRS has been brought to bear on energy matters fairly frequently; it reported on Energy Conservation in 1974 and the Power Plant Manufacturing Industry in 1976. Not all its work is published; for example the CPRS was reported (Raphael, 1978) to be in opposition to the Secretary of State for Energy's view on reactor choice, but nothing has been published to this effect.

The CPRS, from its position within the Cabinet Office, is one of the advisory bodies which has direct contact with the Cabinet and the Prime Minister. The others are the Prime Minister's Office, the Cabinet Office itself, the Civil Service Department and the Treasury. They and the CPRS all have functions which involve the discussion or initiation of policy, but only the CPRS has the time and resources to pursue many thorough investigations. In its present incarnation, the CPRS is headed by Sir Kenneth Berrill, an economist who has previously served in the Treasury. Its staff of fourteen includes C. R. Ross, the second-in-command, another economist who came straight from the OECD in Paris to be a deputy secretary in the CPRS in 1971. There are two under-secretaries, one of whom is the Chief Scientist, Professor J. M. Ashworth, a biologist on a two-year secondment from the University of Essex, and the other is Mrs J. Bridgeman, a career civil servant who has previously worked in the Board of Trade, Department of Economic Affairs, Ministry of Housing and Local Government, and Department of the Environment (and whose husband is a Treasury under-secretary). The eleven advisers who form the rest of the staff tend to have a rapid turnover, as people are brought in for specific studies on a short term basis.

Although there is no actual Prime Minister's Department in this country, the Prime Minister's Office does function as a personal advisory department for the Prime Minister. The Prime Minister's Office has a staff of around eighty (Jones, G. W., 1978) led by the private office, which consists of six private secretaries, all civil servants. The principal private secretary (with the rank of deputy secretary) organizes the work of the private office, which exists 'to do what the Prime Minister would do if he had the time and energy to do it himself' (Jones, G. W., 1978, p. 122).

The private office links the Prime Minister to the Government machine, while the political adviser is the contact with the party political side and the press secretary heads the press and information office, responsible for press relations. The only aspect of the Prime Minister's Office directly concerned with policy is the policy unit, created by Sir Harold Wilson in 1974. James Callaghan inherited the unit and its head, Bernard Donoughue, the senior policy adviser. Donoughue was a political historian at the London School of Economics before he joined the policy unit as a temporary civil servant, heading a team of around seven advisers, a mixture of full-time and part-time workers and consultants. They are all Labour sympathisers with government experience (Jones, G. W., 1978, p. 122). The unit is responsible for medium and long-term policy thinking and can act on its own initiative; it also criticizes departmental papers. Advice from the policy unit is not made public, and indeed the advice is possibly not always given in the form of written reports; the Prime Minister's Office is an unstructured system and works as well as the personal relationships within it can be made to work. The policy unit will clearly have an effect on the Prime Minister's thinking, as Donoughue and his team are allowed to attend ministerial committees, maintain contacts in departments and even help draft White Papers. As far as energy policy is concerned, when decisions reach prime ministerial level the policy unit will already be aware of the strategic implications of various choices, and will advise the Prime Minister; the advice itself remains a secret to those outside the Prime Minister's Office.

The Cabinet Office has the task of briefing the Prime Minister on Cabinet business, and has a great deal of influence at a high level in the government as its members are able to decide which committees see which papers and who is invited to meetings. Their expertise lies in areas of interdepartmental strife, and they try to avoid conflict arising within the Cabinet itself. At the head of the Cabinet Office is the Secretary of the Cabinet, one of the Prime Minister's chief advisers, Sir John Hunt. He has the ultimate responsibility for ensuring that the right officials meet each other at the right time, the heart of interdepartmental coordination and policy-making. For each Cabinet Committee of Ministers there exists a Cabinet Official Committee, usually chaired by a deputy secretary and containing representatives from each department concerned with the subject matter. The committee members are selected each year by the Cabinet Secretariat, and for the Cabinet Official Committee on energy would probably include officials from D.En., DOE, MOD, Home Office, Treasury, FO, DI, DT, and the Scottish and Welsh Offices. Below the Official Committee come various working parties of officials, normally chaired at under- or assistant secretary level. These working parties (or panels, or committees) will have a few members of the Official Committee and several more selected after consultation between the chairperson of the Official Committee and the permanent secretary of the department concerned. All details of these committees are kept secret, but the factual details are probably less important than the personal relationships. As a Cabinet Office official told Heclo and Wildavsky (1974, p. 86): 'Our flexibility is in fact the trick of it all. The Cabinet committee structure can be adjusted to produce the right people working together on anything that is coming up. It includes taking into account questions of individual personality.' Usually these committees are chaired by someone from the Cabinet Office, and the intention behind them is that members will work together as a team, losing some of their departmental identity. The Treasury and D.En. interact on these committees as well as through the PFO.

The Civil Service Department, which was formed as a result of the Fulton Report, is responsible for the management of the Civil Service. Its permanent secretary is the head of the Home Civil Service and has direct access to the Prime Minister. The post is held by Sir Ian Bancroft, previously permanent secretary at the DOE, and at one time private secretary to James Callaghan, while he was Chancellor of the Exchequer. Sir Ian has spent some time in the Treasury, and is an advocate of large departments where officials can share in the argument about expenditure rather than several ministers having to argue it out at Cabinet level (Whale, 1977). His effect as a prime ministerial adviser is likely to be one of moderation, a man who knows how the Whitehall system works and is prepared to defend it. Here again, any advice is not made public, but a man with a Treasury background, and a known moderator, is not likely to support the instigation of any radical new policies. According to Reginald Maudling, for whom he was once private secretary, he is a 'Hell of a nice chap: clear vision, great tact' (Whale, 1977). The final close adviser to the Prime Minister is the Permanent Secretary of the Treasury, Sir Douglas Wass, although G. W. Jones (1978, p. 121) suggests that much depends on the personal relationships between the Prime Minister and the various permanent secretaries; he can go to any department for advice, and can call in professional officials from other fields. The end result is all that is seen by the public, wherever the advice is sought.

Clearly, the mechanisms for discussion of policy in government are complex and indescribable in terms of official functions alone; corridors of confusion rather than corridors of power. (See Figure 2

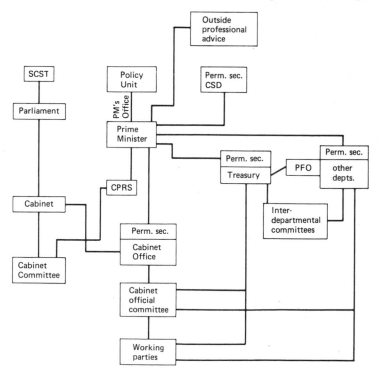

FIGURE 2   The mechanisms for policy discussion in central government

for some clarification of the system.) Energy matters filter through equally convoluted channels within D.En. before they pass through the system outlined above. In conjunction with activity on the departmental side and at Cabinet level, Parliament does discuss energy policy, often at strange hours of the night with correspondingly low attendances in the House. There is a traditional lack of interest in anything related to science or technology in the House of Commons, dating back to the last war. 'On the whole . . . Parliament was uninterested in science during the postwar decade' (Vig, 1968, p. 27). The prestige atomic energy projects of the early sixties drew more parliamentary questions than any other scientific subject, but even so Vig concludes that 'Such questions are of little political significance, except in confirming that scientific programmes are subject to many of the same types of popular pressure as other government activities . . . most [questions] add little to public knowledge of general government policy or the rationale behind it' (Vig, 1968, p. 111). The position today with regard to energy matters is similar, although the standard of questioning and the knowledge of MPs is higher. Debates are still poorly attended and tend to be held late at night. The debate on the Flowers Report (Cmnd 6618, September 1976) on 'Nuclear Power and the Environment' took place over a year after the publication of the report (*Hansard*, 2 December 1977, col. 884) and a debate on EEC energy policy documents began at 11.42 p.m. (*Hansard*, 8 December 1977, col. 1563), whereupon general annoyance was expressed by the few members present that the Cabinet persistently relegated energy debates to late in the day. In this debate Tony Benn, Secretary of State for Energy, floated the idea of a Select Committee on Energy (*Hansard*, 8 December 1977, col. 1564) but was not sure how it could be accomplished. This type of select commitee directly related to a department may become the norm in the future as pressure increases for greater accountability of government to the legislature.

Energy policy is but one aspect of British government policies, and results from the deliberations of interlocking committees, working parties, official meetings and other advisory bodies. It exists in a financial context with worldwide implications – nuclear reactors and solar power research are only two of the many energy technologies where Britain has foreign interests – and in a policy context outlined by the growing pressure for a European energy policy. It is not possible to consider energy policy separately from the rest of Britain's policy, as all expenditure estimates are debated and bargained across departmental lines. There are few policies which will come through the annual spending cycle unscathed, and energy policies often have direct implications in other fields (creation of employment being the main one) which make interdepartmental discussion necessary. Thus energy policy decisions cannot always be taken in relation to their effects on specific energy-related matters. (For example, a new power station may be built earlier than is really necessary for power production on the grounds that the power plant industry must be kept alive.) Energy also involves a high level of expenditure – the UK energy bill in 1977 was about £16 billion (D.En. Press Notice, Ref. No. 25, 24 January 1978) to final users, or £285 per head of population a year – and programmes with high capital costs, thus the Treasury may be reluctant to allow expenditure by D.En. on new programmes which may eventually require high levels of spending but which begin at a low level. Clearly, Treasury, Cabinet and prime ministerial influence on D.En., and in particular on the Secretary of State for Energy, is great but D.En. does have the expertise and advice of the nationalized energy industries to help in the production of policy. The relationship between the nationalized industries and D.En. is almost as complicated as the governmental committee network, final directive powers resting with the Secretary of State who rarely uses them. The nationalized oil, gas, coal, electricity and nuclear industries interact with the government through the Department of Energy. The industries, and the research groups, pressure groups and other interested parties, may also have channels for making their views known outside D.En., for example via the media or through other departments and their advisers, but the initiative for energy policy decisions still emanates from D.En. and it is this department which is considered next.

3 The Department of Energy

The Department of Energy is responsible for the development of national policies in relation to all forms of energy, including energy conservation and the development of new sources of energy. It is also responsible for international aspects of energy policy. The Department's responsibilities include the Government's relationships with the nationalised energy industries (coal, gas and electricity) as well as the Atomic Energy Authority, and the British National Oil Corporation.   (Civil Service Department, 1977, col. 265)

The Department of Energy is a small department by Civil Service standards with only about 1300 staff (including clerical staff), but its responsibilities, in addition to those given above, include areas with very high capital costs such as the nuclear power and oil industries. The ministerial head of the department is the Secretary of State for Energy, Tony Benn, and he is assisted by the Minister of State for Energy and two Parliamentary Under-Secretaries of State. On the Civil Service side, the department is headed by Sir Jack Rampton, the Permanent Under-Secretary of State. Although the Department of Energy as such only came into existence in January 1974, it has had a long history in government under a variety of other names. Areas of responsibility varied, too, as the importance of various energy sources grew or diminished.

THE HISTORY OF THE DEPARTMENT

A minister responsible for mines was a part of the government in the late 1920s, and then was incorporated into the Mines Department of the Board of Trade. The first ministry with energy matters as its sole responsibility was the Ministry of Fuel, Light and Power which lasted from 1942 until 1945, whereupon it became the Ministry of Fuel and Power; the ministers included E. Shinwell and Hugh Gaitskell. In

1957 the title changed again, to the Ministry of Power, which existed for twelve years before being absorbed into the Ministry of Technology in October 1969. Tony Benn had been Minister of Technology since 1966, and took over responsibility for power in 1969. The Ministry of Technology had previously been responsible for the United Kingdom Atomic Energy Authority (UKAEA), so the combination of Power with Technology was a rationalization in the energy area. After the change of government in 1970 when the Conservative Party were elected, Geoffrey Rippon was given the post of Minister of Technology but held it only a month before John Davies took over. The office was then absorbed into the Department of Trade and Industry, still with John Davies as Secretary of State until 1972 when he was succeeded by Peter Walker. The oil crisis took effect in 1973 and combined with the coal miners' strikes to make energy more overtly important, so much so that the Prime Minister, Edward Heath, decided over the 1973 Christmas recess to create a new department, the Department of Energy. He announced this on the first day of the new session of Parliament, 9 January 1974. Heath wanted to create an entirely new department, not just another version of the old Ministry of Fuel and Power (*Review of Parliament*, Issue No. 9, 1973/74 Session, w/e 11 January 1974, col. 241) so he gave the new Secretary of State for Energy, Lord Carrington, a seat in the Cabinet. He made three other appointments: Patrick Jenkin as Minister of Energy, David Howell as Minister of State and Peter Emery as Parliamentary Under-Secretary of State. Several Labour MPs were not entirely happy to have a member of the House of Lords as the new 'energy supremo', but this situation was soon resolved by the February 1974 election when Labour came into power. The first and so far only Conservative Department of Energy had lasted two months.

Eric Varley became the first Labour Secretary of State for Energy on 5 March 1974, and changed office with Tony Benn on 10 June 1975. Benn had been shadow Minister of Trade and Industry from 1970 to 1974, and had taken over as Secretary of State for Industry and Minister of Posts and Telecommunications after the election. His move to Energy appeared to be a result of pressures from the City and Treasury acting upon the government. 'The whispers from the Treasury's contacts grew stronger. Only if Tony Benn was sacked, it was said, would the confidence of British industry be restored. . . . Tony Benn eventually was not so much removed from the chessboard as castled. His departure from Industry to the

Department of Energy was welcomed in the City, but it made not the slightest difference to investment intentions, except that they continued to decline, along with the pound, profits and the stock market' (Haines, 1977, pp. 31−2). However, Benn had been responsible for Power in 1969−70, within Mintech, so it was a reasonably logical move.

THE MINISTERS

Anthony Neil Wedgwood Benn was born in 1925, the son of Viscount Stansgate. He went to Westminster School before becoming an RAF pilot in the last two years of the war, and went on to New College, Oxford, graduating in 1948. He then worked for the BBC as talks producer in their North American service for a year before being elected as Labour MP for Bristol South East in 1950. When he inherited his peerage in November 1960, he had to leave the House of Commons but renounced the peerage and was re-elected in 1963. Since then he has been Postmaster General, Minister of Technology and Secretary of State for Industry. He has held a seat on the National Executive of the Labour Party since 1959 and was Chairman of the Labour Party in 1971/72. He is well known for his radical socialist views, and apparently less than popular with the Civil Service: ' "Novel" is the sort of word civil servants will use about proposals coming from Mr. Tony Benn. It is what "sin" means to a bishop' (Haines, 1977, p. 109). He has a long and consistent record of calling for more socialist measures to be taken by the government, and is also a strong advocate of more open government. This has had its effect on the Department of Energy (D.En.) as is shown by the number of previously confidential papers it publishes. His strongly socialist attitudes sometimes jar with members of his own party: '. . . when Benn invited trade union leaders down to London for talks, he would serve them mugs of tea and hearty sandwiches as if, like gerbils or parakeets, they had a fixed daily diet' (Hoggart, 1977); and he is rarely allowed to forget his upper class background. He has a great deal of grassroots party support, but was defeated in the party leadership election after Harold Wilson's resignation in 1976. The present Prime Minister, James Callaghan, has been quoted as saying of Tony Benn 'I've got him on the end of a rope and occasionally I give a sharp jerk on the noose' (Young, H., 1978). Benn's political ambitions may be thwarted by lack of time; he was President of the Council of the

European Communities (Energy) for six months in 1977, and several decisions involving a great deal of discussion have been necessary in his time as Energy Secretary. Young's (1978) view of Benn is that he is a failed romantic: 'His romanticism runs deep. It encompasses the Labour Party and the whole working class with an unvarnished sincerity which perhaps only a scion of the upper middle classes could summon up.' Benn himself seems to be genuinely involved in the energy debate, initiating, attending and speaking at many meetings and applying his well known principles of openness and account-ability to this area. His view of the complicated technical issues is that experts must be heard but in the end 'These decisions are political' (ITV presentation of Royal Institution Conference on Nuclear Power and the Energy Future, shown 8 November 1977). He quoted a Whitehall report written after the 1973 oil crisis which forecast that oil prices would go down, as evidence that experts were not always right. Benn has now been in the post of Energy Secretary for over three years, and there have been noticeable changes both in departmental style – the new openness – and in forecasts and re-search directions since he arrived.

Until November 1978, Tony Benn's Parliamentary Private Secretary was Brian Sedgemore, MP for Luton West since 1974. Sedgemore is an Oxford man, who had been a civil servant and a barrister before being elected. He is a keen rugby player, has written for *Tribune* and enjoys (according to *Who's Who*) sleeping on the grass. He was sacked from his post as PPS in November 1978 as the result of his action in quoting from a secret Treasury document provided for the Cabinet at a Commons Expenditure Committee session. Sedgemore refused to resign, and was immediately sacked by the Prime Minister. He felt that this raised questions of Parliamentary privilege, concerning the rights of backbenchers who sit on select committees. Although PPS is an unpaid position, it is bound by ministerial rules on confidentiality.

The Minister of State for Energy, who carries responsibility for oil policy, is Dr Jesse Dickson Mabon, MP for Greenock and Port Glasgow. He was born in 1925 and worked in the coal-mining industry before his Army service. He qualified as a doctor at the University of Glasgow where he was President of the Students Union. He was later President of the Scottish Union of Students before being elected MP for Greenock in 1955. He was Minister of State at the Scottish Office from 1967 to 1970 and a member of the Council of Europe in 1970–2 and 1974–6. His Parliamentary

Private Secretary is James White, MP for Glasgow Pollock, famed for his work on the Abortion Bill. Unusually for a PPS, he is older than his minister.

Alexander Eadie, MP for Midlothian, is Parliamentary Under-Secretary of State. He originally worked as a coal-miner, and held various posts on Fife County Council, the Scottish Area NUM and the Scottish Eastern Regional Hospital Board, among others, before being elected. He is now Chairman of the Parliamentary Labour Party Power and Steel Group, and the Miners' Parliamentary Group. The other Parliamentary Under-Secretary of State, with responsibility for the gas industry and all consumer aspects of energy policy, is Dr John A. Cunningham, MP for Whitehaven. Born in 1939 he is the youngest minister in D.En., and is a graduate of Durham University where he took his Ph.D. in chemistry in 1966. He worked as a school teacher and a trade union officer before entering Parliament in 1970, where he became a member of the Select Committee on Science and Technology from 1970 until 1976. He has risen quickly in the party, being PPS to James Callaghan from 1974 to 1976, when he was made Under Secretary. He lists one of his recreations as listening to other people's opinions. Dr Cunningham is the son of Andrew Cunningham, one of the north-east Labour councillors involved in the council corruption cases of the early 1970s.

Before looking at the departmental structure itself, there is one group of people, neither ministers nor civil servants, which deserves a mention. These are the special advisers, or the Whitehall irregulars as they were once known when they began to appear in 1964. Special advisers are temporary civil servants working directly for a minister and having access to all important papers and meetings. Under the present Official Secrets Act, the PPS is not allowed to see highly confidential papers, so that the special advisers are necessary to give ministers advice on policy matters and in general do all the things a minister would like to do but has no time for. Advisers are personally and politically loyal to their ministers, but this is not always the case with a PPS who may be a political rival (Klein and Lewis, 1977). Tony Benn has three advisers: Lord Balogh, who deals with oil policy; Francis Cripps, a Cambridge economist; and Frances Morrell, who met Benn during the policy discussions held by the Labour Party in opposition before the February 1974 election. She was a candidate at Chelmsford, but lost to Norman St John Stevas and became a special adviser to Tony Benn when he was Secretary of State for Industry. Morrell describes one of her first tasks: 'At both the

Department of Industry and the Department of Energy I and my colleague, Francis Cripps, performed exactly the same exercise . . . [this] was working out from the advice that the officials were giving and from the sort of background papers, former White Papers, former studies, any sort of documentary evidence available, what the overall framework of the Department was and how it had grown up over the decades preceding' (*Talking Politics*, BBC Radio 4, 16 April 1977, transcript p. 11). Morrell and Cripps then managed to get the D.En. officials to agree to their version of the department's policy, so that Benn was able to appreciate the significance of policy recommendations and advice. There may sometimes be hostility between civil servants and special advisers – for instance, a D.En. official has been quoted as saying: 'The taxpayer is paying a lot of money for the political education of Frances Morrell; it's trench warfare down here' (*Talking Politics*, BBC Radio 4, 16 April 1977, transcript p. 14), but Morrell herself found that most civil servants were friendly, relaxed and helpful. Tony Benn feels quite strongly that special advisers are necessary: '. . . with the work that I do as a Departmental Minister, Cabinet Minister and political leader, if you like, in the context of future policy it's absolutely essential to me to be able to have the same servicing on that side as I have in advice on the official side in the context of the day-to-day management of the Department' (*Talking Politics*, BBC Radio 4, 16 April 1977, transcript p. 16). Morrell and Cripps produced a paper for Benn, which he then made available for the 1976 National Energy Conference, entitled 'The Case for a Planned Energy Policy' (D.En. Energy Paper No. 13, vol. 2, 1976, pp. 93–6); this showed evidence of broader thinking on energy policy than the sectional interests often produce.

STRUCTURE OF THE DEPARTMENT

Although the Department of Energy only finally emerged as an entity in 1974, most of its staff had performed the same functions in the years previous to its birth. The first and sole head of the department so far is Sir Jack Rampton, the Permanent Under-Secretary of State. He came from the DTI, where he was Secretary for Industrial Development, and has an Oxford and Treasury background, although he had two years in Mintech before going to the DTI. In one of his rare public statements, to the Select Committee on Science and Technology, Sir Jack appeared to share his Secretary of State's concern for the publication and dissemination of information, or as he put it, advice. Answering a question on the disposal of nuclear waste, he said:

> . . . I do think that in general we have a duty . . . to provide the fullest information about things like this to the general public in terms which the non-technical man can understand well enough . . . as a general point, I certainly believe that one wants to ensure that the general public, and particularly people who might feel they were especially affected by something, are given considered advice. Of course, that has its problems; because people do not always believe what nationalised industries or governments or officials tell them; so that even this does not prevent people disagreeing. What I am talking about is trying to give a wider understanding of the actual problems. What you cannot do is to tell other people what they ought to think or that you are right and everyone else is wrong. You can only give the best and most considered view that you can.   (HC534-ii, Session 1976/77, Q. 1805)

Sir Jack's view of energy policy was that judgment of problems had to be continuous as circumstances changed:

> What you have to do is to keep at it and to try so far as possible to keep the options open for as long as you reasonably can so that the margin of error is reduced as far as possible. I have said many times to many people that the one thing that is certain about energy policy . . . is that if you are looking ahead any distance, and you make a prediction, you are going to get it wrong. The only question is how much you are going to get it wrong.   (HC534-ii, Session 1976/77, Q. 1745)

Sir Jack's relationship with Tony Benn has not always been smooth; Benn apparently tried to have him removed in 1977 because of disagreement about the new reactor programme, but the Prime Minister would not agree (Raphael, 1977) and Benn was left to consider creating a post of second permanent secretary, presumably to reduce Sir Jack's influence.

The Permanent Under-Secretary of State heads a department small in number of staff but with a greater proportion of higher civil servants for its size than would be expected; its total staff is only 1300 compared with DOE's 59,200 but DOE has only twice as many deputy secretaries as D.En. The structure of the department is fairly simple, each deputy secretary being responsible for several divisions at under-secretary level (see Figure 3). Although the internal organisation of the department is constantly changing (for example, a new division concerned with energy conservation was created on 12 December 1977), the basic system of responsibility from permanent under-secretary downwards is the same as in other departments. The Information and Establishment Divisions are not strictly related to any one deputy secretary but work for the whole department. The other fifteen divisions are split into five groups, under the four deputy secretaries and the Chief Scientist (who is of deputy secretary rank).

When D.En. started its life in 1974 it had four deputy secretaries plus a post of Chief Scientist and Chief Inspector of Nuclear Installations, but within six months these posts were separated and eventually the Nuclear Installations Inspectorate was transferred to the Health and Safety Executive in 1975, leaving five deputy secretaries again.

FINANCE AND NATIONALIZED INDUSTRY, ENERGY POLICY, ENERGY CONSERVATION, ECONOMICS AND STATISTICS

The group of divisions which might be considered as the most important in D.En. from the point of view of interaction with other departments is the Finance and Nationalized Industry, Energy Policy, Energy Conservation, Economics and Statistics group. The Finance and Nationalized Industry Division contains the Principal Finance Officer (PFO) who negotiates the spending estimates with the Treasury, and thus affects all departmental policy. The deputy secretary in charge of this group is T. P. Jones, the youngest of the five deputy secretaries at 48. An Oxford man, he arrived at D.En. after short spells in Supply, Aviation, the Treasury, Mintech and DTI. At the DTI he was under-secretary for the Electricity Division, which was moved in its entirety to D.En. in 1974. Officials of this rank rarely have the chance to speak in public, but Jones was called to give evidence to the SCST in May and June 1976. He was introduced by his permanent secretary as having the main responsibility for coordination of energy policy, and he too went on record as agreeing with Benn's advocacy of open government: 'I think generally as a Department our record on publishing is good. We try to publish as much as we can; and it is the

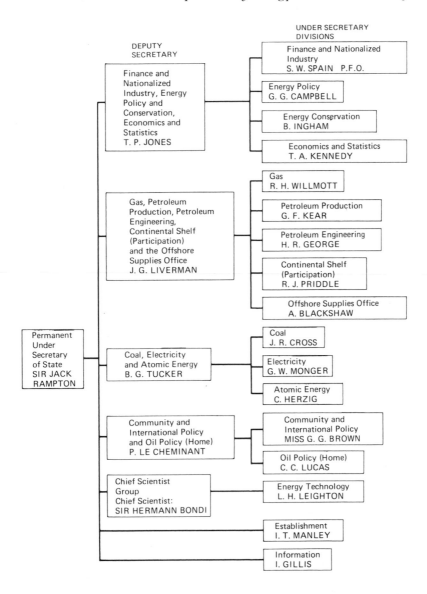

FIGURE 3 The Department of Energy

wish not only of our Secretary of State but of the Department as a whole that we should make available as much work as we can' (HC 534-ii, Session 1976/77, Q. 2004). Jones is the chairman of the

Working Group on Energy Strategy (WGES) which was set up by the Secretary of State for Energy in 1975 with membership at board level from the nationalised energy industries and from government departments. It exists to discuss a more coordinated approach between government and industries to the formulation of energy strategy and energy policies. Very little of its proceedings are published, the exception being Energy Commission Paper No. 2 (D.En., 1977) which dealt mainly with forward planning methods. The WGES has a technical group under the chairmanship of D.En., with both industry and D.En. members, which looks at forecasting and planning methodology. There are several other D.En. members of the WGES, all of lower rank than Jones, and one Treasury man, under-secretary C. W. France, the Establishment Officer.

(a) *Finance and Nationalised Industry Division*

Jones did spend two years in the Treasury, and will thus have some idea of its inner workings. His Finance and Nationalized Industry Division is headed by the PFO, under-secretary S. W. Spain, and is split into two branches. Before becoming D.En. PFO in 1974, Spain was under-secretary in the Oil Policy Division of the DTI, and assistant secretary in Mintech. He has never worked in the Treasury, but was honorary secretary of the First Division Association (the higher civil servants group) in 1961 – 4, and director of the Central Computer Agency (in the Civil Service Department) in 1971 – 3. He is a member of the WGES. Branch 1 of the division (assistant secretary J. E. W. d'Ancona), is responsible for submissions to the Parliamentary Accounts Committee, estimates, PESC (the Treasury method of expenditure forecasting), major projects, new expenditures and the internal audit. In other words, this branch has the task of liaison with the Treasury and keeping track of the internal departmental finances. The assistant secretary has only held the post since early 1977, being preceded by P. S. Ross who had previously worked in the branch of the Coal Division concerned with finance. All departmental PFOs sit on the Public Expenditure Survey Committee (PESC) which controls the yearly round of forecasting and interdepartmental haggling. This has led to a greater sense of unity between PFOs in the face of Treasury pressure to limit spending, but has not resulted in money being voluntarily left for one department at the expense of another; departmental self-interest is still the basis on which the system functions. The PFO and his officials in Branch 1 have less contact with the profusion of energy related committees, inside and outside government, than officials in other divisions, as their work is mainly internal to D.En. Branch 1 has recently been made responsible for corporate planning methods and standards, energy sector industry plans, guidelines, assumptions, appraisal and monitoring. This was a result of one of the frequent internal reorganisations of the department, which reduced the division from three branches to two, although with the same duties.

Branch 2 of the Finance and Nationalized Industry Division (assistant secretary G. Hadley) is responsible for nationalized energy industry policy, financial objectives, pricing policy and policy on pay and non-financial issues. The corporate planning adviser to Branch 2 is M. H. Cadman, the secretary of WGES. Thus the main Treasury—D.En. contacts are made between PFO Spain, assistant secretary d'Ancona and their staff in Branch 1, and the Treasury Energy Division (PE1) of the Public Enterprises Group (PE), under assistant secretary E. P. Kemp.

(b) *Energy Conservation Division*

Two of the other divisions under T. P. Jones were part of a single division, Energy Policy and Conservation, until December 1977, when a new Energy Conservation Division was set up under Bernard Ingham, previously D.En. Director of Information, to add weight to the newly announced energy conservation measures. This promotion to under-secretary came after four years as Director of Information. This division is divided into two branches: Branch 1 (assistant secretary W. K. Pryke), deals with policy development, planning and coordination on energy conservation. Pryke is the secretary of the Advisory Council on Energy Conservation (ACEC). Branch 2 is responsible for energy conservation in the public sector and in industry, and for regional energy conservation activities. Its senior principal is W. G. J. Denness. As energy conservation principles can be applied to almost all forms of industrial activity, there are a great many interdepartmental and non-governmental committees in this area. One of the first of these was the Committee of Ministers on Energy Conservation (MEC), under the chairmanship of Dr John Cunningham, the D.En. Under-Secretary of State, mentioned in the joint D.En./DOE/DoT memorandum to the SCST (HC534-iii, Session 1976/77, p. 617). This was set up to promote energy conservation within and outside government, and was backed by several Civil Service groups: 'Contact at official level takes place through regular liaison arrangements, in *ad hoc* committees established to deal with particular issues and in the course of normal interdepartmental dealings between officials. There are regular exchanges between senior officials of the Departments to review matters of major common policy interest' (HC534-iii, Session 1976/77, p. 617). The work of these groups is not made public, but one of them at least was given a more permanent basis in June 1977 when an interdepartmental group of officials was established to consider energy saving in various sectors (D.En Press Notice, Ref. No. 427, 12 December 1977, notes). The government departments responsible for elements of conservation are many and varied, as listed, for instance, in the SCST report on Energy Conservation (HC487, Session 1974/75, p. 59) which mentions D.En., DOE, DI, DT, Treasury, DHSS, Home Office, MAFF, MoD and the Scottish and Welsh Offices. Clearly there is great scope for interdepartmental committee work in this area. Research into energy conservation is overseen by the Interdepartmental Committee on Energy Conservation R and D (ENCORD), which works under the Committee of Chief Scientists. Its membership comprises departmental representatives and some representatives from ACORD and ACEC, and its function is to liaise with departments to ensure that necessary R and D is carried out and to review the progress of energy conservation research funded by D.En.

D.En. runs three schemes for industry to help with energy saving: the Energy Survey Scheme (ESS) helps with the cost of a fuel consultant's survey; the Energy Saving Loan Scheme whereby loans are available for certain energy saving projects in industry; and the Energy Quick Advice Service (EQAS), dealing mainly with telephone enquiries. DI runs the Industrial Energy Thrift Scheme (IETS), in which selected companies are visited and advised and the Energy Audit Scheme (EAS), which gives more detailed advice. EAS and IETS are managed by the Energy Unit at the National Physical Laboratory. The main body where D.En., industry and academics meet is the Advisory Council on Energy Conservation (ACEC), chaired by Professor Sir William Hawthorne, Master of Churchill College. ACEC was set up by Eric Varley, then Secretary of State, in October 1974 to 'advise and assist the Secretary of State for Energy in carrying out his duty of promoting economy and efficiency in the use and consumption of energy'. It works mainly through small working groups on particular subjects such as buildings and transport, and its membership (now 25) is drawn from a wide range of areas, trade unions, universities, industry, as well as D.En. and a strong DI representation. Their reports are published through D.En., and there are D.En. members on MISER (Methodology of Industrial Sector Energy Requirements), a standing committee looking at problems in the energy audit field, and SLICE (Committee for Studies Leading to Industrial Conservation of Energy) which advises on energy use in industry. MISER is run by D.En., DI and the CBI. Clearly all the research groups and committees have an interest in energy conservation, and the International Energy Agency (IEA) is taking greater interest in energy-saving measures. There is increasing activity in the energy conservation field, as reflected in the announcement of the energy conservation programme in December 1977, and this has meant most other government departments taking a more active role. Thus there are a large number of interdepartmental committees and working groups outside government coming under the aegis of the Energy Conservation Division (see Figure 4).

(c) *Energy Policy Division*
The Energy Policy Division, newly split from the old Energy Conservation Unit, is the third division for which deputy secretary T. P. Jones is responsible. It is headed by G. G. Campbell, who worked in Fuel and Power, Power and the DTI before his division moved to D.En. in 1974. He attends meetings of the WGES. He gave evidence to the SCST in 1976 concerning the D.En. views of future energy policy, in particular the role of pricing policy in the nationalized energy industries (HC534-ii, Session 1976/77, Q.1989), but was rather overshadowed by his deputy secretary and the Chief Scientist. The Energy Policy Division has two branches: Branch 1 (assistant secretary Miss S. M. Cohen), deals with general energy policy. She explained the division's role to SCST in June 1976: 'The Energy Policy Division is charged with looking at the development of all possible sources of energy and the way in which that might match with demand. . . . We look on our work as administrative and policy making. We rely on our colleagues for technical assessments and for the progress of the work at the technical level' (HC534-ii, Session 1976/77, Q. 1897 and Q. 1898). They later went on to discuss the thorny question of who actually decides policy, and in answer to the question 'So where does the policy lie?', she replied: 'The policy lies in the joint evaluation from all wings of the Department going up to the top management of the Department and, of course, eventually to Ministers, to Ministerial committees if necessary, to inter-Departmental discussion, in the normal way that government policy

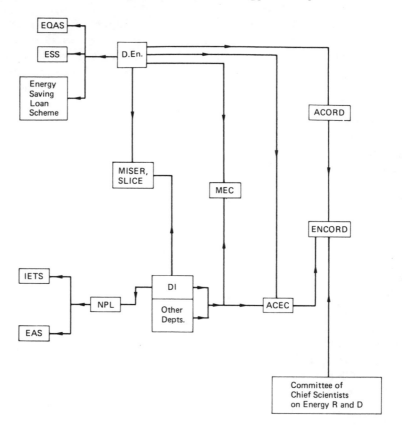

FIGURE 4   Government bodies concerned with energy conservation

is formulated' (HC 534-ii, Session 1976/77, Q.1940). Branch 2 (assistant secretary K. C. Price), is responsible for environmental aspects of energy policy (including international aspects), coordination of land-use planning and international aspects of energy conservation, including liaison with IEA, OECD and EEC.

(d) *Economics and Statistics Division*
The fourth division under T. P. Jones is the Economics and Statistics Division, brought into his group during 1977. Its under-secretary is T. A. Kennedy and it is responsible for statistical services for the whole department. Kennedy is an economist who has worked in the Treasury, the FO, DEA and DTI, and was also Economic Director of

the National Economic Development Office from 1967 to 1970. He attends WGES meetings. Until mid 1977 the division had a Chief Economic Adviser, F. J. Atkinson, but he is now working in the Treasury as Head of the Government Economic Service and Chief Economic Adviser to the Treasury. The division has five branches: Branch A (chief statistician J. Draper) deals with basic data coordination and development. Draper moved to this post in late 1977, and previously had been chief statistician in the Ministry of Defence statistical system division, where he was responsible for computer systems for defence statistics and research into manpower planning systems. Branch B (chief statistician F. W. Hutber) is responsible for forecasts and analyses for energy and the electricity industries, including the nuclear industry. Hutber was a member of the Working Group on Energy Elasticities, an interdepartmental group set up to report on the relationship between energy consumption and price. Its membership was drawn from the Treasury (1), CPRS (1), DOE (3) and D.En. (8), and T. A. Kennedy was the chairman. It reported in February 1977, and the report was published as Energy Paper No. 17. The working group was a successor to the interdepartmental Working Group on Oil Prices, which was formed as a response to the oil crisis and the effect of expanding gas supplies on the electricity industry. Branch C of the division (senior economic adviser J. M. Barber) deals with general economic questions, and forecasts and analyses for petroleum other than from the North Sea; Branch D (senior economic adviser G. A. C. D. Houston) is responsible for forecasts and analyses for the North Sea gas and petroleum industries. Branch E (senior economic adviser Professor N. J. Cunningham) deals with special studies on medium and longer term aspects of the energy sector, economic problems of the nationalized industries, and forecasts and analyses for the coal industry. Professor Cunningham was a member of the Working Group on Energy Elasticities.

GAS, PETROLEUM PRODUCTION, PETROLEUM ENGINEERING, CONTINENTAL SHELF (PARTICIPATION) AND THE OFFSHORE SUPPLIES OFFICE

The group of divisions headed by T. P. Jones has a heavy load, not only having to ensure the department maintains its share of total government expenditure but in directing energy policy as a whole. The group also has responsibility for energy conservation, the latest growth area in the energy field. An equally important group, perhaps, is that headed by deputy secretary J. G. Liverman and concerned with North Sea oil and gas production. Liverman, a Cambridge graduate, served in the Treasury, Power, Mintech and DTI before moving over to the D.En. when it was established in 1974. He has been Director of the British National Oil Corporation (BNOC) Organizing Committee since 1976, but serves on BNOC in an ex-officio role, not as an individual member; he is there to ensure BNOC take due account of the government's overall energy policy in making its decisions. The group is split up into five divisions: Gas, Petroleum Production, Petroleum Engineering, Continental Shelf (Participation) and the Offshore Supplies Office.

(a) *Gas Division*
The Gas Division, headed by under-secretary R. H. Willmott, a WGES member previously in charge of the Continental Shelf Policy Division, is split into three branches. Branch 1 (assistant secretary S. W. T. Mitchelmore) deals with the organization of the gas industry, its tariff policy, industrial relations, appointments, land use, including underground gas storage, and gas safety measures. Branch 2 (assistant secretary S. W. Fremantle) is responsible for corporate planning, finance, natural gas absorption policy, international matters, the purchase of gas from the UK part of the continental shelf and from abroad, and gas gathering pipelines. Thus Branch 2 deals with D.En. relations with Gas Gathering Pipelines (North Sea) Ltd, the joint public/private sector company which is studying the viability of a gas gathering system in the Northern Basin of the North Sea. It also deals with the examination of the annual corporate plan of the British Gas Corporation (BGC) which forecasts activities and programmes planned for the following five years. This, along with an estimate of probable developments over a further ten years, is submitted to D.En. in March of each year, and is eventually discussed by BGC, D.En. and Treasury representatives. The corporate plan originates from the operating plans prepared in the previous year by all regions of BGC. Branch 3 of the division is the Gas Standards branch, based in Wigston, Leicestershire, and is responsible for gas safety, standards and examination, and meter standards and safety.

(b) *Petroleum Production Division*
Until 1977 the Petroleum Engineering Division was a part of the Petroleum Production Division (PPD), but now both exist in their

own right. The Petroleum Production Division is headed by under-secretary G. F. Kear, an Oxford graduate with a varied background. He has worked in Supply, Aviation, MOD and the Cabinet Office as well as having two years in Paris with NATO and spending 1972— 3 as a Fellow at the Harvard Centre for International Affairs. He sits on the Offshore Energy Technology Board (OETB), set up to advise on R and D in the field of offshore oil and gas technology. The division has two branches: Branch 1 (assistant secretary P. H. Agrell) handles liaison with offshore operatives concerning their petroleum production plans and programmes, and deals with questions on the United Nations Law of the Sea Conference (UNLOSC); Branch 2 (assistant secretary A. R. D. Murray) is responsible for UK petroleum production licensing.

(c) *Petroleum Engineering Division*
The Petroleum Engineering Division (director H. A. George) contains four branches and the Diving and Pipelines Inspectorates. Branch 1 (assistant secretary B. D. Emmett) deals with gas flaring, pipeline authorization, pollution, the issue of safety and health regulations and the protection of offshore installations. Branch 2, under deputy director J. A. Thornton, is responsible for the assessment of petroleum discoveries and prospects, conservation, the monitoring of field behaviour and the publication of records. Branch 3 (deputy director P. Selwood) deals with safety, including advisory functions in day-to-day operations, safety inspections and accident investigations. Branch 4 (assistant director engineer W. R. Street) deals with R and D related to continental shelf exploration and the safety of offshore installations. The Diving and Pipelines Inspectorates deal with the safety of diving operations and land and submarine pipelines respectively.

(d) *Continental Shelf (Participation) Division*
The Continental Shelf (Participation) Division (under-secretary R. J. Priddle) has the complex task of looking after UK interest in the North Sea. Branch 1 (assistant secretary C. E. Henderson) deals with BNOC, North Sea policy on depletion, oil sharing and refineries, North Sea aspects of UK energy policy and international policy discussions. Branch 2A (assistant secretary C. C. Wilcock) is responsible for oilfield financing policy and financing and partici-pation negotiations with banks and oil companies. Branch 2B (assistant secretary P. T. Harding) deals with oilfield participation

policy and participation and financing negotiations with oil companies. Harding, previously in the Community and International Policy Division, took over this post in late 1977 because of the promotion of R. J. Priddle to under-secretary of the division.

(e) *Offshore Supplies Office*
The fifth and final division of the group is the Offshore Supplies Office (OSO) which is based in Glasgow and headed by Director General A. Blackshaw. This is a rather unusual area of the Civil Service, as it was set up in 1973 to make sure that British industry was given its fair share of work stemming from the North Sea. It has six branches, and Branch 1, the Venture Group, takes a very positive role in its task of identifying opportunities for greater British involvement. 'It will seek out weaknesses in British capability, select a suitable firm and then try and arrange a joint venture with an American firm that has the product or the technology to fill the gap. . . . Much of this work has to go unpublicised if firms are to reveal confidential information to OSO' (Eglin, 1977). Branch 2 is the Establishment and Publicity branch; Branch 3 deals with economic analysis of opportunities, and R and D (there is an OSO member on the OETB); Branch 4 liaises with the Offshore Operating Companies (OOCs); Branch 5 is the London representation, including parliamentary work, PESC and industrial strategy (for example, relations with the NEB and British Shipbuilders); Branch 6 is the Export branch, which coordinates OSO's work on exports, including the identification of major offshore related activities overseas and the provision of advice to industry. A seventh branch, the Platform Sites Directorate, was disbanded during 1977. OSO has been successful in its short life, both encouraging firms to compete for North Sea contracts with financial and research support, and acting as a clearing house for information. The oil companies send their quarterly purchasing returns to OSO, which enables officials to spot trends early and so warn companies about changing patterns of demand. A trust has been built up between officials and companies, and the companies are now more willing to provide OSO with details of their future plans. OSO's readiness to intervene in private industry is rare for a government department; Eglin (1977) quotes an OSO official: 'It's rather untypical for civil servants but we have found several cases where our prodding has greatly speeded things up. Going in as a department of government has certainly helped impress some firms how important the North Sea is, something sub-

contractors are not always aware of.' OSO officials are said to think their tactics would work just as well in other areas of British industry.

COAL, ELECTRICITY AND ATOMIC ENERGY

The third group of divisions in D.En. is the Coal, Electricity and Atomic Energy group, under deputy secretary Brian G. Tucker. Tucker entered the Civil Service as a clerical officer in 1939 and was posted to Africa, the Middle East and Hong Kong until being promoted to assistant principal in the Ministry of Power. He then rose via the Ministry of Power, the government of Northern Rhodesia, Mintech, the Cabinet Office and DTI to his present position as deputy secretary in 1973. He has been a part-time member of the United Kingdom Atomic Energy Authority since 1976.

(a) Coal Division
The Coal Division is led by under-secretary J. R. Cross, a WGES member who had several spells abroad before moving to the DTI in 1972. He was the Senior British Trade Commissioner in Montreal in 1968–70 where he was kidnapped and held by terrorists for 59 days in late 1970. His division is divided into two branches. Branch 1 (assistant secretary G. W. Thynne) deals with financial matters relating to the coal industry; supply, distribution and demand for solid fuels; the NCB corporate plan; and defence planning and civil emergencies. Branch 2 (assistant secretary C. N. Tebay) is responsible for international organizations including the European Coal and Steel Community (ECSC); imports and exports of solid fuel; environmental matters, opencast coal working and mining subsidence; redundancy benefits and other social costs; and manpower and industrial relations.

(b) Electricity Division
The Electricity Division is headed by under-secretary G. W. Monger (a member of the WGES), and has four branches, dealing with pricing policy (Branch 1, assistant secretary J. L. Cohen); investment programmes, energy policy and EEC matters (Branch 2, assistant secretary D. I. Morphet); corporate planning (Branch 3, assistant secretary B. Hampton); and pollution, amenity matters, appointments and consumer relations (Branch 4, assistant secretary Miss J. A. M. Oliver). Branch 3 examines the yearly plans put forward by the electricity industry, in the form of proposals from the Central

Electricity Generating Board and the area boards, and a background memorandum from the Electricity Council. The estimates are prepared in February/April of each year and stretch five or six years forward. The division also contains the Engineering Inspectorate, which is responsible for public inquiries on power station and overhead line proposals.

(c) *Atomic Energy Division*
The Atomic Energy Division is led by under-secretary Christopher Herzig who previously worked in Fuel and Power, Aviation, Mintech and the DTI (a common combination for D.En. senior officials), before moving to D.En. in 1974. He is a member of the WGES. The four branches of his division have the complex task of dealing with the British nuclear industry, but are no longer responsible for the Nuclear Installations Inspectorate (NII), now a part of the Health and Safety Executive (HSE). Branch 1 (assistant secretary W. E. Fitzsimmons) takes care of British Nuclear Fuels Ltd (BNFL), uranium enrichment and procurement policy, physical security and relations with HSE. Branch 2 deals with overseas aspects of atomic energy policy, including EURATOM, the International Atomic Energy Agency (IAEA), the Nuclear Energy Agency (NEA) and the International Energy Agency (IEA). Branch 3 (assistant secretary R. T. J. Wilson) is responsible for the United Kingdom Atomic Energy Authority (UKAEA) and the National Nuclear Corporation (NNC). Branch 4 (assistant secretary P. G. D. Fullerton) deals with all safeguards aspects of the nuclear trade, non-proliferation policy and the international fuel cycle evaluation programme, INFCEP.

The present Atomic Energy Division had its origins in the postwar Ministry of Supply (MOS) where it was known as the Atomic Energy Department. When the UKAEA was formed in 1954 many civil servants were transfered from MOS to the AEA, initiating the close relationship between the UKAEA and the government depart-ment responsible for overseeing its performance. It was decided not to attempt to duplicate the technical bureaucracy of the UKAEA on the Civil Service side, so that the normal government functions of checking budgets and controlling policy were beyond the small resources of the Atomic Energy Division, which became more of a mouthpiece for the UKAEA than a brake on its expansionist ideas. The UKAEA in the sixties had a high reputation based on its pure research and this, combined with its ability to produce convincing long term plans which appealed to the growing body of economic planners within the Civil Service, meant that UKAEA estimates passed through the Treasury net relatively unscathed. Burn says of the civil servants in the Atomic Energy Division in 1967 that: 'They appeared to believe that all AEA judgements and assessments were right, all critics of the AEA wrong, and all AEA answers to criticism right' (Burn, 1978, p. 176). There was some unease within the Ministry of Technology concerning the lack of impartial advice and the need for more economic analysis of decisions, and the Programmes Analysis Unit at Didcot was set up to provide 'techno/economic assessments of problem areas'. It was staffed jointly by the UKAEA and the responsible government department, and had a wide remit which included the consideration of the environmental and social effects of technology. The director was Dr P. M. S. Jones, a strongly pro-nuclear radiation chemist who had previously worked in the Atomic Weapons Research Establishment. The Programmes Analysis Unit also gave advice to the UKAEA on its non-nuclear research programme, but it disappeared in Autumn 1977 and Dr Jones became head of the Economics and Programmes Branch of the UKAEA. His views on nuclear power were stated in a recent article:

> In conclusion it can be said that there is no technical obstacle to nuclear energy becoming the workhorse of the UK and world energy system. Furthermore with the continued evolution of the fast reactor programme there is no technical reason why this happy situation should not persist throughout the great part of the next century with thermal energy requirements also being met at least in part from nuclear sources.   (Jones, P.M.S., 1978, p. 29)

It is no surprise that criticism such as Bugler's concerning the lack of money for alternative energy research: '. . . the nuclear establishment in the Department of Energy fixes the allocations' (Bugler, 1977, p. 872), is growing. The ingrained policy of nuclear expansion and the general secrecy of nuclear affairs combine to produce an atmosphere where even genuine decisions on the allocation of finance for non-nuclear research are regarded with extreme suspicion. The only solution to the unproductive situation is more openness on both the UKAEA and D.En. sides; there is still no neutral body to provide advice to ministers on nuclear matters.

COMMUNITY AND INTERNATIONAL POLICY AND OIL POLICY (HOME)

The fourth group of divisions is the Community and International Policy and Oil Policy (Home) group, headed by deputy secretary P. le Cheminant. He was a member of the UK delegation to the ECSC in 1962/63 and private secretary to Harold Wilson, the then Prime Minister, in 1965–8 before taking the usual route through Power, Mintech and the DTI to D.En. He is a member of the General Policy group of ACEC. He is responsible for two divisions, Community and International Policy and Oil Policy (Home).

(a) *Community and International Policy Division*
Miss G. G. Brown is under-secretary in the Community and International Policy Division; she has a long record of posts abroad with the Diplomatic Service in Washington, Budapest, Berne and Paris where she was first secretary for the UK delegation to the OECD. She has been an under-secretary since 1975, and is responsible for two branches. Branch 1 (assistant secretary J. Whaley) is responsible for EEC energy policy and oil matters in the EEC and other West European countries. Branch 2 (assistant secretary R. A. Custis) deals with IEA, OECD, Economic Commission for Europe (ECE; a UN body) and world energy matters other than those handled by Branch 1.

(b) *Oil Policy (Home) Division*
The Oil Policy (Home) Division, OP(H), is headed by under-secretary C. C. Lucas, a WGES member, and has three branches. Branch 1 (assistant secretary L. F. Barclay) is responsible for oil emergency planning, oil stocks and OP(H) interest in international energy policy. Branch 2 has as its assistant secretary W. C. F. Butler who until late 1977 was the assistant secretary for Branch 2 of the Atomic Energy Division. This branch deals with refinery policy, the disposal of North Sea oil and petrochemicals. Branch 3 (assistant secretary Mrs D. E. F. Carter) deals with oil pricing, marketing and distribution.

CHIEF SCIENTIST GROUP

The final large D.En. group is the research group known as the Chief Scientist Group. The present Chief Scientist is Professor Sir Hermann

Bondi, appointed in August 1977, from his previous post as Chief Scientific Adviser to the Ministry of Defence. He is an astrophysicist and has been on leave of absence from King's College, London, where he is Professor of Mathematics. He is also a Fellow of the Royal Society. His predecessor in the post was Dr Walter Marshall, sacked by Tony Benn in June 1977. Marshall never received a salary for his Chief Scientist post, keeping on his position originally as director of the Harwell laboratory of the UKAEA and then as deputy chairman of the AEA, which he became in December 1975. When Marshall entered D.En., he was viewed with suspicion by the officials because 'he does not have the bureaucrat's way of doing things' (Kenward, 1977a), but he soon won over the administrators enough to be able to complete his R and D package (see D.En. Energy Paper No. 11, 1976) before he left. It would appear that Marshall was sacked, or '...asked to resume full-time work in the Authority as soon as possible' (Official D.En. statement quoted in Kenward, 1977a) because of his strong advocacy of nuclear power.

Bondi has not proved as forthcoming with the press as Marshall; his first interview with *New Scientist* came to an end early because he insisted on reading the article before it was published (Kenward, 1977b), but he did say that he had been visiting important establishments in order to acquaint himself with energy research. He approved of Marshall's R and D strategy, and the scenario approach used by D.En., but he thought it might be necessary to consider scenarios not covered in the original study. On alternative energy sources, he said, 'I do not believe alternatives are being held back by lack of money. They are not in competition with anything else for funds.' He sees wave energy as an attractive option for Britain but 'any fool can build a windmill' while wave energy calls for large scale complex engineering techniques.

Energy Technology Division
Bondi is in charge of one division of D.En., the Energy Technology Division (ENT) headed by under-secretary L. H. Leighton. Leighton is an Oxford man and a Fellow of the Institute of Fuel who has served in the NCB, Power, Mintech and the DTI. Branch 1 of his division is concerned with electrical technology and project assessment, and is led by Deputy Chief Scientific Officer D. C. Gore. Gore, an engineer, attended the SCST hearing concerned with the D.En. attitude to tidal power and the Severn barrage in particular. G. A. Goodwin, a principal scientific officer, was also at that meeting and is presumably

in Branch 1 and deals specifically with tidal power research, although he said nothing at the hearing. Gore was forced to defend the D.En. policy of low priority for tidal power research, and confessed he took rather a harsh view of the possibilities of tidal power. In answer to a question concerning the energy gap around the year 2000, he said: 'I think that the Department has said clearly that, as do other countries, we see an energy gap opening there; but in common with other countries we see the only major way of filling the gap as being nuclear' (HC534-ii, Session 1976/77, Q. 879). Branch 2 consists of three sections, each headed by a senior principal scientific officer (SPSO). The sections deal with coal technology, gas technology and energy conservation technology; H. F. Ferguson, G. S. Dearnley and Charles Ryder are the respective SPSOs.

Branch 3 deals with divisional administration, and acts as the secretariat for the Advisory Council on Research and Development for Fuel and Power (ACORD); its principal is M. Hewett. ACORD is a non-statutory body set up in 1960 as a successor to the Ministry of Fuel and Power Scientific Advisory Council. It is responsible for reviewing the research programmes of the nationalized fuel and power industries, and serves as a Requirements Board for R and D programmes funded by D.En. in non-nuclear and non-marine areas. There is also an ACORD Programme Committee to support the work of ACORD. There are at present seventeen members of ACORD, the number having been increased recently to include more independent members. The chairman is the D.En. Chief Scientist, and there are representatives of the NCB, BGC, CEGB, Electricity Council, UKAEA and various academic and industrial institutions, such as the Science Research Council (SRC), Esso, BP, ICI and GEC. Although no civil servants (apart from the chairman) are officially stated as belonging to ACORD, it is clear that they do attend meetings. Miss S. M. Cohen revealed this in her evidence to the SCST on Alternative Sources, saying that the Energy Policy Division was '. . . represented through our Deputy Secretary, Mr. Philip Jones, . . . on ACORD. We see all the papers that are coming forward to ACORD and we are enabled to comment on them' (HC534-ii, Session 1976/77, Q. 1897). Although ACORD's membership has been expanded, it is still rather an inappropriate body to examine ideas for national energy R and D policy; it is composed of establishment producers and users of energy, with no input from interests more directly concerned with alternative energy sources. As a body overseeing the R and D programmes of the nationalized energy industries in times of little change, it was adequate, but a broader membership or a different committee altogether would be more useful in the present unsettled situation.

One of the areas considered by ACORD is the work of the Energy Technology Support Unit (ETSU) at Harwell. This was formed in April 1974 to give attention to the increasing number of non-nuclear energy projects. ETSU and MATSU (the Marine Technology Support Unit) are directed by the Research Director (Energy) at the Atomic Energy Research Establishment (AERE) at Harwell, Dr F. J. P. Clarke. Clarke explained the relationship between D.En. and ETSU to the SCST as follows: 'The Energy Technology Support Unit is funded by the Department of Energy and carries out work from time to time, such as they may require' (HC534-ii, 1976/77, Q. 1321). He later went on in answer to a question concerning the independence of ETSU:

> We, I am sure, are required by the Department to give as honest and professional an appraisal of the various topics that they refer to us as we can. I think that we do that. On the question of publication, that is entirely a matter for the Department. We submit our reports, we give our views of the situation as we see it, and these are submitted to the Chief Scientist and to ACORD, and the subsequent publication of those is a matter for the Department. We cannot control that. I repeat again, we are agents of the Department and we have to do as they require us to do.   (HC 534-ii, Session 1976/77, Q. 1390)

The head of ETSU, Dr. J. K. Dawson, was at the same SCST hearing and spoke on the ETSU research programme: 'The programme is determined by a committee of which the Chief Scientist is the chairman, and it is entirely open to us to suggest to that committee new studies to be carried out from time to time; and in fact we do that' (HC534-ii, Session 1976/77, Q. 1389). Dawson also said that ETSU tried to take a wide perspective in its work, considering not only technical factors relevant to the energy needs of the country. ETSU's research programme is guided by the Committee of Chief Scientists on Energy Research and Development, whose membership includes the chief scientific advisers from all departments concerned with energy. It is responsible for liaison between the various departments and the Cabinet Office in the energy field. Through its standing sub-committee it oversees the work of the national steering groups on energy R and D programmes, and also UK representation on various international working groups. There are steering committees on geothermal energy and wave energy, with relevant organizations and sections of D.En. having representation. The Wave Energy Steering Committee (WESC), for example, is chaired by Dr F. J. P. Clarke and there are two D.En. members, D. C. Gore and G. A. Goodwin. Gore is head of the electrical technology branch and Goodwin works in that branch. These interdepartmental steering committees exist to coordinate the national R and D programmes in areas which ACORD has recommended should be investigated. At a lower level than the steering committees are advisory groups responsible for certain aspects of the programmes; for example there is a D.En. Advisory Group to deal with generation and transmission systems in the wavepower programme.

The D.En. Chief Scientist also sits on the Committee of Departmental Chief Scientists and Permanent Secretaries, chaired by the Secretary of the Cabinet, which reviews research and development and other scientific matters, and brings questions before the appropriate ministers where necessary. This committee was set up as part of the reorganization of the government scientific advisory machine in 1976, and replaced the post of Chief Scientific Adviser. This was abolished as the range of work had become too wide for one person to cover adequately. At the same time the Science Group, formerly within the Cabinet Office, was transferred to the CPRS, and a chief scientist appointed to the CPRS in October 1976.

ACORD itself also has responsibility for the Combined Heat and Power Group (CHPG) chaired by Dr Walter Marshall, the ex-D.En. Chief Scientist, which reports to the Secretary of State on the economic role of heat and power in the UK. The CHPG was set up towards the end of 1974 under the aegis of ACORD, and has already spawned the District Heating Working Party, chaired by a CEGB engineer. D.En. representatives are D. C. Gore and W. Macpherson, a senior principal scientific officer second in command to Gore in the electrical technology branch. (See Figure 5 for the organization of non-nuclear energy R and D.)

Branch 4 of the Energy Technology Division is the Chief Scientist Branch, headed by deputy chief scientific officer Dr R. G. S. Skipper. Skipper works directly for the Chief Scientist and his branch is responsible for day-to-day contact with ETSU, managing the energy R and D budget on the non-nuclear, non-marine side, and the general coordination of the various programmes on novel forms of energy in

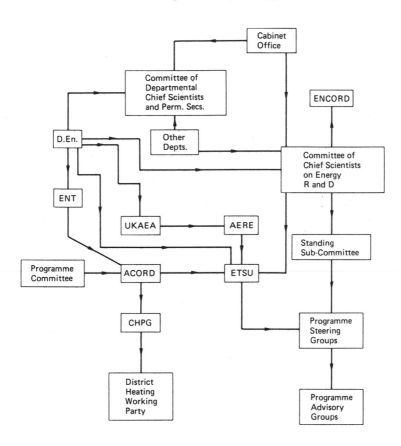

FIGURE 5   The organization of non-nuclear energy R and D

particular. Dr G. Preston, one of the two SPSOs in Branch 4, deals with D.En. contacts with EEC research. The final section of the Chief Scientist Group is the Offshore Technology Unit, lead by senior principal scientific officer M. S. Igglesden. This provides administrative and technical support to the Chief Scientist and acts as the secretariat for the Offshore Energy Technology Board. The OETB advises D.En. on the priorities and objectives of R and D relating to oil and gas policy. Its members include senior executives of major oil companies and the BGC. It is assisted by an OETB Programme Committee.

ESTABLISHMENT AND INFORMATION

There are two other divisions in D.En.: the Establishment Division and the Information Division. The Establishment Division is headed by under-secretary I. T. Manley, who was private secretary to Tony Benn when he was Minister of Technology. The division is responsible for all matters concerned with staffing, management and pay. The Information Division is led by the Director of Information (a rank roughly equivalent to under-secretary), and deals with press relations, information services and the department's own library. The director of information since March 1978 has been Ian Gillis, who was previously deputy director of information at DHSS. He was originally a news editor on the *Bristol Evening Post* before joining the government information service in the Ministry of Housing and Local Government in 1966; he moved to DHSS in 1969.

Tony Benn's term as Secretary of State for Energy has been remarkable for the number of public meetings and conferences at which energy policy has been discussed, and the openness of the department in publishing its working papers. The National Energy Conference held on 22 June 1976 was the first of these open forums, and was attended by about 400 people. The SCST were not convinced that a one-day conference would produce any useful discussion, as nobody would be able to speak for more than five or six minutes (HC534-ii, Session 1976/77, Q. 1981–1988), but there were a number of position papers produced which were then published (D. En. Energy Paper No. 13, vols 1 and 2, 1976). The Conference drew representatives from all the nationalized energy industries, the political parties, the trade unions, pressure groups and private industry, and provided the initiative for the formation of a permanent body to discuss energy policy matters. This was to be the Energy Commission, announced on 28 June 1977 (D.En. Press Notice, Ref. No. 348, 13 October 1977) in reply to a parliamentary question. Its terms of reference are: 'To advise and assist the Secretary of State for Energy on the development of a strategy for the energy sector in the United Kingdom, and to advise the Secretary of State on such specific aspects of energy policy as he may from time to time refer to them.' The Commission is chaired by the Secretary of State for Energy and both its working papers and minutes are published. The membership of twenty-four consists of seven energy industry representatives (NCB, Electricity Council, BGC, UKAEA, BNOC, SSEB, Petroleum Industry Advisory Committee), seven union representatives from the TUC Fuel and Power Industries Committee, eight representatives from other industries and consumer interests, the Secretary of State for Energy and the Minister of State, Scottish Office. Membership is at a high organizational level, for example the nationalized industries are all represented by their chairmen, so that the Commission is intended to consider general policy rather than the complexities of forecasts and analysis. The first meeting of the Commission was held on 28 November 1977, and it will meet about four times a year.

There are three other bodies, all administered through the Department of the Environment, which have a bearing on energy policy. The Royal Commission on Environmental Pollution (RCEP) under the chairmanship of Sir Brian Flowers produced the report *Nuclear Power and the Environment* (Cmnd 6618, 1976) which advised great caution in the development of the fast breeder reactor. It also suggested the establishment of two more committees, the Standing Commission on Energy and the Environment (CENE) and the Radioactive Waste Management Advisory Committee (RWMAC). The CENE first met in June 1978, under the chairmanship of Sir Brian Flowers, (no longer RCEP chairman), its terms of reference being 'to advise on the interaction between energy policy and the environment'. It has a membership of sixteen, four of whom are also on the RCEP and five on the Energy Commission. Two are also ex-RCEP members, and three are members of ACEC. The CENE has decided not to publish its working papers or minutes, and will not concentrate at present on nuclear power because of the work already done in this area by the RCEP. RWMAC has a membership of eighteen, including academics, nuclear industry representatives and one union representative. Its chairman is Sir Denys Wilkinson, a nuclear physicist, and it met for the first time in September 1978. The chairman of RCEP is now Professor Hans Kornberg, a biochemist. Several people hold office on more than one committee or commission, and this is intentional in the case of the overlap between Energy Commission, RCEP and CENE membership as they are expected to work closely. There are personal connections to a wide variety of committees. For example, Professor T. J. Chandler of the CENE was a member of the RCEP, is on the Natural Environment Research Council and the Health and Safety Commission; Dr A. W. Pearce is the chairman of Esso, and is a member of the CENE, ACEC and the Energy Commission. Many committee members are also members of the research councils and boards.

Other conferences also took place in 1977; the Sunningdale Seminar on Nuclear Policy was held on 13—14 May 1977 to allow ministers and officials to hear the various points of view on forthcoming policy decisions. D.En. participants included Sir Jack Rampton, B. G. Tucker (in charge of the Coal, Electricity and Atomic Energy Group), C. Herzig (under-secretary of the Atomic Energy Division) and both Benn's special advisers, but apparently none of them spoke in the seminar, according to the condensed 14-page version of the proceedings made available by D.En. There were also participants from other government departments, industry, the academic world and Friends of the Earth (FOE). Another conference, the Royal Institution Forum on Nuclear Power and the Energy Future, was held on 11—12 October 1977 and part of the proceedings was eventually televised. This was attended by all the usual sectional interests — nationalized energy industries, FOE, other pressure groups, D.En., academics — and happened at the end of a year when D.En. officials had been questioned in public about their assumptions and methods of working, at the Windscale inquiry on the reprocessing plant.

Thus the Department of Energy is seen to be an extremely open department as compared with most of the other British government departments. Criticisms of D.En. tend to hinge on its inflexibility and unwillingness to entertain new policies. For example, Anthony Tucker (1975) wrote '. . . it is becoming difficult to believe that Mr. Benn's department is capable of grasping the importance of any energy source that is neither nuclear nor written into elderly and theadbare policies'. Since 1975 policy options advanced by D.En. have changed quantitively rather than qualitatively, in spite of a great deal of well-researched criticism. Even the open government policy is still not always accepted as advantageous; Tony Benn intends to publish the transcripts of Energy Commission meetings '. . . so long as I can carry the Commission with me' (*Hansard*, 9 January 1978, col. 1244), which indicates some reluctance on the part of the commission. Although Benn does not appear to share his officials' views on nuclear policy, they do support his stance on publishing information, but whether a public debate will ensue is uncertain. At present, participation in discussions seems limited to the same set of industrial/government/pressure group interests, and even the Windscale inquiry received little popular media coverage.

The multiciplicity of organizations within D.En. and their

interrelationships means that it is difficult to locate a centre of power or decision-making. Clearly, though, two important groups are ACORD and WGES. ACORD sees all information relating to the initiation and conduct of research, and itself suggests new areas for investigation. Its chairman is the D.En. Chief Scientist, who has great personal influence over the department's research programme, merely by virtue of his presence on so many committees and working groups. WGES is the forum where the nationalized energy industries meet their nominal controllers at a level where policy and priorities can be discussed in detail, rather than in terms of generalized objectives as on the Energy Commission. The power of personal opinion inside the department is, to a great extent, an unknown factor; the most which can be deduced from the existence of particular working groups or the presence of the same people on a series of committees is a possible consistency of thinking in different policy areas. There are only a limited number of occasions on which D.En. officials are allowed to speak in public – for example, the SCST hearings – and these are invariably the higher civil servants. At least the profusion of committees, sub-committees, working groups, steering committees and advisory groups gives the impression of a thorough coverage of the whole complex energy field.

The intention behind the formation of the Department of Energy was to create a department which could look after energy interests as a whole, so that energy policy would be a coordinated entity rather than a piecemeal collection of short and medium term policies applied separately to each nationalized industry. D.En. has only been in existence four years, and took its original structure from the DTI divisions concerned with energy. It has made internal reorganizations, some very recent, and has had to cope with the enormous financial and international complexities of North Sea Oil with a small staff. It also has to deal with the nationalized energy industries via tenuous and vague forms of control, which in the main imply control through consensus rather than directive. The objective of D.En., as set out in the official definition, is to be responsible for '. . . the development of national policies in relation to all forms of energy. . .'. The adequate development of policy depends to a great degree on the methods available for control of the various energy industries, the degree of accountability of the multinationals and the financial resources of the department itself. Legislation can change the relationship between nationalized industries and the responsible minister, while multinationals can be induced to cooperate with a variety of tax controls and other incentives. The finances of the department help determine the amount and direction of the research effort, which has important implications for future policy; policy decisions and research priorities tend to reinforce each other. To understand further the internal workings of D.En., it is necessary to know how the spending application cycle of government functions, so that any analysis of D.En. is made with an awareness of the effects of government and Treasury pressures which may not have direct relevance to energy policy.

4 The Tools of Public Expenditure Control

> The examination, control and planning of public expenditure are facets of the same process, and include the subsequent verification that expenditures have in fact been carried out in accordance with the intentions of Parliament and of the government.   (From a Treasury memorandum to the Select Committee on Expenditure [HC549, Session 1970/71, p. 17])

The process referred to by the Treasury is the annual and continuing cycle of expenditure estimates, bargaining and allocation. The present method of allocation, the Public Expenditure Survey System (referred to as PESC from the Public Expenditure Survey Committee), was instituted in 1961. Its use results in the annual White Paper published around the turn of the year, the latest one being *The Government's Expenditure Plans 1978–79 to 1981–82* (Cmnd 7049, vols I and II, 1978). The spending plan is split up into individual programmes, and energy related matters feature in three of these. The Trade, Industry and Employment programme contains the estimates for energy research, including the separate nuclear allocation; some support for the nationalized industries also come under this heading. The main bulk of spending on the nationalized energy industries comes under the programme for government lending to nationalized industries, while any energy research financed by, for example, the Science Research Council, comes within the Education and Libraries, Science and Arts programme. The programmes themselves are not given in any great detail, so it is impossible to judge, for example, how much money is being spent on R and D for novel energy sources. After publication of the expenditure plans they are discussed in Parliament and when eventually they are passed the public money is paid into the Exchequer account at the Bank of England. The Treasury alone can draw on this account, and it releases funds to each department at the same time as checking up on how the funds are spent.

PESC came about as a result of Treasury dissatisfaction with the fragmented, short term picture of public expenditure which the old system provided. In the 1950s the Treasury found that it had great difficulty in controlling future departmental expenditure commitments; as control could only be exercised year by year, a small initial outlay on a project could lead irretrievably to eventual high expenditure. The stop-go policies of governments throughout the 1950s also spelt further difficulty for the Treasury as it tried to cut budgets immediately to tally with periods of worsening financial conditions, and found departments resisting because their plans dealt with longer term requirements. The House Select Committee on Estimates was set up as a result of Treasury unhappiness, and its report was followed by the formation of the Plowden Committee on the Control of Public Expenditure in 1959. It reported in July 1961, and recommended a system of forecasting of expenditure represented by costings of existing policies which would enable comparisons to be made between policies. The system was to cover all public expenditure irrespective of how it was financed, and expenditure was to be analysed by function (health, for example) and by economic category. Most importantly, the estimates were to cover a period of five years.

The first PESC exercise was carried out in 1961, and the method was used without basic changes until 1967, possibly in a spirit of discovery, as two observers have pointed out: 'It is sufficient now to observe that no one, not even those in charge of making the new procedure a reality, understood precisely how it would turn out. They improvised for several years, sometimes buffeted by events, other times seizing on an unexpected opportunity' (Heclo and Wildavsky, 1974, p. 209). By 1967 PESC appeared to be failing because it concentrated on expenditures in the current year and projections for five years hence, leaving the years between to look after themselves. The estimates needed to be made complete, by planning exact targets for the second, third and fourth years as well, and this innovation began in 1968. Since 1968 further refinements have been added, most of them reducing the length of time between estimates or increasing Treasury monitoring. The results of PESC are now published as the White Paper on public spending plans, and analyses by spending authority and broad resource area have been added.

The annual timetable for PESC is as follows (HC549, Session 1970/71, p. 20):

December	Instructions on the conduct of the coming year's survey are issued by the Treasury.
end February	Spending departments submit preliminary expenditure returns to the Treasury.
March–April	Discussions take place between the Treasury and individual spending departments to reach agreement on figures and underlying policy and statistical assumptions – agreement here meaning no more than an identity of view on what present policies are and on the probable cost of continuing them.
May	A draft report on public expenditure is drawn up by the Treasury and considered by the PESC.
June	The report is submitted to ministers.
July–October	Decisions are taken on the aggregate of public expenditure and its broad allocation to the major functional heads.

Thus when the January White Paper is published, the PESC process for the following year is just beginning. The timetable is clearly a simplification of actual events, and the March/April period of discussion between the Treasury and the spending departments conceals a great deal of haggling and bargaining. The basically simple PESC proposition of looking at present policies and projecting them into the future is immediately confused when there is disagreement about the content of present policy. When the Treasury and the departments have settled their differences (after referral to a higher level if necessary), the draft report is passed on to the Public Expenditure Survey Committee itself. This committee is composed of the department principal finance officers and Treasury officials, and is chaired by a Treasury deputy secretary. When the PESC report is complete it goes to the Cabinet along with the Treasury estimate of economic prospects for the coming year, whereupon further bargaining and (often) cutting takes place to produce the final White Paper. Although PESC has worked fairly well in that it has enabled both the Treasury and the departments to see the future implications of present spending policies, events still combine to make the PESC figures differ dramatically from the Treasury economic forecasts. In the late 1960s several emergency cuts in public expenditure were necessary, much to Richard Crossman's annoyance:

The PESC meeting has become our regular July exercise. Its job is to keep the growth of public-sector expenditure in line with the growth of the economy. This year it had been found that although the rate of economic growth had declined, the growth of Government expenditure had jumped from $4\frac{1}{2}$ per cent, the level at which we wanted to keep it, to something like 10 per cent. As part of our regular process of Government, therefore, there had to be something of a cut-back. What was clear to me was that it was useless to attempt this regular annual cut-back until we had seen the crisis measures which were being prepared behind our backs. It took most of my colleagues a full hour before they grasped that official Whitehall was busy quietly working out a precise package of cuts for announcement on Wednesday while we Ministers were sitting round the table blithely discussing the remote possibility of retrenchment. . . . It was already clear that over the weekend the centralized mandarin machine had once again been put to work, working out a desperate programme without Cabinet knowing about it.   (Crossman, 1975, pp. 572–3)

The problem in the late 1970s has more often been one of underspending, caused by difficulties in forecasting due to the high inflation rates and by the introduction of cash limits on spending. These limits were introduced in 1977 and resulted in a 4 per cent underspending, as departments were careful not to reach their projected figures, which have now changed from plans to effective ceilings. The Treasury deputy secretary responsible for PESC, J. Anson of the General Expenditure section, was cross-examined by the Select Committee on Public Expenditure (General) Sub-Committee in January 1978 concerning underspending. He said that it was a normal tendency for people who came under spending controls to undershoot, and the object of the exercise was to provide a figure in the knowledge that there would be a shortfall. He went on to say that it was not possible to counteract this tendency by increasing spending totals, as different areas underspent each year, and that '. . . more experience of the new system and lower inflation should make for more accurate estimates' (Carvel, 1978). So although PESC is certainly seen to be an improvement on the previous short term methodology, it still requires constant modification to suit particular circumstances.

The other main control mechanism within the Treasury is Programme Analysis and Review (PAR), which originated as an idea put forward by the businessmen drafted into government as consultants by Edward Heath's new Conservative government in 1970. PAR was announced in January 1971, and the Select Committee on Public Expenditure (Steering Sub-Committee) had the details explained to it a year later by the businessman who had spent most time working on the concept, R. J. East, a special adviser to the Chief Secretary to the Treasury. He said '. . . Programme Analysis and Review is not a technique; it is, in this day and age of accelerating change, a systematic approach to general management' (HC147, Session 1971/72, Q. 57). He went on to explain that PAR was introduced to improve government effectiveness in five areas:

1. Collective decision-making; government needed to be able to compare major programmes both within and across departmental boundaries.
2. Selection of issues for depth study; this would facilitate the development of strategic options before the passage of time eliminated most of them. It was especially useful at a time when problems were becoming more complex, there was an accelerating rate of change in the environment, good policy analysts were scarce, and it was felt necessary to reduce the time taken by decision making while increasing the amount of public participation.
3. Development of programme objectives; this would '. . . help highlight and contrast the real nature of the subjective political choice facing society' (HC147, Session 1971/72, Q. 57).
4. Creating time at top management level for reviewing strategic analysis; this was necessary as governments exist for five years at the most but many decisions are of a truly long term nature.
5. The need to structure basic information systems; it was necessary to identify key emerging issues, as '. . . one of the great hazards of strategic planning is the danger of disappearing under irrelevant information' (HC147, Session 1971/72, Q. 57).

A Treasury official, under-secretary K. E. Couzens (now second permanent secretary of the Treasury), was also present at the Select Committee hearing, and he said that: 'PAR is essentially about objectives and alternative ways of achieving them' (HC147, Session 1971/72, Q. 58). He stated that a powerful impact was made on the effort given to PAR work by the fact that it was being done for collective consideration by ministers. He described it as an approach to review of policy which uses all the techniques available, and said that it was intended to provide a more informed basis for political judgement rather than act as a substitute for it. Of course, analytical studies of particular topics had always been carried out within departments, but PAR was more directly related to financial problems not catered for within PESC, such as policies which had no initial effect on expenditure and matters which exceeded the five year PESC term.

At first PAR was not accepted by the departments because it was the responsibility of the Civil Service Department (CSD), not the Treasury, thus there was no obvious incentive for departments to cooperate. PAR is now run by the Treasury, using a PAR Committee (PARC) of departmental representatives and Treasury under-secretaries, and the system is working, although quite how still remains a mystery: '. . . the myth . . . is intensified by the secrecy which lays down that no mortal in the ordinary public should know how PAR actually works. The fact is that there is little agreement on the nature of analytic studies. If men have difficulty defining what is good policy, then they are likely to be hard-put to state precisely the ingredients of a good analysis leading to better policy' (Heclo and Wildavsky, 1974, p. 281). Thus the formal definition of PAR requirements as given by R. J. East (see above) is subject to negotiations between Treasury and department officials.

When PAR reports are finally prepared, they are supposed to be useful at a ministerial level to help in decision-making across departmental barriers, but in practice they are little read or thought about. At Cabinet level there are two committees dealing specifically with PAR: the Steering Committee which is concerned with the selection of issues for PAR, and the Management Committee which looks after progress. Apart from within these committees, PAR reports are not regarded as very important: 'The actions of one Cabinet committee – which placed a PAR report at the bottom of its agenda for two months and eventually concluded an hour's half-hearted discussion by calling for further studies – is characteristic' (Heclo and Wildavsky, 1974, p. 296). Ministers and top officials do not have the time to read the reports, and they seem to have done nothing to enhance collective decision-making. A good PAR can change the direction of a department in a way which the yearly PESC cannot do, as it is concerned with spending as well as cutting. The Treasury, naturally, is not enthusiastic about PARs which represent new expenditure. PAR seems to have had less overall effect than PESC because it is aimed at improving a task somewhat alien to British government, collective decision-making. PESC, with its mass of yearly and monthly figures, provides ample opportunity for spending ministers to battle for their departments' allocation in Cabinet; PAR often emphasizes spending and new programmes, which to ministers from other departments simply means cuts in their own budgets. Thus the backbone of the government spending cycle is provided by PESC and its timetable as it runs throughout the year. PAR is merely an additional layer, perhaps used fully only when the results agree with some programme in need of extra support.

The spending cycle moves on, year after year, with each year's cuts and new programmes affecting the next year's, within and between departments. It is reasonably easy to explain the theoretical workings of PESC and the objectives of PAR, but far harder to actually find out what happens during, say, the months of March and April when discussions take place between the Treasury and the spending departments. The inner workings of Whitehall are relevant not only to Treasury matters but to all departments; most of the proceedings of the D. En. committees and working groups are kept secret, as often is the existence of the groups and committees themselves, and this occurs even in D. En. with its growing reputation for openness. Brittan condemned this 'obsession with secrecy' because one result was that: 'It becomes more important to keep one's thoughts on policy confidential than to get them right' (Brittan, 1969, p. 33). Secrecy is encouraged by the Official Secrets Act, which makes it a criminal offence for a civil servant to communicate any information to an unauthorized person, and by the doctrine of ministerial responsibility for policy which means that '. . . the advice given to them is on a par with the confessional' (Brittan, 1969, p. 32). It is important to try and understand what actually goes on in government departments, to see how the basic rules of the spending cycle and the committee structures are interpreted and modified by personal contacts.

5 Unofficial Government

. . . it is possible for a major Whitehall Department, the Treasury above all, so to ordain events as to drive Ministers to adopt policies which they find repugnant but to which there is, apparently, no alternative. (Haines, 1977, p. 228)

Joe Haines was not alone in his judgement of the effect of Whitehall on Labour governments in particular. Haines was Press Secretary to Harold Wilson from 1969 to 1976, and his feelings echo those of Richard Crossman, who was a member of Wilson's government, and Marcia Williams, Wilson's Personal and Political Secretary. The Conservative view of the Treasury is similar; Jock Bruce-Gardyne and Nigel Lawson, who have both had experience as Conservative MPs, felt that Treasury influence endured whatever the outcome of its policies, and ministers continued to be overawed by its reputation (Bruce-Gardyne and Lawson, 1976). One of the few books to illuminate the reality behind this fearsome reputation is Heclo and Wildavsky (1974). They talked to many high ranking civil servants and quoted them (anonymously) at length, concentrating mainly on treasury officials. It is impossible to portray the Treasury atmosphere without going into great detail, but a few illustrations should suffice to give an idea of what happens on the inside.

Departmental PFOs are the link between the department and the Treasury; they negotiate the yearly budget. Their position is difficult, as the needs of their departments require that they should obtain as good a deal as possible, without incurring the wrath of the Treasury, which may produce cuts or lack of cooperation in years to come. They need to be trusted by both parties:

Conflict with department policy people can be mitigated if the finance officer is able to show them he is looking after their interests. He tells them what the financial pressures are likely to be, whether they should be prepared for decreases or can plan on the expectation of increases. He advises them of the specific view on policies held by Treasury officials. Yet his departmental colleagues may not always like what they hear, and, what is worse, they may not believe it. One way of overcoming this distrust is to take policy officials along for discussions so that they can see you are not selling them down the river to the Treasury. (Heclo and Wildavsky, 1974, pp. 123–4)

The PFOs have to emphasize their honesty at all times, and not ask the Treasury for too much and impair their credibility. They have to be tough with their departments in order to encourage the Treasury to trust them, hoping in the long run that this will be to their advantage and the Treasury will agree with the PFOs' judgements. A good PFO can considerably increase the departmental budget, as one permanent secretary commented: 'If he inspires confidence at the Treasury, the range of difference might be 85 to 125 per cent' (Heclo and Wildavsky, 1974, p. 121).

PFOs are often concerned in deals with the Treasury, which may, for example, guarantee budget growth at a certain rate in return for a limit on programme expansion. Deals are worked out by going to see the 'right chap' at the Treasury, and convincing all parties involved that it is to their advantage. Sometimes the bargaining is less about money than principles, as one former Treasury official and permanent secretary said: 'To the uninstructed it will seem like sheer rubbish to argue about £0.5 million out of £100 million. But the purpose is not the figure – arithmetically it may not matter. What does matter is to keep the idea of discipline and control' (Heclo and Wildavsky, 1974, p. 89). At all times there is an interchange of views between department and Treasury. A top Treasury official says: 'There is a necessary ritual dance. He inflates to enable you to cut and you bargain him down to show you can cut.' (Heclo and Wildavsky, 1974, p. 89) Even in mechanisms such as PESC, with its timetable and clear objectives, haggling is rife. Simply to continue existing policy without argument may be impossible; a PFO said 'Existing policy is one of those delightful phrases that one exploits as well as one can' (Heclo and Wildavsky, 1974, p. 217). Once again it is the general nature of the argument that is important, rather than specific figures; a Treasury official: 'If people fuss that the figures aren't good, I don't care and I never did care. What is important is the framework – creating habits of mind' (Heclo and Wildavsky, 1974, p. 234). Overall the Treasury is a highly suspicious and critical institution, highly politically sensitive and with a culture of its own. Personal contact is very important, and although there is a constant flow of papers around the Treasury, 'the chat' is frequently used to settle issues. Heclo and Wildavsky refer to the chat as 'one of the most vital phenomena of British Government' and pinpoint the incessant gossip as one of the compensations for arduous Treasury work. The stream of personal contacts mean that Treasury officials take account of their opinion of other officials as well as what is actually said in meetings. 'Co-ordination in the Treasury is based, above all, on a never ending round of personal contacts among people who know each other and who have a strong professional interest in talking about their work' (Heclo and Wildavsky, 1974, p. 71).

It is not simply the Treasury as such which has an influence over government affairs, it is their great range of contacts: 'Amidst the "magic circle" of the Permanent Secretaries in Whitehall the former Treasury men are rightly regarded by the rest as almost a mafia – a "family" whose members are to be found at the key points in the whole Civil Service network' (Bruce-Gardyne and Lawson, 1976, p. 162). Sir Jack Rampton, the D.En. Permanent Under-Secretary, was a Treasury Under-Secretary in 1964–68, so presumably he is to be regarded as a part of this 'mafia'. Marcia Williams felt that the Civil Service in general were remote from reality, unaccountable, and given to following their own policies. The classic account of a new minister's meeting with a department was given in the Crossman *Diaries*:

> The whole Department is there to support the Minister. Into his in-tray come hour by hour notes with suggestions as to what he should do. Everything is done to sustain him in the line which officials think he should take. But if one is very careful and conscious one is aware that this supporting soft framework of recommendations is the result of a great deal of secret discussion between the civil servants below. There is a constant debate as to how the Minister should be advised or, shall we say, directed and pushed and cajoled into the line required by the Ministry. There is a tremendous esprit de corps in the Ministry and the whole hierarchy is determined to preserve its own policy. Each Ministry has its own departmental policy, and this policy goes on while Ministers come and go.   (Crossman, 1975, p. 31)

Thus there is certainly a pattern of Treasury influence through other departments, and departmental influence in government, often acting through personal contacts. Indeed it would be strange if this pattern did not exist, given the small number and common backgrounds of top officials. According to Sheriff (1976, p. 13), two thirds of the administrators in the higher Civil Service have Oxbridge backgrounds, and this figure is rising. This lack of variation in the Civil Service world view sometimes produces a situation where top officials seemingly become insular and more attached to the functioning of policy than its content. In fact: 'What they do affects the real world mightily, but they know little of it at first hand' (*The Economist*, 3 September 1977, p. 24).

The inherent overwork associated with the small number of higher officials does nothing to alleviate the slightly incestuous nature of civil service life. Lord Strang, Permanent Under-Secretary in the Foreign Office in 1949–50, described his daily routine as follows:

> Experience tends to show that, if the job is to be done with due conscientiousness, the hours must normally be twelve or upwards a day. . . . I look back on my mornings as times of stress, when the day's work loomed up like a mountain in one's path . . . the routine files would be arriving on my desk. . . . These were disposed of in the intervals between interviews and other consultations. . . . By about five o'clock the back of the most arduous part of the day's work was usually broken. . . . I could look forward to a relatively undisturbed period in which to dispose of papers . . . [which] began to flow in from about six o'clock onwards. . . . It was less of a strain to spend an extra hour or two quietly working at night than to face an accumulated residue in the morning, in addition to the pressing problems of the new day. . . . The major restriction was naturally the concentration of one's working attention almost exclusively upon one's job.   (Rose, 1969, pp. 137–42)

The pressure of work is the same for ministers as for their officials; soon after Richard Crossman became Minister of Housing he complained that his department '. . . have begun to insulate me from real life with the papers and the red boxes that I bring home with me' (Crossman, 1975, p. 30).

Treasury influence, overwork and the general effect of government by a group of people with much the same background prevail in all departments, but there is little specific evidence of how D.En. works. Tony Benn has been described as: '. . . one of the most hard-working people I've met, rising at an early hour and entering his office at the crack of dawn, much to the astonishment of his civil servants. This quickly instilled in them the idea that they were perpetually late for work. For Tony it was not an act of pretence or a demonstration, it was how he operates' (Williams, 1975, p. 254); and he also: '. . . has a passion for drawing up plans. His office is awash with them. Visitors gaze with wonderment at the latest home-made wallchart, depicting the organisation of the energy industry . . .' (Young, 1978). Thus D.En. appears to be as overworked as any other department, with disagreement between Benn and his Permanent Secretary, Sir Jack Rampton, over the reactor choice issue in early 1978. Sir Jack told the SCST in 1976 that he had had eight Secretaries of State during the four years in which he had been responsible for energy matters. He appeared to agree with Crossman's view that departmental policy endured despite changes of minister: 'In practice, I think there has been a very real element of continuity about energy policies which have been the policies of successive Governments and successive Ministers' (HC534-ii, session 1976/77, Q. 1742). He did not see the constant ministerial changes as any problem, except for the initial period required while ministers gained a feel for the subject if they had had no previous experience in the field.

The Civil Service clearly has an effect on policy-making, mainly by virtue of its continuity in the face of changes of government. This point is felt more strongly by incoming Labour governments – which are likely to want radical changes in policy – than Conservative governments which fit in more easily with the inherent official conservatism. Ministers and top officials are overworked and therefore have little time to think about the implications of changes in policy, especially those with long term effects which are so important at D.En. The basic system of government, with its maximum five year span, does nothing to encourage putting forward thinking into practice, especially in fields where there is no immediate and apparent electoral gain. The Civil Service trend appears to be towards consolidation of positions within the department and with respect to the Treasury. Official efforts in some cases concentrate more on the provision of finance than its ultimate destination, an attitude encouraged by the network of relationships and the premium placed on compromise and agreement. There is also a lack of personal responsibility for the outcome of decisions, leading to what has been termed 'the unimportance of being right' (Henderson, 1977, p. 190); the special advisers have been brought in specifically to provide high level personal advice to ministers. Administrative control proceeds via a system of bargaining, compromise and high level huddles indulged in, as a Treasury official put it, ' . . . by a small group of people who grew up together' (Heclo and Wildavsky, 1974, p. 76). This incessant incestuous discussion is bound to have an inhibiting effect on innovatory policies. In the case of D.En., the discussions and negotiations have added complications as they occur with the nationalized industries as well as within the department. The many organizations, from the nationalized energy industries and the research councils to the pressure groups and European energy bodies, all have to liaise with each other and with the government, often through a D.En. committee or official. Here again, the structure, roles and responsibilities of the various groups are complex, but pressure from outside the government certainly has a profound effect on energy decision-making, especially where the nationalized energy industries are concerned. To understand how energy policy finally evolves, the role and function of each organization connected with the energy industry needs to be considered, as viewed by the organization itself and by the D.En. and the other organizations. Perspectives on energy policy differ according to the sectional interests involved, and policy may develop as a response to the power of the interest groups.

6 The Energy Industry

Energy supply and distribution in Britain is largely controlled by nine public enterprises, some of which have holdings in private firms. In England and Wales, electricity is supplied by the Central Electricity Generating Board (CEGB), and policy is formulated by the Electricity Council. In Scotland, electricity supply is the responsibility of the South of Scotland Electricity Board (SSEB) and the North of Scotland Hydro-Electric Board (NoSHEB), while in Northern Ireland a new authority, the Northern Ireland Electricity Service (NIES), is responsible. This started operating in 1973. The British Gas Corporation (BGC) and the National Coal Board (NCB) are both fully nationalized bodies, while the United Kingdom Atomic Energy Authority (UKAEA) and the British National Oil Corporation (BNOC) have varying degrees of holdings in private industry. BNOC is the newest public corporation, having been set up in January 1976. These corporations form the basis of the energy industry, here taken in its broadest sense as meaning all semi- or non-governmental organizations in the energy field. Apart from the bodies directly interested in energy supply, there are various research boards, such as the Science Research Council (SRC) and the National Research Development Corporation (NRDC), which include energy research in their activities, and the plethora of interest and cause groups concerned with energy and the environment. One of the most active of these is Friends of the Earth (FOE) but new ones such as SCRAM (Scottish Campaign to Resist the Atomic Menace) are continually forming and older groups, for example the Town and Country Planning Association (TCPA), are finding that their interests are now affected by energy policy decisions. There are also groups within the British political system, such as the party energy groups, which have no direct influence on government decisions, as well as trade union interest groups. At a higher level, British energy policy is affected by all the European bodies concerned with energy; the European Coal and Steel Community (ECSC) and the EEC Energy Council, to name but two.

Most of these organizations relate to each other by way of common representation, official lines of responsibility or through governing bodies. They all have a particular view of energy policy and their role in its formulation and execution, and these views are often conflicting. Most organizations have a perspective on policy which extends well beyond their actual responsibilities, and alliances of groups may form and reform as new questions arise and specific sectional interests gain in importance. One role of the Department of Energy is to reconcile the differing opinions and come up with a policy acceptable to all interests which still meets the requirements of national energy policy. However, D.En. can also impose its own views if it thinks fit; D.En., or any of the other organizations for that matter, may take differing roles to deal with different organizations, or change roles over the various stages of policy-making. The relationship between the government and the nationalized industries has undergone many changes over the years, and the initial reasons for the nationalization of an industry have not always been made clear. The purpose of bringing an industry into public ownership can be to achieve political, social or economic objectives, and it is rarely that specific reasons have been made explicit, or the objectives of an industry have been clearly defined.

The nationalization of the energy industries (coal, gas and electricity), between 1945 and 1950 under the Labour government was prompted by the need to set up some form of centralized planning for these industries. The nationalization acts did not give each industry any clear objectives, financial or otherwise, but the Conservative government of 1951−64 made few changes in their constitutions. The Select Committee on Nationalized Industries (SCNI) was established in 1957 to increase the accountability of the industries to Parliament, and in 1961 a White Paper was produced, *The Financial and Economic Obligations of the Nationalised Industries* (Cmnd 1337, 1961). This was a response to criticisms made by the SCNI concerning the lack of economic discipline within some of the nationalized industries. The White Paper suggested that certain financial objectives should be set for each industry, and that investment decisions should be discussed more thoroughly between the industry and the sponsoring department of the government. After the production of the White Paper, specific financial targets were agreed for most of the nationalized industries, but the system was found to be imprecise and rather irrelevant to the needs of the economy as a whole.

The Labour Party returned to power in 1964, and considered the state of the nationalized industries in a White Paper: *Nationalised Industries – a Review of Economic and Financial Objectives* (Cmnd 3437, 1967). The idea of financial targets for each industry was condoned and strengthened, although the role of the industries in the economy as a whole was ignored. A standard test discount rate (TDR) of 8 per cent was suggested, so that investment proposals could be assessed on the same criteria throughout the nationalized sector. The government did take a broad view of investment policy, saying that social as well as financial returns should be considered when making investment decisions; this attitude was a development of the 1961 White Paper view that commercial, economic and social considerations could be reduced to one financial target. The 1967 White Paper was an improvement on the previous system of financial guidance, as it took into account a wider range of problems than the 1961 White Paper, and showed that the government realized that financial targets were an imperfect form of control. To compensate for this, the government stated that it would have no objections if an industry failed to meet its target in a particular year, providing there were good long term economic reasons. The 1967 White Paper was a first attempt to let the management of the nationalized industries work towards specific financial targets, with as little government intervention as possible.

The next official pronouncement on the nationalized industries was the July 1968 report of the SCNI (HC371-i, ii, iii, Session 1967/68) concerning ministerial control. Their inquiry was thorough, the evidence – from the industries, the sponsoring departments and ministers, and interested academics – running to 700 pages, and the main conclusion reached was that the efficiency of the nationalized industries was deteriorating due to a confusion of purposes between their management and their sponsoring departments. Their suggested remedy was a Ministry of Nationalized Industries, which would take over responsibility for ensuring the efficiency of all the nationalized industries. Policy-making functions would be retained by the original sponsoring departments. The new ministry would be able to make better use of the staff available – one of the criticisms in the report concerned departmental staff movements, which the SCNI felt were too rapid to produce any continuity of experience or development of expertise. They realized that this point was similar to that made by the Fulton Committee on the Civil Service, and recommended that the government should bear the

SCNI views in mind when discussing the Fulton Report (Cmnd 3638, 1968). They also felt that the arrangements for exchanges of staff between industries and ministries were useful and should be continued, although the Civil Service view of the matter appeared to be that it was a complex process, requiring much planning if it was to be of any real benefit to either side.

The government reply to the SCNI was published in a White Paper (Cmnd 4027, 1969) nearly a year later, and the main recommendation for a Ministry of Nationalized Industries was rejected on the grounds that it would be less efficient than the present system of control. The government felt that the SCNI had not realized the difficulties of dividing the sector and efficiency responsibilities between two ministries; problems might include the need for two ministers to be involved in discussions rather than one, and the chance of conflicts of interest within departments becoming conflicts between departments. Some smaller points were accepted in the White Paper, such as the proposals for more discussions on common problems between the industries and their sponsoring departments, and between the Treasury, the Department of Economic Affairs and the sponsoring departments concerning investment control. Thus there was little real change in the organization of the sponsoring departments after the SCNI report, and little change in the structure of the Civil Service after the Fulton Report, which was produced a month earlier.

After a period of Conservative government, the next inquiry into the nationalized industries was launched by Labour in June 1975 when the National Economic Development Office was asked to investigate 'their role in the economy and control in the future'. Their report was published just over a year later (NEDO, 1976) and contained two main recommendations which they hoped would increase the accountability of the industries. These were to be the introduction of policy councils and corporation boards. NEDO saw the policy councils (for each industry) as being responsible for the general aims, objectives and strategies of the industry, while the corporation boards would be the executive authorities. Policy councils were to be composed of representatives of the main interest groups, sponsoring departments and the Treasury, while corporation boards would consist of people working in the corporation. These recommendations, similar in theory although set at a different level in the management structure to those of the SCNI, resulted from the same type of criticism — inadequate accountability and confused responsibilities – as those contained in the SCNI report. NEDO felt that the relationship between the industries and the departments was deteriorating because of too much government intervention. They suggested that financial controls and targets should be tailored to suit individual industries, and that the minister's ability to intervene should be more closely regulated by the introduction of specific powers of direction and less restrictive general powers of direction. NEDO looked closely at the staffing of the sponsoring departments, and was dissatisfied, again for the same reasons as the SCNI eight years previously; they felt that a greater degree of job continuity was necessary, and that needless misunderstandings arose through confusion over the exact role of the civil servants. The staff of the sponsoring departments were described as performing several functions, including ensuring that broad social, industrial and national considerations were taken into account by the industries; advising on government policies for whole sectors such as energy; safeguarding public funds; advocating the corporations' interests in Whitehall; and answering parliamentary questions. They added that: 'While many functions are derived directly from provisions of the nationalisation statutes and subsequent legislation, it is a universal assumption among civil servants that these statutes cannot be interpreted in a restrictive or legalistic manner for the purposes of defining their precise functions and relationships with corporations' (NEDO, 1976, p. 25). There were several criticisms from corporation board members that civil servants were unaware of the consequences for an industry of a change in policy, that departmental disagreements were left to the industries to reconcile, and that although there was a lack of long term policies (especially in the energy sector), too many short term interventions were made, which were then out of context with any overall strategic plan. The NEDO report also made the point that the roles and aims of the corporations were rarely made public, even though they were normally to be found in the corporate plans. The boards appeared to see themselves as performing an essentially commercial role, but the ministers and civil servants were not always agreed on this, therefore more uncertainties appeared.

A year and a half later, the government published their reply to the NEDO report, a White Paper entitled *The Nationalised Industries* (Cmnd 7131, 1978). Earlier in the year, the SCNI had had a much publicized row with the British Steel Corporation, in which they eventually forced BSC to provide confidential information on its finances, an unusual victory for a select committee. The White Paper began by rejecting the main NEDO proposals for policy councils and corporation boards on the grounds that they would slow down decision-making — a similar reason to that given for rejecting the SCNI's proposed Ministry of Nationalized Industries. The government did, however, agree to the introduction of specific powers of direction for ministers, and stated that the corporate plan should have a central place in the relationship between each industry and its sponsoring department. One result of the NEDO criticisms of the lack of a long term energy policy, along with other developments in this field, was that strategic planning in the energy sector was now seen to be at a more advanced state than in any other area. The government felt that the benefits of the planning process were

. . . already becoming apparent in the energy sector where over the past year or so a joint Working Group on Energy Strategy (with membership drawn at board level from the nationalised industries and from government departments) has contributed materially to the harmonization of planning timetables and procedures, to the understanding of the industries' and Government's medium-term forecasting methods, and in particular to the joint examination of the implications of alternative energy sector strategies for the plans and prospects of the industries.   (Cmnd 7131, 1978, para. 43)

The White Paper made one important change in the financial framework for the industries, namely developing the 1967 principle of the TDR into a required rate of return on investment (RRR). The advantage of the RRR was that it was more flexible than the TDR, as it focused on the return from an industry's investment as a whole, rather than from specific projects. The RRR was set at 5 per cent, from a consideration of the average recent rates of return obtained by private companies. The White Paper also suggested more indicators for monitoring the performance of the industries, such as the publication of forward projections; the whole of the financial and economic section of the paper was taken up with refining and improving the previous system of controls, but with few basic procedural changes. In spite of the amount of criticism of Civil Service staffing arrangements and responsibilities contained in the NEDO report, no mention was made of changes in sponsoring departments.

Although the White Paper stated that it set out: '. . . proposals designed to reconcile the purposes of public ownership with the independence needed for vigorous and enterprising management; and to ensure that the nationalised industries employ resources efficiently to the benefit of the whole community' (Cmnd 7131, 1978, para. 2), the purposes of public ownership were not given. This is consistent with other government papers on the national industries, but does not assist the attempt to formulate objectives; the publication of the corporate plans may reveal more government thinking in this area. The overall view of the White Paper was that a flexible approach was necessary because of the diversity of the industries involved, and that this approach should include financial targets and give the industries the opportunity to reach those targets without government intervention, such as the price restraint of the early 1970s. Not all the nationalized industries have been given their particular targets as yet, but it seems that the Labour government wants a fully commercialized approach to the market from each industry. Although overall sectoral planning is to be encouraged, there is still to be a great deal of freedom for each industry, particularly in the matter of pricing, where the White Paper comments: '. . . it is primarily for each nationalised industry to work out the details of its prices with regard to its markets and its overall objectives, including its financial target' (Cmnd 7131, 1978, para. 68). Pricing in the energy sector was the subject of heated discussion between the coal, electricity and gas chairmen in early 1978, showing that the interests of individual industries have not yet been resolved. The production of an overall energy policy has made little impression on the pricing argument as yet, showing the difficulty of reconciling commercial and strategic interests of the various industries.

The nationalized industries, their sponsoring ministers and departments and the Treasury are not the only bodies with responsibility for formulating energy policy, although they carry a great deal of weight in discussion because of their financial commitments and influence in government. There is a continuous discussion, both within government and between D.En. in particular and various concerned groups, ranging from unions to interest groups and academics. Discussion occurs at all levels of policy-making, and it is difficult to know the precise effect which any one group will have on the system as a whole. However, it is necessary to understand the internal workings of each organization in order to ascertain their view of energy policy and their role in its formulation.

NATIONAL COAL BOARD

The history of the British coal industry is not a happy one, with its strikes, contractions and expansions. Before the First World War Britain was the world's leading coal exporter, and in spite of the loss of some export markets due to the war, there was a coal shortage during the war years because of demand for fuel from the navy. After 1918, demand was still high even though oil was beginning to challenge the dominance of coal as the leading energy source, and in 1920 the Mines Department of the Board of Trade was set up to cope with the organization of the industry. The early 1920s were boom years, but the slump of 1926 culminated in the General Strike; this lasted for only one week of 1926, but the coal-miners were out for nearly seven months. The slump continued until the start of the Second World War, and Britain's share of the world coal market decreased. The war itself caused a coal shortage, and in 1942 the government took control of the industry by setting up the National Coal Board. This was not full nationalization, but dual control, whereby the government was responsible for supervising the affairs of the industry but ownership was left in private hands. In 1943, the coal shortage was so severe that conscription was introduced for miners (the Bevin Boys), and by 1945 the reserves were becoming depleted. The seams were not being worked out so much as deteriorating in quality, thus the cost of coal production increased and productivity fell. There was a strong political and union movement for full nationalization of the mines, and this took place on 1 January 1947, with the NCB as the controlling body.

The NCB was meant to be largely independent of the government, as it had no civil servants on its board, but it was given specific instructions by the government on issues such as the machinery for consultation with the miners and with consumers. The minister responsible for the industry also had final control over investment plans, but the Board was left to itself to decide how to carry out the bulk of its duties concerned with the supplying of coal and developing the industry. The NCB inherited a serious coal crisis, with low coal stocks in the hard winter of 1946–7, and another crisis occurred for the same reasons in 1950–1. The NCB *Plan for Coal* produced in 1950 suggested an investment plan for the industry, and this was revised upwards in the 1956 review of the plan (NCB, 1956), because of the constant coal shortages of the early 1950s. There was a fall in demand in 1957, which heralded the start of the substitution of alternative fuels for coal, and recruitment to the industry was restricted. By 1959 the industry's investment plans had to be scaled down, and a *Revised Plan for Coal* (NCB, 1959) was published. The industry contracted in the 1960s, and there was a severe reduction in consumption after 1964; between 1965 and 1969 over 200 pits were closed. At this time, however, the coal industry was not convinced that the closures were necessary in the long term. E. F. Schumacher (of *Small is Beautiful* fame), Economic Adviser to the NCB, gave the first warning of the rise of OPEC in 1962, and although the NCB and its chairman, Lord Robens, argued for preservation of a larger coal industry, the government disagreed. Robens (1977, p. 5) feels this was because '. . . fundamentally the assurances of the oil companies about oil supplies and price were more acceptable to Whitehall than the warnings of the NCB'. Richard Marsh, the Minister of Power in 1966, is quoted as saying: '. . . at that time nobody outside the coal industry saw any future for coal, and the men at the Ministry regarded some of the advocacy as hysterical. All the advice from all expert sources outside coal was that oil was plentiful, that oil prices would not rise as fast as those of coal, and that the future of oil supplies was secure' (Berkovitch, 1977, p. 137). So during the 1960s, therefore, the contraction continued, until by the end of the decade the coal stocks declined for the first time in 15 years. The NCB slowed down the rate of contraction and then produced a new five-year plan in 1971, and the government took steps to increase coal supplies by encouraging open-cast mining and removing the subsidy from the electricity and gas industries for burning extra coal. They also urged the CEGB to burn more oil, as they had wanted to do in previous years. This was a strange decision, coming just after the 1970 break in the Trans-Arabian pipeline had allowed Libya to raise its oil prices; a small taste of things to come. Coal consumption decreased again in 1972, partly as a result of shortages due to industrial action, and in 1973 an agreement was reached between the CEGB and the NCB for an increased coal burn.

In mid 1973 the coal industry's luck changed when OPEC began to increase its oil prices and limit supplies; oil was still coal's most important competitor, and the home-produced energy source was suddenly seen in a different light. The miners capitalized on coal's greater competitiveness in the market during their strike in early 1974, which eventually caused a change of government. Jackson (1974, p. 147) rates the change in attitude towards different sources of energy as more important than the physical effects. Yet another new

Plan for Coal (NCB, 1974) was produced which aimed to expand the industry by creating new mining capacity, and this again was revised in 1977, being published as *Coal for the Future* (D.En., 1977).

The NCB itself has up to fourteen members, some part-time, all of which are appointed by the Secretary of State for Energy. The full-time members are each responsible for a specific area of the Board's activities, such as finance or marketing. At the moment the chairman of the NCB is Sir Derek Ezra, who has been a board member since 1965 and deputy chairman from 1967 to 1971, when he became chairman. He has represented the NCB on various European committees, and was a regional sales manager and then NCB director general of marketing before joining the Board. He is a member of ACEC and the Energy Commission. The deputy chairman since 1973 has been Norman Siddall, a mining engineer who joined the Board after a long career in the then East Midlands Division. There are also five full-time board members, including an accountant, a mining engineer and a colliery manager, and six part-time members. The regional organization is comprised of twelve areas, each with a local headquarters. The NCB was established to 'work and get coal in Great Britain' (D.En. Fact Sheet 4, February 1977, p. 2) but is also allowed to set up subsidiary companies and form joint enterprises with other industries providing these activities relate to the primary duty of working and getting coal and securing the development of an efficient coal industry. The NCB is financed mainly by a combination of sales revenue and borrowing from the National Loans Fund and foreign lenders. It is not allowed to raise money on the domestic market, and is limited in the amount it may borrow. The government has the power to make grants to the coal industry to help in financing coal and coke stocks, and also to contribute to the deficiency in the Mineworkers Pension Scheme.

The current statutory financial objective of the NCB is to break even, but in the past certain financial targets have been set, and this may again be the case in the future as a result of the review of the relationship between the government and the nationalized industries. At the present time the Board's finances are healthy and they have a high self-financing ratio; in 1976/7 they were able to provide 40 per cent of the funds necessary for fixed asset formation from internal sources (NCB, *Report and Accounts 1976/7*, 1977, p. 17), which they felt was almost a high enough level bearing in mind the earlier low levels of investment in the industry. A higher self-financing ratio would penalize present consumers for the current expansion in capacity.

The coal industry's own plans for the future are assessed by the Joint Policy Advisory Committee (JPAC) of the Coal Industry National Consultative Council (CINCC), which is made up of representatives from the NCB and the three mining unions, the National Union of Mineworkers (NUM), the National Association of Colliery Overmen, Deputies and Shotfirers (NACODS) and the British Association of Colliery Management (BACM). Government, management and unions make up the Joint Coal Industry Examination which agreed with the NCB's 1974 *Plan for Coal*, and this effective tripartite grouping is seen by Sir Derek Ezra to be very important for the future of the coal industry. Liaison with other nationalized industries occurs in the Working Group on Energy Strategy, where F. B. Harrison, the NCB member responsible for finance, and M. J. Parker are the NCB representatives. There are, of course, many other committees and groups concerned with the coal industry. On the research side there is representation at Board level on ACORD, and within the NCB the Mining Research and Development Establishment (MRDE) deals with coal extraction and the Coal Research Establishment (CRE) is responsible for research into coal utilization. There is a Coal Industry Tripartite Group Working Party on R and D, which reports occasionally, and the NCB attends the International Committee for Coal Research (ICCR). The main European coal organization is the European Coal and Steel Community (ECSC), which was established in 1952 and exists to promote national expansion and modernization of coal and steel production and to ensure an orderly supply of coal and steel to member countries. Britain became a member in 1973, on joining the EEC; the ECSC provides loans to members, and in 1976/7 the NCB received £3.0 million for research and development. The Association of the Coal Producers of the European Community, CEPCEO, exerts pressure on the EEC for action in matters relating to coal, and the Association for Coal in Europe (CEPCEO plus the Spanish coal industry) fulfils much the same purpose. Other international connections include British representatives on the West German coal industry R and D committee. The NCB has two wholly owned subsidiary companies, NCB (Ancillaries) Ltd and NCB (Coal Products) Ltd. The directors of these companies are mainly NCB members, and NCB (Coal Products) Ltd is chaired by L. Grainger, previously a full time NCB member responsible for research. This group has interests in smokeless fuels and chemicals, while NCB (Ancillaries) Ltd is concerned with solid fuel distribution, building materials and computer services amongst other things.

The NCB's day-to-day relationship with the government is handled by the Coal Division of D.En., headed by under-secretary J. R. Cross. It is not easy to discover what the D.En. officials actually do; relationships between the nationalized industries and their sponsoring departments change, in terms of official functions and human relations. The *Civil Service Year Book* merely lists the responsibilities of the branches of D.En., and even when senior civil servants are called before select committees their evidence tends to concern generalized policy rather than everyday control. However, Lord Robens was able to give his opinion of NCB contact with government when he was called before the Select Committee on Nationalized Industries in 1967, when he was NCB chairman. Initially, the questioning concerned financial incentives set for the NCB by the government, and Robens was asked how much influence the board were able to exert over the people in the Treasury who made the decisions. He replied that: 'There have been many occasions on which I would like to have seen the people who make the decisions. On one occasion I was point blank refused permission' (HC371-ii, Session 1967/68, Q. 464). This is consistent with the Treasury policy of only corresponding with the outside world through other departments. Robens was equally critical of the Ministry of Power which at that time was responsible for the NCB, particularly on its handling of small scale decisions. 'I do not believe that any Ministry is adequately staffed with the right kind of people to examine these individual projects. So far every project submitted has come back without change. This is because they have not the technical people to indicate any changes' (HC371−ii, Session 1967/68, Q. 489). Robens called for an Energy Board with permanent staff who would be able to take a 'total sum approach' to energy, and he criticized the frequent staff changes within the ministry. Lord Robens has been a consistent supporter of the idea of an Energy Board or Commission for some time; in an article in *Nature* (Robens, 1974) he suggested a commission staffed by experts to deal with the long term planning functions which Whitehall, with its inadequate resources, cannot carry out properly. On the same theme in 1977 he criticized the 1976 National Energy Conference as window-dressing and accused the department of making the same old mistake again − that is, being concerned with each energy industry separately rather than seeking the collective advantage. He criticized the membership of the new Energy Commission, and restated his original suggestion of a '. . . powerful, independent energy commission upon which will sit people who are completely independent of the energy industries themselves. Representatives from the energy industries would be able to make submissions and to appear before the Commission and give some oral evidence. But only people with no axe to grind but only the national interest to serve can actually produce an energy policy that makes sense' (Robens, 1977, pp. 7–8).

Since Tony Benn has been Secretary of State for Energy, more public statements of policy have been made by the coal industry, including the NCB and the unions at the Tripartite Energy Consultations of 20 February 1976. This was a forum of coal and electricity management and unions, held to help the two industries understand each other's aims and intentions. There was a public disagreement between the NCB and the CEGB about the amount of consultation which should take place between them, but Sir Derek Ezra continued Lord Robens' tradition of pursuing cooperation with rather than competition between sectional interests in his speech. He insisted that '. . . our policy now is to explore with the CEGB to our mutual advantage ways in which more coal can be consumed, but in high efficiency plants so that the CEGB can gain the price advantage which coal can offer' (D.En. Energy Paper No. 14, 1976, p. 10). The NCB felt that their main problem was to reconcile short-run variations with long-term expectations in energy policy: there was insufficient modern coal-fired power station capacity available to burn coal at high efficiency, and if coal production was to be cut back for this reason, it would impair the industry's ability to respond to increased demands in the future. Joe Gormley, the NUM president, supported the NCB line which he said had previously been agreed with the unions. He went on to say: 'Without the electricity industry, and God knows we say enough harsh things to one another, but without the electricity industry there's no great future for the coal industry, and vice versa . . .' (D.En. Energy Paper No. 14, 1976, p. 13). Later in 1976 the NCB paper to the National Energy Conference stated that: 'Coal has by far the largest ultimate reserves of fossil fuels in the UK, and will assume increasing importance in the longer term' (D.En. Energy Paper No. 13, 1976, vol. 2, p. 25). Sir Derek Ezra, in his speech to the conference, said he felt coal had a vital role to play in the immediate future to help reduce imports, in the medium term to help release resources for export and in the longer term to close any energy gap which emerges as the reserves of other fossil fuels are reduced. In order that the coal industry would be capable of fulfilling these roles, there was a need for the development of new capacity beyond the range of the existing *Plan for Coal*, for investment in new plant for effective coal burning and for sufficient funding for research into new coal conversion technologies. Sir Derek continued to press for a long term energy policy within which the individual fuel industries could work.

The latest statement of coal industry policy is contained in *Coal for the Future*, a review of the 1974 *Plan for Coal* issued in February 1977 by the Coal Industry Tripartite Group. Tony Benn was the chairman and, apart from the NCB, NUM, NACODS and BACM representatives, the three government members were Alex Eadie, the Under-Secretary of State responsible for coal, Harold Walker, a Minister of State in the Department of Employment, and Joel Barnett, the Chief Secretary to the Treasury. The Chief Secretary is a minister of cabinet rank who argues the Treasury case with the spending ministers, and has a great deal of power by virtue of office, not merely as deputy to the Chancellor. The Tripartite Group found that the objectives of *Plan for Coal* remained valid, but that it was now necessary to look further ahead than 1985. The government pledged its support for *Plan for Coal* and stated that it would consider providing temporary support for the industry in order that long term viability could be maintained. The group was in favour of a planning agreement being entered into between the government, the NCB and the unions, and this was confirmed in February 1978. The general support of the mining unions for the NCB has meant that the industry has been able to present a united front to government when policy discussions are taking place. Even during the 1972 and 1974 strikes, the NCB was clearly seen to be merely a tool of government policy, and the same could be said for its position during the era of mine closures. The mining unions have a strong political effect on Labour governments in particular, with a number of sponsored MPs, and the alliance between the unions and the NCB has helped to put coal into the prominent position it enjoys in British energy plans.

The latest coal industry statement, contained in the *Report and Accounts 1976/7* (NCB, 1977), emphasized the main points of its 'Plan 2000' as suggested in *Coal for the Future* — that is the expansion of output combined with generation of new productive capacity. Annual output was to rise to at least 135 million tons by 1985, which would be achieved by creating 42 million tons of new colliery capacity and increasing opencast production to 15 million tons from its previous rate of 10 million tons. On energy policy, the NCB felt that '. . . increasing general acceptance was shown of their view of the essential issues' (NCB, 1977, p. 24). The only slight disagreement between the NCB and the government at present is the NCB's wish for planning objectives to work towards within the time-scale of 'Plan 2000'. Although the government recognize the need for planning objectives, they are not willing to settle on any specific targets before the national energy policy nears completion. There does indeed seem to be general acceptance of the need to expand the coal industry, but unfortunately production in 1976/77 was down on the previous year. This was due to a variety of causes, one of which was the lack of financial incentives, but the introduction of productivity schemes in early 1978 has stimulated production.

The NCB seems fairly well placed to profit from the change in energy costs and attitudes caused by the oil price rise. Although they have a legacy of aging pits, the government is backing their new investment programme and tripartite cooperation continues to be successful. The coal industry's view of other energy sources and national energy policy has been consistently non-sectional, and Leslie Grainger, chairman of NCB (IEA Services) Ltd, an ex-Board member who has worked in both the coal and nuclear industries, has continued this tradition. Writing in an individual capacity, he said: 'For some years now too much emphasis, pseudo-accuracy and dramatisation has centred on the apparent competition between coal and nuclear power and their respective costs of generating electricity. I believe coal – or more properly fossil fuel – and nuclear power to be complementary, not competitive. They have different but interlocking destinies, and humanity will need all the energy it can get at a sensible price' (Grainger, 1977, p. 22).

There are, of course, problems with both the increased coal burn at power stations and increased coal production, particularly opencast coal. The OECD has claimed that sulphur dioxide and other pollutants from British power stations are falling as acid rain in Scandinavia, but the Board feels that its policy of dispersal of emissions by tall chimneys is effective. 'It is beyond question that it is a very economic method of ensuring that ground level concentrations of sulphur dioxide and other pollutants emitted from industrial plants and power stations do not constitute a health risk' (NCB, 1977, p. 19). Experts are still debating the exact amount of pollution caused by Britain, and available methods of sulphur reduction are regarded as too costly. Environmental considerations have slowed down the growth of opencast mining; *Plan for Coal* (NCB, 1974) required a 50 per cent increase in opencast production, but this has not yet been achieved, partly because of difficulties in opening up new sites. The NCB say in their *Report and Accounts 1976/7* (NCB, 1977) that they regard environmental matters as central to the industry's main activities, and that the Opencast Executive face environmental difficulties possibly greater than anywhere else in the world because of British conditions. However, opencast coal is cheap to produce and often of high quality, so that it helps the viability of the industry as a whole though penalizing localized opencast mining areas. In spite of the environmental difficulties, the industry is to develop further new capacity, and the government has stated its intention of keeping open ready markets for coal (D.En. Press Notice Ref. No. 52, 13 February 1978, p. 10).

CENTRAL ELECTRICITY GENERATING BOARD

In England and Wales the Central Electricity Generating Board (CEGB) are the producers and wholesalers of electricity; retail electricity sales are handled by twelve area boards. The CEGB has only existed since 1957, when it and the Electricity Council, the policy-making body for the industry, were set up.

The legislative history of public electricity supply began in 1882 with the Electric Lighting Act which laid down the terms on which private enterprises would supply electricity, and made provisions for local authorities to purchase the undertakings after a period of 21 years, later extended to 42 years. By the turn of the century there were a large number of small companies and local authorities supplying electricity; some supplied direct current, some alternating current and the voltage and frequency also differed. Legislation at this time prohibited companies from supplying electricity outside their prescribed areas, but the Electric Lighting Act of 1909 authorized bulk suppliers to act outside the original small areas. Central coordination was introduced in 1919 but proved ineffective, and the Central Electricity Board was established in 1926 to construct a national grid of main transmission lines. The grid system was operative by 1934, and the amount of spare generating plant was slowly being reduced. The consequent reorganization of the distributive network occurred in 1947 when the industry was nationalized. The 1947 Electricity Act created twelve area electricity boards in England and Wales and two in Scotland, and the British Electricity Authority to act as the coordinating body. The 1947 Act defined one of the duties of the Authority as ensuring that an economical supply of electricity was maintained, and this principle has remained the same ever since, although the most economical use of energy would combine the generation of electricity and the sale of heat as a by-product. In 1955 the British Electricity Authority was renamed the Central Electricity Authority, but its responsibilities did not change until 1957 and the passing of the Electricity Act. The Authority was replaced by two bodies, the Electricity Council and the CEGB, and the twelve area boards were given more autonomy. These measures were designed to decrease the centralization of the industry, and each board was made directly responsible to the Secretary of State, none of them being required to cooperate with each other or act for the good of the industry as a whole. The Electricity Council had no powers of control over the boards, and merely acted in an advisory role as a forum for disagreements. Because of the lack of central direction within the industry, a Bill was introduced in 1970 to strengthen central policy-making functions, but this lapsed on the change of government. In 1974 the Labour government set up the Plowden Committee to inquire into the structure of the electricity supply industry in England and Wales, which reported in January 1976 (Cmnd 6388, 1976). They felt that the weakness of the Electricity Council was responsible for the general lack of direction in the electricity industry, and recommended that a Central Electricity Board (CEB) should take over the responsibilities of the Electricity Council, the CEGB and the area boards. They felt that the duties of the industry should be enlarged to cover energy conservation, and that the CEB should be able to initiate combined heat and power (CHP) schemes, which meant changing the restriction on selling heat which is not directly the by-product of electricity generation. On presenting the report to Parliament, Tony Benn said he felt there had to be adequate safeguards against the dangers of excessive central-ization, but that he intended to bring in legislation abolishing the Electricity Council and the boards as constituted at present and creating a new central body. He went on to say that: 'Although a stronger centre is required to deal with the major strategic issues facing the industry I believe it is equally important to find a solution that also preserves vigorous and effective local boards enjoying statutory authority under the initial order' (*The Times*, Parliament report, 20 July 1977, p. 9). Legislation has not yet been introduced concerning the electricity industry, but a White Paper was published in April 1978 containing the suggestion of a central body for the industry, the Electricity Corporation (EC). Although the intention was to introduce legislation during the 1977/78 session of Parliament, this was frustrated by the opposition of the Liberal Party to the degree of centralization suggested. The Lib–Lab pack was then in operation, so this effectively deferred the entire Bill and the White Paper was produced instead.

The CEGB itself consists of a chairman and between seven and nine members, all appointed by the Secretary of State for Energy. The chairman since May 1977 has been Glyn England, an engineer who has worked in the electricity industry since the war, and was previously chairman of the South Western Electricity Board, as well as being a part-time member of the CEGB since 1975. There are five full-time members at present, one of whom is deputy chairman, and they form the executive of the CEGB. One CEGB member attends the WGES. There are four part-time members, including Lord Kearton who was on the Plowden Committee and is chairman of BNOC and the Electricity Supply Research Council and a part-time member of the UKAEA. He also worked in the atomic energy project during the Second World War. Apart from maintaining the supply of electricity to the area boards, the CEGB is allowed to sell in bulk to certain consumers, for example, the UKAEA. It is also responsible for planning the future development of the generating system, the pricing policy, the bulk purchase of fuel and the direction of research.. National Grid Control oversees the deployment of power station capacity as the load varies, and for administrative purposes the stations are split into five regions each headed by a director general, directly responsible to the executive. The design and construction of power stations is the responsibility of the Generation Development and Construction Division, and the design and construction of transmission schemes is carried out by the Transmission, Development and Construction Division. Both the directors general of these divisions are directly responsible to the executive. The twelve area boards are responsible for the electricity distribution networks and the retail sale of electricity, and each board consists of a chairman, deputy chairman and from four to six other members all appointed by the Secretary of State for Energy. In each area there are electricity consultative councils, which are consumer councils having no powers of direction; their chairmen are all ex-officio members of the appropriate area boards.

The research functions of the CEGB are carried out at three separate laboratories and there are CEGB members on various research groups and working parties, such as the District Heating Working Party of the CHP Group, ACORD (where the representative is the CEGB Controller of Research, Dr D. J. Littler), WESC (where the representative is CEGB Strategic Planning Officer Dr J. K. Wright, the chairman of the District Heating Working Party) and of course WGES, where the representation is at board level. ACORD's relationship with the CEGB is very much on the advisory level; Mr D. R. R. Fair, in 1976 the CEGB member responsible for operational work, told the SCST about it at one of their hearings on alternative sources of energy: 'I would not judge that ACORD had the power to tell us not to do something; they can advise but we are a Corporation set up by Statute and I do not believe they have the power to direct accordingly without first going through the Secretary of State to do so' (HC534-ii, Session 1976/77, Q. 967).

Strangely, there is no CEGB representative on the Energy Commission, although the chairmen of both the Electricity Council and the SSEB are members. This is because the CEGB is officially a subsidiary of the Council, but it has led some CEGB executives to feel that their views were not being put across to the Commission, particularly in the debate about reactor choice at the first Commission meeting. There appeared to be some disagreement on policy between the CEGB and the Council (which represents it), which resulted in a CEGB member saying: 'We are not getting the right representation at the right level' (Cook, 1978c). This is a clear case of what the Plowden Committee saw as the industry's difficulty in speaking with a single voice.

As with the other nationalized industries, the CEGB has financial objectives laid down for it by the government, but its ability to reach these targets has often been impaired in the past by developments emanating from outside the electricity industry itself. The capital investment programme is often a source of acrimony between the CEGB and the government, particularly in the case of the latest coal-fired power station, Drax B. The Central Policy Review Staff study, *The Future of the United Kingdom Power Plant Manufacturing Industry* (CPRS, 1976) recommended the advance ordering of Drax B in order to help maintain a viable power plant industry, but the CEGB initially said that this would increase electricity prices and asked for financial compensation for placing the order early. Unfortunately the CEGB record on power plant ordering plans is a little erratic and estimates for the number of nuclear reactors required varied wildly throughout the early seventies. In August 1972, Arthur Hawkins (later Sir Arthur), the then chairman of the CEGB, told the SCST about his plans for the next ten years, firstly with a 5 per cent load growth rate: 'That would mean starting ten or eleven new stations, of which we would probably suggest that four would be nuclear stations, one probably a fast reactor.' Secondly, with a $3\frac{1}{2}$ per cent load growth rate, which was higher than the average over the previous three or four years: 'That would mean in this period for commissioning until after 1980 only three new station starts, of which one would be probably nuclear – and probably the fast reactor' (HC117, Session 1972/73, Q. 104). However, in December 1973, Hawkins told the SCST that the CEGB plan: '. . . means provisionally eighteen new reactors to be ordered between 1974 and 1979 inclusive, subject to the rolling review which goes on year by year' (HC145, 73i–vii, Session 1973/74, Q. 253), although the load growth estimates were unchanged since 1972. He explained the discrepancy between his two statements to the committee by saying that eighteen months was a long time in planning, and that they had misunderstood his previous remarks about the urgency of the situation. By October 1976 the plans had changed again, and Sir Arthur told yet another SCST hearing on nuclear policy: 'We do not need to place an order for a new power station even under our energy case 1 – that is the more optimistic load growth – until at least 1979. If the load growth is less than that, it could be into the 1980s before we need to order any new power station. We have a very substantial margin of capacity at the moment' (HC623, Session 1975/76, Q. 116). Energy case 1 entailed a growth of electricity demand of 3.4 per cent per annum, only 0.1 per cent different from the 1972 lower estimate, and the 1973 unchanged estimates. Thus the reactor requirements until 1980 had changed from 1 to 18 to 0 in four years, during which the load growth estimates had remained roughly constant, in spite of the oil crisis. Thus although the CEGB has suffered from outside pressures concerned with employment in the coal-mining and power-plant industries, government indecision and changes of decision over reactor policy, the sudden and drastic changes in scale of reactor ordering on the part of the CEGB have not improved their relationship with other organizations.

Within D.En., CEGB affairs are handled by the Electricity Division, but the CEGB view of civil servants has been fairly abrasive, as Sir Arthur put it to the SCST in 1976: 'I am always happy to condemn any committee dominated by civil servants who know nothing about the situation at all' (HC623, Session 1975/76, Q. 145). He went on to say that the CEGB had eliminated committee structures and tried to work on the basis of personal accountability. The relationship between the coal industry and the CEGB has also been somewhat unhappy; at the Tripartite Energy Consultations Sir Arthur accused the NCB of being as bad as the sheikhs in raising the cost of energy, and of being absorbed with the poor pawns of the electricity industry rather than looking at energy requirements on a broad front. He did, however, say that it was: '. . . in the national interest to have a strong, viable coal industry, and coal can count on the continued goodwill and cooperation of its best customer, the electricity industry' (D.En. Energy Paper No. 14, 1976, p. 5). This advocacy of the national interest seems to be the basic CEGB attitude on energy policy, as Sir Arthur has repeated it in other circumstances, for example at the National Energy Conference: 'It is the national interest, not that of any group in the energy field, that must come first in any national energy strategy' (D.En. Energy Paper No. 13, vol. 1, 1976, p. 10). In spite of frequent references to the 'national interest' by the chairmen of the nationalized industries, it is rare for them to actually define it in anything other than vague terms relating to freedom of choice and competitive pricing policies. Sir Arthur put his views on cooperation into practice when discussing with Sir Derek Ezra advancement of the completion date of the Drax power stations to match the development of the Selby coalfield, and pointed out a weakness in national energy planning on this point: 'The only difficulty is that we need some subsidy so that the electricity consumer is not, in effect, subsidizing still further the coal industry' (HC623, Session 1975/76, Q. 122). The interdependence of energy supplies and the costs of development of advanced technology both have cost implications for the consumer of energy, and only the production of a comprehensive national energy policy can take into account the vast variety of factors; meanwhile, the arguments between sections of what is basically one industry, the energy industry, will continue.

Perhaps because of the amount of criticism levelled at the CEGB in recent years, the Board's attitude to the public has been to advocate giving people as great a freedom of choice as possible in the energy-consuming area, but to ignore them where decision-making as regards choice of generating and technology was concerned. Sir Arthur Hawkins stated his views plainly to the SCST when questioned on the viability of public hearings for issues of nuclear policy: '. . . I would say that in our view these important matters are best dealt with by experts and by the procedure laid down by Government and not debated before the world until decisions are made' (HC145, 73-i–vii, Session 1973/74, Q. 347). The chairman replied, rather mildly, 'That is hardly a democratic procedure.' The present chairman of the CEGB, Glyn England, has only been in office since May 1977 and has had few chances to make public statements on CEGB policy. He did, however, reply to a Tony Benn article on energy policy, and his remarks may herald a change of CEGB attitude to public participation in decision-making: 'In the interests of the country we want to avoid the alienation of public opinion and the violent opposition to the nuclear industry that has occurred in some other countries. We welcome public debate and accept our obligation to take part in it' (England, 1977, p. 734). He endorsed earlier remarks by Hawkins to the effect that consumer choice was an efficient mechanism provided that energy pricing was consistent and took into account all aspects of fuel costs, and, of course, was in favour of an energy policy which would benefit 'UK Ltd'. Thus the CEGB seems to see itself as something of a pawn in a game played between the fuel suppliers and the government, the butt of decisions taken for the good of other industries which may then adversely affect the electricity supply industry. In spite of frequent disagreements with the coal industry in particular, it would seem to be in the best interests of the CEGB that a national energy policy was formulated which could look beyond sectional interests, and England appears to realize that the previous CEGB attitude on public participation is not only untenable now but bad for public relations.

SOUTH OF SCOTLAND ELECTRICITY BOARD

Scottish electricity supply has been nationalized since the 1947 Electricity Act, but the SSEB itself did not come into existence until 1955. It differs from the CEGB in that it is responsible for the generation, transmission and distribution of electricity, combining the functions of the CEGB and its area boards. The headquarters of the SSEB is in Glasgow and the Secretary of State for Scotland appoints its members, a chairman and from four to eight members.

The present chairman is Roy Berridge, who took over from F. L. Tombs (now chairman of the Electricity Council) in 1976, having been deputy chairman for two years. He is an engineer with experience in nuclear reactor design, and was the SSEB's director of engineering from 1972 to 1974. He is a member of the Energy Commission and the North of Scotland Hydro-Electric Board (NoSHEB). The part-time Board members include the chairman of NoSHEB, Sir Douglas Haddow, and the chairman of the Electricity Consultative Council, Jack Kane. Kane is a JP and was South East of Scotland District Secretary of the WEA for 21 years, and in 1972/5 was Lord Provost of the City of Edinburgh and Lord Lieutenant of the County of the City of Edinburgh. The Director of the Business School at the University of Strathclyde, Professor A. J. Kennerley, is also a part-time Board member.

Two SSEB representatives attend WGES meetings, on behalf of both the Scottish boards.

The SSEB and the NoSHEB plan and operate their plant on a 'whole Scotland' basis in order to provide power economically. The Mackenzie Committee of 1962 recommended that the two boards should be merged, but this suggestion was rejected; some planning functions were combined in 1965, leading to the 'whole Scotland' arrangement which now exists. The SSEB is also required to cooperate with the Electricity Council when necessary, and the CEGB and SSEB exchange electricity to achieve the lowest cost generation over the whole of Britain. Financially, the Board is responsible to the Secretary of State for Scotland, who has to approve their capital investment programme and give consent for new power stations; he also has similar powers of direction to those exercised by the Secretary of State for Energy with respect to the CEGB.

The CEGB's generating capacity is about nine times that of the SSEB; SSEB's territory has a population of about four million, while the CEGB is responsible for supplies to about forty-nine million people, thus SSEB has a higher ratio of generating capacity to population than the CEGB. Although the SSEB is supposedly free to make its own decisions in, for instance, matters of choice of reactor type, the then chairman, Frank Tombs, told the SCST: 'It is very difficult to envisage Scotland choosing a reactor which is different from the nationally chosen reactor' (HC145, 73-i—vii, Session 1973/74, Q. 97). He later defended the independence of the SSEB, saying that although they found the CEGB useful for research information, the SSEB had the highest reliability Magnox station and the largest coal-fired station in the country, 'So I would not be in any way unduly reticent about the resources and capabilities of the SSEB' (HC623, Session 1975/76, Q. 479). Tombs felt that it was better to leave more responsibility to the manufacturers during the building of nuclear power plants than was the CEGB practice. He also advocated nuclear power more openly than the CEGB, saying at the Tripartite Energy Consultations in 1976 that he had no doubt that an energy gap would arise in the 1990s and it would have to be filled with nuclear power. He saw coal and nuclear power as having a secure future together. Tombs and the CEGB ex-chairman Hawkins shared much the same views about public participation in nuclear decision-making. Tombs told an SCST hearing: 'The issues are extremely complex. I think it would be difficult to expose them in a general public hearing, because what people tend to do at public inquiries is to seize on out of the way aspects and blow them up out of proportion' (HC145, 73-i–vii, Session 1973/74, Q. 130). Clearly the boards do have a great deal in common, but the SSEB endeavours to be one step ahead of the CEGB in power station efficiency.

Roy Berridge, the SSEB chairman since 1976, has attended some SCST hearings as deputy chairman but his replies were confined in the main to detailed engineering matters. His most recent chance to speak in public came after the accident at the Hunterston B nuclear power station when sea water leaked into the base of the reactor in 1977, causing up to £20 million damage (Kerr, 1978a). Berridge was able to announce that the cost of repairs would be met out of reserve funds, making the accident less embarrassing for the Board which had been advertising the stability of its prices due to efficient nuclear generation (Hetherington, 1977). The Board expects about 40 per cent of its supplies to be nuclear-based by the mid 1980s (Electricity Council, 1975, p. 34).

NORTH OF SCOTLAND HYDRO-ELECTRIC BOARD

The North of Scotland Hydro-Electric Board (NoSHEB) was established in 1943 and nationalized in 1947; it is responsible for generation, transmission and distribution of electricity in the north of Scotland, an area including about 2 per cent of the population of Britain. The Board has its headquarters in Edinburgh and is responsible for 54 main hydro-electric stations as well as a few oil- and diesel-fired stations. It exchanges power supplies with the SSEB, and the construction of new generating capacity in Scotland is planned between them on the basis of total Scottish needs. The Board itself consists of a chairman and from four to eight members, all of which are part-time except for the deputy chairman who is also the chief executive. Appointments to the Board are made by the Secretary of State for Scotland, who is responsible for the NoSHEB. The present chairman is Sir Douglas Haddow, an ex-civil servant who was Permanent Under-Secretary of State at the Scottish Office from 1965 until 1973, when he became NoSHEB chairman. He is an ex-officio member of the SSEB, and the SSEB chairman is likewise a member of the NoSHEB. The chairman of the local Electricity Consultative Council, D. D. S. Craib, is also a Board member. Craib is a farmer and company director who sits on various committees with agricultural interests, notably the Potato Marketing Board of Great Britain. The deputy chairman is K. R. Vernon, an engineer who has worked in both the SSEB and the NoSHEB.

The total installed capacity of the NoSHEB stations is about a fifth of that of the SSEB; clearly it is not a large concern compared with the CEGB. It is extremely non-controversial; very little is heard from it in public, it took no part in the 1976 National Energy Conference and it has no representative on the Energy Commission. To a great extent, its needs in national energy planning are cared for by the SSEB representatives. Interestingly, it is the only utility with an obligation to carry out measures for the economic development and social improvement of its district, as far as its powers and duties permit. It shares with the SSEB the obligation to preserve the beauty of the scenery in Scotland, and is also the only British authority using an alternative energy source, hydro power, for electricity generation.

NORTHERN IRELAND ELECTRICITY SERVICE

An electricity board was established in Northern Ireland in 1931 to coordinate generation and transmission and to acquire existing undertakings. By 1951 the process was complete, apart from those areas supplied by the Londonderry and Belfast Corporations, and overall coordination was carried out by the Northern Ireland Joint Electricity Committee. This committee was replaced in 1967 by the Northern Ireland Joint Electricity Authority, with increased powers, and all four bodies were merged into the Northern Ireland Electricity Service (NIES) in 1973. The NIES total installed capacity is about twice that of the NoSHEB, and about threequarters of it is oil fired.

The NIES paper to the National Energy Conference pointed out the difficulties faced by NIES in keeping their prices down to the level of the rest of the UK in the face of rapid oil price escalation. As a long term strategy NIES wanted to reduce its dependence on oil, but ruled out coal because of high transport costs. The present size of nuclear power plants was thought to be too large, and NIES suggested interconnection with the UK using direct current submarine cables. The Service saw no prospect of a reduction in tariffs unless interconnection was possible, and this clearly had an adverse effect on industrialists making investment decisions, and thus on employment.

Like the NoSHEB, the NIES has a small voice rarely heard at national level in energy policy discussions.

THE ELECTRICITY COUNCIL

The Electricity Council came into existence on 1 January 1958 as a result of the 1957 Electricity Act. Its brief is 'to promote and assist the maintenance and development by Electricity Boards in England and Wales of an efficient, coordinated and economical system of electricity supply' (Electricity Council, 1975, p. 21). It acts as a forum where general policy is formulated, and advises the Secretary of State for Energy. It has particular responsibility for finances, research, industrial relations and consultations with outside organizations, including select committees. Various financial objectives have been agreed between the Council and the government, which has often restricted the industry's ability to reach targets by freezing prices. From 1973, the government compensated the industry for limiting its price increases, but in 1974 those subsidies began to be phased out in favour of higher tariffs. The Council has overall responsibility for the investment plans of the CEGB and the area boards, and each year a programme for the whole industry is agreed and sent to the Secretary of State for approval. Finance for investment comes from profits and loans, both from the Treasury and overseas. At present the industry is in a healthy position financially, being able to provide about half its capital needs from profit.

The Plowden Report of 1976 proposed amalgamating the Council, the CEGB and the area boards, to provide greater central control in the industry, but no legislation has yet been passed on the recommendations. The Electricity Council were in favour of legislation bringing about a Central Electricity Board (CEB), provided that the generating and area boards continued to carry out their normal functions consistently with strategic policy decisions made by the CEB. The Plowden Committee had found a lack of a central force in the electricity industry, loyalty to individual boards often prevailing in Council discussions. Decisions were sometimes not made in the best interests of the industry as a whole but were compromises. They found that the yearly demand forecasts made by the Electricity Council tended not to be reasoned decisions but compromises which reflected the individual interests of the Boards rather than the merits of the arguments. The committee felt that the industry was lagging behind other nationalized industries in planning, although this had now been rectified to some degree by the production of a Corporate Plan.

The Council itself consists of the twelve area board chairmen, three members of the CEGB (including the chairman) and up to six independent members, including the chairman and two deputy chairmen. The chairman since April 1977 has been Sir Francis Tombs, who had previously been chairman of the SSEB. He is a Birmingham-educated engineer who has spent his entire career in the electricity industry, becoming director of engineering with the SSEB in 1969, their deputy chairman in 1973 and chairman in 1974. He is a member of the Energy Commission, and one of his first tasks as chairman was to attend the Sunningdale Seminar on Nuclear Policy in May 1977, where he reiterated his view that there would be an energy shortage in the UK by the end of the century. The full-time deputy chairman of the Council since December 1976 has been A. W. Bunch, (previously CEGB deputy chairman), and the part-time deputy chairman is Sir Samuel Curran, a nuclear physicist who has worked for the UKAEA and is now vice chancellor of the University of Strathclyde and a member of various committees. There are two other full-time independent Council members, R. W. Orson and W. J. Prior. Orson is a statistician who became head of the Council's Economics and Forecasting Branch in 1963, deputy commercial adviser in 1968, commercial adviser in 1972 and was appointed to Council in 1976. He is the Council representative on the WGES and on ACORD. Prior was a power station superintendent at Berkeley and Hinkley Point before becoming director general of the SE region in 1972. He was appointed to Council in 1976. The three CEGB members on Council are Glyn England, the CEGB chairman who was previously on the Council by virtue of being chairman of the South Western Electricity Board, the deputy chairman F. E. Bonner (a WGES member) and G. A. W. Blackman. The Electricity Council meets every month and has three standing committees – on Industrial Relations, Commercial Policy and Research – to look at matters in detail. The Council has responsibility for research in the electricity industry, and oversees the CEGB's laboratories and the Electricity Council Research Centre (ECRC) at Capenhurst. Research planning is dealt with by the Council's Research Committee (technological) and Commercial Policy Committee (commercial and economics). The Electricity Supply Research Council is an advisory body to the Council and is composed of scientists and experts from inside and outside the industry; it is chaired by Lord Kearton. The Electricity Council representative on ACORD is R. W. Orson. There is also a Power Engineering Research Steering Committee which brings together people from the manufacturing and supply sides of the industry and D.En. observers.

The Council is an active member of several acronymous international organizations, such as the European Centre of Public Enterprises (CEEP), the International Union of Producers and Distributors of Electrical Energy (UNIPEDE), the World Energy Conference (WEC) and the International Conference on Large High-Voltage Electric Systems (CIGRE). CEEP and UNIPEDE have the strongest formal connections, with a direct line of communication at European government level.

The Electricity Council is and always has been strongly in favour of reliance on nuclear power for future electricity generation. Sir Peter Menzies, the chairman until 1977, said at the Tripartite Energy Consultations:

. . . the future, the long term future for electricity is in the main, not fully, in the main atomic . . . so, although I do have a very great deal of sympathy with Sir Derek Ezra and his short term problems . . . I think we do really need a long term plan and if the only outlet for coal in the future is to power stations, I think we've got to recognize that it will be competing against something in which I personally would put my entire effort: the development of the technologies that will be required to introduce atomic power.   (D.En. Energy Paper No. 14, 1976, p. 16)

This attitude contrasts with the CEGB's attempts to form long term working arrangements with the NCB, and the CEGB view of the coal and electricity industries needing each other to remain profitable. Later in 1976, at the National Energy Conference, Sir Peter advocated a new basis for the national discussion of energy policy; a set of guidelines which would consider the public interest and give each industry the power to plan within them. This point was extended in the Council's paper to the conference which set out ground rules which the energy industries could use as a planning basis. They included standards for preserving safety and the environment, required rates of return on resources, pricing principles and degree of freedom of consumer choice (D.En. Energy Paper No. 13, vol. 2, 1976, p. 43). The Council felt that these ground rules would help in decentralizing decision-taking and in allowing society to understand and approve the long term energy planning framework. This call for some sort of guidelines for the nationalized industries to work along seems to be a continuation of the pressure for the setting of financial targets, which other industries have advocated.

The Electricity Council's planning mechanism still continues to function, despite the criticism of it contained in the Plowden Report; the Council themselves are not happy about their planning role, as their commercial adviser R. Forman told the British Association for the Advancement of Science: 'The implementation of corporate plans by the industry is difficult, though by no means impossible, owing to the statutory independence of the constituent Boards and the federal, advisory nature of the Electricity Council' (Forman, R., 1977, p. 9). The medium term planning process for the industry begins with the production of a set of assumptions about UK economic performance, under guidance from the Treasury. These assumptions then go to the Boards, each of which responds with their estimate of demand for the years of the planning period. This mechanism is duplicated by the Council's own staff. The Council then considers the sets of estimates and adopts one for use by the whole industry. Forman goes on to emphasize the uncertainties of the planning process, commenting that '. . . we must not expect any energy estimates to be right, except by coincidence' (Forman, R., 1977, p. 11). It is clear from his paper that the Electricity Council sees the future of the UK as one involving a high degree of dependence on electricity, and: 'As seen at present, the choice lies essentially between, on the one hand, developing nuclear power rapidly and improving the standard of living or, on the other hand, not developing nuclear power rapidly and accepting a lower standard of living' (Forman, R., 1977, p. 6). In their Annual Report, the Council confirm their views of nuclear power stating: '. . . unless the government are prepared to accept a substantial risk of a prolonged energy supply crisis in about 20 years time, with all that this would entail for the general economy, decisions on a nuclear programme are needed very soon' (*The Electricity Council Annual Report 1976–77*, p. 4). Their view of the importance of electricity to the economy and of nuclear power to generate the electricity has remained consistent over the last few years, and is unlikely to change with the coming of the new chairman, Sir Francis Tombs. Sir Francis was always a firm advocate of nuclear power when SSEB chairman, but perhaps to a lesser extent than the CEGB of that time.

There is less heard from the Council than from the other energy industries about the importance of the national interest in energy planning. Sir Peter Menzies' idea of guidelines for planning seem to have disappeared, and the Council persistently advocates its role as the provider of an increased nuclear electricity supply for the UK. Perhaps one reason for the unpopularity of public policy discussion in the Council is the chairman's attitude to the public, which appears to be unchanged since his days with the SSEB. He told a recent meeting of the Institution of Electrical Engineers: 'The majority of the objectors [to nuclear power] appear to be people with only a superficial knowledge of the subject. Nuclear power was the only assured source of energy that can meet our future needs' (Cook, 1977c). The Council has overall, if indirect, control of research for the electricity industry, and so its view of the future is important in determining research priorities. It would be unfortunate if options were closed because of lack of research in areas thought by the Council to be unimportant, for example renewable sources. Sir Francis Tombs feels that: 'Most of [the renewable energy sources] are wildly uneconomic and likely to remain so. For this reason, they are unlikely to contribute as much as 10 per cent of the nation's energy demand by the year 2000' (Cook, 1978b, p. 14).

Sir Francis has other problems apart from defending the industry's opinions on nuclear power; energy pricing is the current cause for concern, with gas prices being held down compared to both electricity and coal. He presented a paper to the second Energy Commission meeting in February 1978 saying that consumers were being misled about prices they would eventually have to pay for gas; gas was dominating the market and thus investment in electricity and coal would be limited by low income. Sir Derek Ezra, the NCB chairman, backed the Council view, which went on to suggest pricing fuels by heat content so that the equivalent heat from any fuel would cost much the same. The British Gas Corporation chairman, Sir Denis Rooke, not surprisingly defended his industry, saying that gas prices would move smoothly upwards as depletion continued, and that pricing should reflect real costs. This argument appears to be another reason for the formulation of a national policy which would take into account factors such as depletion rates, reserves and pricing for the energy industries as a whole, thus avoiding the incessant attacks by one industry on another. Within the electricity industry, the National Joint Co-ordinating Council for Great Britain, the NJCC(GB), was set up in 1977 and is the equivalent of the coal industry's tripartite group, being a body of board and trade union officials. This may enable the electricity industry to speak as a whole in the way that the coal industry has already achieved, giving a better foundation for planning at a high level and allowing statements by the industry to be treated with a greater level of confidence.

BRITISH GAS CORPORATION

The British gas industry was nationalized in 1948 under the Gas Act, which gave the Gas Council a duty to advise the appropriate minister on questions affecting the gas industry. There were twelve area gas boards at that time, and the Gas Council had to assist them in their duties and raise any capital required by the boards or the Council. The area boards and the Council were independent of each other and accountable directly to government, via their departmental minister. The Gas Act of 1965 extended the functions of the Gas Council to enable gas supplies in Great Britain to be developed on a national basis, in view of the arrival of North Sea gas. The financial position of the Council was that the revenue from one year had to balance the expenditure of the following year – that is, it was required to break even.

The Gas Act of 1972 reorganized the industry under one central body, the British Gas Corporation (BGC), which was charged with the duty of: '. . . developing and maintaining an efficient, coordinated and economical system of gas supply for Great Britain and of satisfying as far as it is economical to do so all reasonable demands for gas . . .' (D.En. Fact Sheet 3, 1976, p. 3). The BGC is a unified body taking the place of the Gas Council and the area boards; within the BGC, the country is divided into twelve regions for administrative purposes, two of those regions being Scotland and Wales. The original chairman of the BGC since its inception on 1 January 1973 was Sir Arthur Hetherington, who had spent his entire career in the gas industry, and he was succeeded on 1 July 1976 by Sir Denis Rooke, who had previously been deputy chairman. Sir Denis Rooke is an engineer who worked with liquefied natural gas, and was a member of the technical team which sailed in the *Methane Pioneer* on its first voyage bringing liquefied natural gas to the UK in 1959. He joined the Gas Council in 1960 as a development engineer and was appointed director of production and supplies in 1966. He became deputy chairman of the Gas Council in 1972 and then of the BGC in 1973. He is a member of the OETB, the NEDC and a part-time member of BNOC. He is also chairman of the nationalized industries' chairmen's group, and '. . . is a stern champion of the right to run his industry with a minimum of Government interference' (Cook, 1978a).

The deputy chairman of the BGC is J. H. Smith, a chartered accountant who had been chief accountant with the Southern and East Midland Gas Boards before becoming deputy chairman of the East Midland Gas Board in 1968. He was appointed Member for Finance of the Gas Council (and then BGC) in 1972 and he is the BGC representative on WGES. There are five other full-time board members, each with special responsibility in either finance, economic planning, production and supply, marketing or personnel. The member for marketing, B. C. Smith, is a member of ACEC. There are at present nine part-time members of the BGC, including Alistair Macleod Matthews (who held a senior post with BP until 1973 and is a member of the Scottish Industrial Development Board and the Scottish Economic Council), R. Greenbury (a director of Marks and Spencer Ltd) and Hugh Scanlon (ex-president of the Amalgamated Union of Engineering Workers and a member of the National Economic Development Council). Research contact with other energy industries and the academic world is maintained via ACORD, of which Dr J. A. Gray, the BGC director of research, is a member. Coordination of planning between the nationalized energy industries is carried out by WGES, and apart from the BGC deputy chairman, the director of corporate planning, J. V. Licence, also attends the meetings.

The finances of BGC are subject to restrictions imposed by

government similar to those of other nationalized industries. The Corporation is limited in its borrowing power by the 1972 Gas Act, but during the 1976/77 financial year was granted permission to operate in the commercial market, thus gaining access to surplus funds from commercial companies. As far back as 1961 the government set financial objectives for the nationalized industries in order to improve their financial performance. In 1967 government opinion was that objectives had proved their worth, and targets were set up in discussion with each industry. The targets were to cover approximately five-year periods but were to be combined with a flexible approach to cater for changing circumstances. Targett (1977), who reviewed the record of BGC in reaching its given objectives, concluded that policies were decided in discussion between senior management and ministry officials, but that these policies were not then linked with financial objectives at an operational level. He felt that the process of setting objectives fell between two stools, being conducted at a high level and yet ignoring wider policy issues. The objectives were not made explicit and they did not act as incentives to good management. One of the problems peculiar to BGC was the dependence of the return on assets on the depletion policy and accidental changes in the depletion rate. This uncertainty made nonsense of tightly calculated financial targets. Finally Targett felt that the need for flexibility in the setting of objectives had not been met, giving as an example the five-year objective set in 1969, after which oil prices rose dramatically and North Sea gas extraction fell behind schedule. He commented:

> If it takes greater changes than these in 'events inside and outside the industry' for financial objectives to be adjusted, one can only pray devoutly that they will not budge in our generation. It is very hard to escape the conclusion that the Treasury and the sponsoring ministry had thought through no operational process or mechanism of any kind for systematic review of the financial objectives.   (Targett, 1977, p. 179)

Interference by the government on non-commercial grounds is still taking place: a 10 per cent price increase was imposed on BGC in 1977/78 in order to repay an International Monetary Fund (IMF) loan, although this came about as a result of IMF pressure on the government.

The BGC is highly profitable at the moment, and the 1977/78

figures are expected to be greater than the 1976/77 figures which themselves prompted an inquiry by the Price Commission into BGC's profitability. The government imposed price increase during the 1977/78 year explains some of the increase in profits, but even so gas prices are the subject of complaints by the chairman of the NCB and the Electricity Council. One of Sir Denis Rooke's problems at the BGC stems from the contracts signed with the oil corporations stating the rate of gas extraction to be maintained in the Southern Basin of the North Sea; the BGC has to sell the gas it has contracted to buy, thus low pricing is advantageous for the Corporation at present, even though it may present a misleading picture in the overall energy policy context. The Corporation does not want to be forced to sell its Southern Basin gas to non-premium customers at lower prices. The formation of a long term depletion strategy for gas is a complex process because even the reserve estimate is not a universally agreed figure; as the assistant director (planning) of the Corporation put it:

> The size and expected life of indigenous natural gas reserves seems to concern a lot of people. We in British Gas are not without interest in the subject. However, we are by no means in a position to assume a single figure – there must be a range of assumptions about reserves and a corresponding range of possibilities for their use and for the eventual development of replacements and substitutes.   (Lewis, 1977, pp. 2–3)

The Corporation has several subsidiary and associated companies concerned with exploration and development in the UK sector of the Continental Shelf, and their estimates of reserves tend to be greater than estimates made by the other energy industries. The Corporation feel that there are strong hopes of more major fields being discovered to sustain gas supplies into the next century.

At the 1976 National Energy Conference Sir Denis Rooke advocated substitute natural gas (SNG) as an insurance policy for Britain's future energy prospects ' . . . because the most efficient way of getting the energy in coal applied in our homes to produce space heating and hot water will be through SNG rather than electricity generation' (D.En. Energy Paper No. 13, vol. 1, 1976, p. 46). He stated that gas was a most effective and efficient way of transporting energy from source to the point of utilization, and advocated conservation, exploration and R and D to extend fuel resources as far as possible. The BGC paper to the Conference continued in the same vein, replying to a combined NCB/CEGB attack on low gas prices and asking for more freedom from government price controls. On general energy policy, the paper took a different line to the other nationalized energy industries, questioning the assumption of an energy gap and pressing the case for increasing the number of options available. The Corporation felt it would be bad policy to enter into any commitments before it was absolutely necessary, and attacked the combined coal and electricity industries' view of the future: 'This caution must apply to proposals to expand coal capacity beyond the level at which costs can be covered by a competitive price, to the adoption of highly uneconomic depletion policies for gas or oil, or to investment on a dramatic scale in nuclear power' (D.En. Energy Paper No. 13, vol. 2, 1976, p. 30). Thus the gas industry view of the future and the national interest is rather different from the coal/electricity view; it stems from the highly commercial attitude of the Corporation, wishing to obtain maximum return from the capital investment in the North Sea. This implies more effort in research and conservation to extend the life of the resources, and more exploration to increase the level of known reserves, which the Corporation already assume to be high compared with estimates made by other interests. They also see an alternative use for coal in the future to produce SNG rather than as a fuel for electricity generation. Clearly, although the gas industry will naturally defend its own interests in the face of pressure from coal and electricity, its perspective on the future may be equally viable, merely advocated less often. As with the other industries, the BGC plans try to combine the national interest with an extension and expansion of their own sector: 'In short, we must not be obsessed by the realisation that any local reserves of hydrocarbons have a finite life — the contribution which the gas industry is able to make to the fuel economy of Great Britain is a continuing one' (Lewis, 1977, p. 4). The BGC has not been criticized as much as the electricity and nuclear industries for secrecy in decision-making, as few of their projects are particularly controversial: their attitude to public discussion of energy policy is welcoming, but consistent with their commercial ethic: 'However there is always a danger that if every discussion ranges too widely, important decisions may be delayed and the opportunity to embark upon the most economic course of action may be lost' (BGC, *Annual Report and Accounts 1976–77*, p. 24).

UNITED KINGDOM ATOMIC ENERGY AUTHORITY AND THE NUCLEAR INDUSTRY

The United Kingdom Atomic Energy Authority (UKAEA) was established on 1 August 1954 by the Atomic Energy Authority Act 1954 to take over defence and civilian atomic projects from the Ministry of Supply. The UKAEA mandate was 'to produce, use and dispose of atomic energy and carry out research into any matters connected therewith'. The world's first large scale nuclear power station began operations in October 1956 at Calder Hall, Cumbria, and the nuclear establishment expanded to cope with the increasing amount of research and design work allotted to it. Research facilities were built at Harwell, and design and production facilities at Capenhurst, Springfields and Risley. From the engineering group at Risley came many of the reactor designers who began working in the five reactor building consortia of the 1950s. Another organization created at that time was the Nuclear Installations Inspectorate (NII), which was part of the D.En. from its beginnings in 1959 until 1975, when it was transferred to the Health and Safety Executive (HSE). In 1971 the UKAEA responsibilities for weapons research were transferred to the Ministry of Defence, leaving the UKAEA its civil atomic functions only. Also in 1971 two commercial undertakings which had developed in the Authority since 1965 as the Trading Fund were established as private companies with all shares held by the Authority on behalf of the state. These were the Radiochemical Centre Ltd (TRC) at Amersham which manufactures and sells isotopes, and British Nuclear Fuels Ltd (BNFL) which has four plants at Risley (fuel cycle services), Springfields (uranium processing), Capenhurst (uranium enrichment) and Windscale (plutonium fuel fabrication).

The Authority has prime responsibility for carrying out R and D on all aspects of nuclear power, although reactor research is also carried out by the CEGB and SSEB. The chairman of the Authority since 1967 has been Sir John Hill, and he is to be chairman until 1981 when he reaches retiring age. He is also chairman of BNFL and TRC, in which the Authority are the sole shareholders, has been a member of the Nuclear Power Advisory Board since 1973 and is a member of the Energy Commission. Not surprisingly, Sir John is a staunch advocate of the need for a substantial nuclear power programme in the UK, but he is also in favour of increasing coal production and R and D for alternative energy sources. His many speeches tend to concentrate on refuting what he believes to be the over-emotional opposition to nuclear power, in particular to the fast breeder reactor. At the 1976 National Energy Conference he pleaded for continuity in the ordering of nuclear plant to ensure a viable nuclear industry, and the Authority paper to the conference pressed the case for nuclear power as a result of growing electricity demand. Sir John is sure that there will be a major world energy shortage in 25 years' time, and sees the fast breeder as the one sure way of providing for the energy needs of the UK and avoiding the problems of uranium shortage. He told the SCST that he did not think the amount of money devoted to nuclear research was excessive compared with that spent on alternative sources: 'I would not accept that there is a vast expenditure on nuclear development. Certainly the expenditure is significant, but by comparison with the importance of assuring our energy supplies for the future I do not think the development expenditure on nuclear power is in any way out of line with what is sensible' (HC534-ii, Session 1976/77, Q. 1003). In contrast to his usual stance of sticking to the facts of nuclear power matters as the Authority sees them, Sir John made a public relations error, if nothing more, in a 1977 television programme discussing the evidence for a nuclear waste explosion in the Southern Urals in the 1950s. His attitude was that the Authority was not interested in the claimed explosion, felt that it could not have happened, and that it did not matter anyway. As Sir John put it, 'What if it did happen?' His unfortunate remarks received less publicity than they deserved, especially at a time when several important debates on energy matters were coming to a head.

The deputy chairman of the Authority is Dr Walter Marshall, who until July 1977 was also the D.En. Chief Scientist. He too is well known for his advocacy of nuclear power, and is a research physicist who worked at AERE Harwell, the University of California and Harvard before becoming director of the Research Group of the Authority in 1969. He was made an Authority member in 1972 and deputy chairman in 1975. Dr Marshall took part in the May 1977 Sunningdale Seminar on Nuclear Policy, and the record of the second session states: 'After observing that the problems of developing fusion power were staggering, Dr Marshall went on to say that the safety arguments ought not to be significant in reactor choice' (D.En., Sunningdale Seminar on Nuclear Policy, 1977, p. 5). Interestingly, the seminar took place only a couple of months before Tony Benn sacked Marshall from his post as Chief Scientist, apparently on the grounds of their disagreements over nuclear power.

The only other full-time Authority member is A. M. Allen, the member for Finance and Administration since 1976. He is an ex-civil servant who worked in the Treasury before becoming director of the Reactor Group at the UKAEA from 1959 to 1963, general manager of the British Waterways Board from 1963 to 1968 and then returning to the Authority in 1968 to fulfil various personnel capacities. He is a member of the NRPB, and was formerly secretary of the Authority. There are eight part-time board members: Lord Kearton, the BNOC chairman; Sir Leslie Williams, an ex-civil servant and deputy chairman of the Civil Service Appeal Board; Professor Sir Brian Flowers, Rector of Imperial College and chairman of the Royal Commission on Environmental Pollution, 1973–6; Dr Ned Franklin, the Nuclear Power Company chairman; W. B. S. Walker, a partner in the management consultancy firm of Peat, Marwick, Mitchell and Co.; Con Allday, the managing director of BNFL; R. A. Peddie, a CEGB member; and B. G. Tucker, the D.En. deputy secretary responsible for the coal, electricity and atomic energy divisions. The Authority representative on the WGES is R. L. R. Nicholson, the principal economics and finance officer.

The Authority is financed by a parliamentary grant which covers the cost of both nuclear and non-nuclear R and D, the largest single amount going to the fast reactor programme at the moment. The Authority receives a substantial income for its R and D services, services to BNFL and isotope production. Authority research takes place at the Atomic Energy Research Establishment (AERE) Harwell and at the various laboratories of the Northern Division. The Northern Division is concerned mainly with the research, development and demonstration of nuclear reactors while AERE work concentrates on nuclear fuels, wastes, radiation damage and so on. Harwell is also the base for the Energy Technology Support Unit (ETSU) and the Marine Technology Support Unit (MATSU), and AERE research is under the overall direction of Dr Lewis Roberts. Before becoming director of AERE in early 1976 he was AERE Research Director (Energy), in charge of all non-nuclear projects at Harwell including ETSU and MATSU. The Authority representative on ACORD is Dr T. N. Marsham, the managing director of the Risley Nuclear Power Development Establishment. International contacts are maintained with the relevant bodies such as the EEC Joint Research Centre (JRC) which has a programme including work on reactor safety and the management of fissile materials, and leads the International Energy Agency (IEA) research effort in these fields. The IEA was established in November 1974 under the auspices of the OECD, and has a committee on Research and Development on which the UK representative is the D.En. Chief Scientist. International nuclear safeguards – that is the system whereby nuclear materials are accounted for and inspected – are applied through the European Atomic Energy Community (EURATOM), of which the UK is a member, and the International Atomic Energy Agency (IAEA).

EURATOM was formed as a result of discussions by the European Coal and Steel Community (ECSC) concerned with increasing co-operation between the ECSC partners. A treaty was signed in March 1957 setting up EURATOM, which had as its main task the creation within a short period of the technical and industrial conditions necessary for the utilization of nuclear discoveries and the production of nuclear power on a large scale. It was also responsible for the supply and security of nuclear fuel, the establishment of a nuclear industry and the training of necessary specialists, the control of fissile material and several other related functions. A EURATOM Supply Agency was set up to ensure the supply of reactor fuel, but has never been needed as uranium has always been easily available. EURATOM itself has not proved to be very significant, as a Community reactor design was never developed; France was unwilling to exchange technical information with other members, and German industrialists saw their best interests as lying in the exploitation of US designs. The UK joined EURATOM on 1 January 1973, but the function of EURATOM is now solely research, although in a number of joint ventures rather than in true Community projects. The International Atomic Energy Agency (IAEA) was formed in July 1957 to encourage the peaceful uses of atomic energy. It is a United Nations agency, having over 100 members, and its General Conference meets annually. Executive functions are carried out by the Board of Governors consisting of 34 members and a Secretariat in Vienna, under Director-General Sigvard Eklund, a Swedish nuclear physicist. The IAEA has set up a system of international safeguards to prevent the diversion of fissile materials which includes inspection by IAEA inspectors. There are also IAEA standards for containers for the transport of radioactive materials and radiation standards based on the International Commission on Radiological Protection (ICRP) standards.

Several UKAEA research programmes involve international cooperation, such as the Joint European Torus (JET) fusion research project and the fast breeder reactor research effort. (The British Parliament occasionally has difficulty with the technical terms of the energy debate, as the *Guardian* (10 January 1978, p. 3) reported Kenneth Warren MP having to explain that his question was about Joint European Taurus (sic) not Joint European Tours as printed in the list of questions!)

British Nuclear Fuels Ltd (BNFL) has responsibility for the manufacture and supply of uranium and plutonium-based fuels and the provision of fuel cycle services for nuclear power stations. It is a state-owned company whose shares are held solely by the UKAEA, and it came into existence in 1971, since when its chairman has been the Authority chairman, Sir John Hill, and its managing director Con Allday (also a part-time Authority member). Allday is a chemist who worked for ICI from 1939 until joining the UKAEA in 1959, where he was in turn chief chemist, technical director, commercial director and managing director. BNFL take a strictly commercial view of waste management problems. The Windscale inquiry into the construction of a new waste-reprocessing plant held up their plans to finalize a contract for reprocessing Japanese nuclear waste and although Allday wanted to sign contracts on a provisional basis before the end of the inquiry, Tony Benn refused permission. The deputy managing director of BNFL, Donald Avery, was interviewed on television (BBC2, *Newsday*, 21 October 1977) about the profitability of waste reprocessing, and said he felt that the single most worrying aspect of nuclear power was proliferation, but also that: 'I'm in business and I'm quite satisfied I'm making money.'

BNFL has holdings in various subsidiary and associate companies, including some registered abroad. It owns one third of URENCO Ltd, based at Marlow, Buckinghamshire, which markets enriched uranium; the remaining two thirds of the URENCO shares are held by Ultra Centrifuge Nederland (UCN) and Uran-Isotopentrennungs GmbH (URANIT), a West German firm. The consortium resulted from the 1970 Treaty of Almelo, signed by the UK, West Germany and the Netherlands, whereby the three countries decided to collaborate on a single centrifuge design which would become the basis of the European enrichment industry. CENTEC GmbH was set up at the same time as URENCO to coordinate R and D. BNFL also owns one third of United Reprocessors GmbH (Uni Rep), set up in 1971 to market reprocessing techniques. The other partners in this consortium are the French state atomic energy agency CEA (through its subsidiary COGEMA) and a West German combine with several

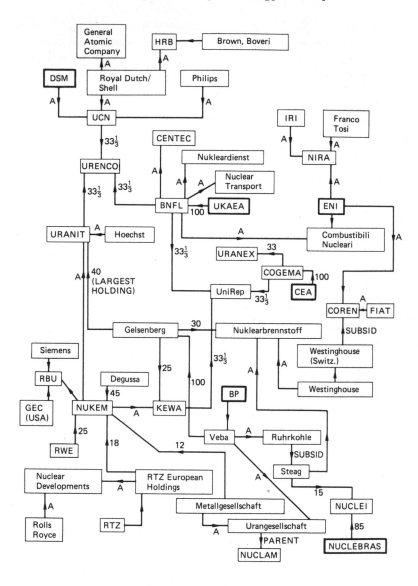

FIGURE 6   BNFL and its international connections

BNFL	British Nuclear Fuels Ltd
BP	British Petroleum
CEA	Commissariat à l'Energie Atomique

shareholders (KEWA), based in Frankfurt. As may be seen from Figure 6, it is impossible to separate the functions of the various European and world state atomic energy agencies as many of their subsidiary and associate companies are interconnected. The UK, through the AEA and BNFL, has common interests with the Dutch government via URENCO, UCN and DSM, the Dutch state-controlled chemicals company. The UK and France both have holdings in Uni Rep (through BNFL and COGEMA), and BNFL also has an Italian-registered associate, Combustibili Nucleari, of which Sir John Hill is chairman and Con Allday is technical director. Several of the large multinational corporations are involved in the nuclear industry, including RTZ, GEC, Royal Dutch/Shell and Philips.

The international ties of the nuclear industry mean that decisions taken in the course of purely commercial ventures as seen by the companies involved may rebound upon governments. For instance, the export of enriched uranium to the Brazilian state nuclear

COGEMA	Compagnie Generale de Matieres Nucleaires
COREN	Combustibili per Reattori Nucleari
DSM	Naamloze Vennootschap DSM
ENI	Ente Nazionale Idrocarburi
HRB	Hochtemperatur-Reaktorbau GmbH
IIR	Istituto per la Ricostruzione Industriale
KEWA	Kernbrennstoff-Wiederaufbereitungs-Brennstoffen mBH
NIRA	Nucleare Italiana Reattori Avanzati
NUCLEBRAS	Empresas Nucleares Brasileiras
NUCLEI	Nuclebras Enriquecimento Isotopico
NUCLAM	Nuclebras Auxiliar de Mineracao
RBU	Reaktor-Brennelemente GmbH
RTZ	Rio Tinto-Zinc
RWE	Rheinisch-Westfalisches Elektrizitatswerk
UCN	Ultra Centrifuge Nederland
UKAEA	United Kingdom Atomic Energy Authority
UniRep	United Reprocessors GmbH
URANIT	Uran-Isotopentrennungs GmbH

☐	State-owned or state holding.
→—	Owned by/shares held (number indicates percentage of shares held).
A	Associate—company owning 10—50 per cent of shares in another company.
Subsid	Subsidiary company—over half shares owned or controlled by parent company.

company, NUCLEBRAS, by URENCO has been the cause of much recent concern, particularly in the Netherlands where large demonstrations have taken place. Brazil is not a signatory to the Non-Proliferation Treaty (NPT), and the Dutch Parliament were originally of the opinion that no enriched uranium from Almelo, the Dutch enrichment plant, should be exported to countries which had not signed the NPT unless strict safeguards were agreed in advance. A small demonstration took place at the British URENCO plant at Capenhurst, near Chester, in June 1978, when it seemed likely that URENCO would supply NUCLEBRAS from their British plant, but British interest in the problem has been slight. The main cause for concern is that commercial expediency in the form of West German exports of reactors, and the possible sale of a reprocessing plant to Brazil, will override the possibility of Brazil eventually achieving a nuclear weapons capability by using the reprocessing plant to produce weapon-grade plutonium. Britain is nominally in favour of non-proliferation, being a signatory to the NPT, but the BNFL view (and, implicitly, the British government view) is that the safeguards requested by URENCO concerning the use of uranium are adequate. The mix of secretive government agencies and multinational companies in the nuclear industry means that international dealings are very opaque, and often constitute agreements between governments rather than simply private companies. Most of the large oil companies have diversified their holdings into nuclear power (and various alternative energy sources), thus nuclear power has brought an increase in corporate and international control of energy resources, as opposed to individual state control.

The evolution of the single nuclear power plant design and construction company which now exists in Britain is long and complex. At the time of the placing of contracts for the first nuclear power programme in 1955 there were five consortia of companies in the running, many of their engineers having come from the UKAEA group at Risley. By the end of the first programme of nine stations in 1963, the number of consortia had shrunk to three, due to problems with the construction of the stations, each of which had different designs. The three consortia were the English Electric Group, the Nuclear Power Group (TNPG) and Atomic Power Construction (APC).

APC had been formed partly at government behest as the last of the original five consortia, and was composed of Crompton Parkinson, Richardsons Westgarth, International Combustion and Fairey, with the General Electric Company Ltd (GEC) involved for a few years in the early 1960s. The English Electric Group was made up of English Electric and Babcock and Wilcox (the boilermakers) amongst others, and eventually was transformed into British Nuclear Design and Construction (BNDC) after GEC's merger with English Electric in 1968. This government-encouraged merger heralded the entrance of Sir Arnold Weinstock into the British nuclear industry. He had been managing director of GEC since 1963, having begun his career as a financier and property developer by taking a degree in statistics at London University. Within four years of the AEI–EE–GEC merger, he had cut the GEC labour force by 72,000 – closing 67 production units in the process – and gained a reputation in government circles for good management. The third nuclear consortium, the Nuclear Power Group, was made up of two of the original consortia, Parsons and AEI. Thus GEC had an interest, at one time or another, in all three groups which began bidding for the second round of nuclear power plant contracts.

The second programme, announced in 1964, was to consist of a different type of reactor, the advanced gas-cooled reactor (AGR). The Magnox reactors used for the initial programme were considered to be outdated, but the choice of the AGR was preceded by much discussion on the merits of the American light-water reactors. APC undercut the BNDC and TNPG estimates for the Dungeness AGR and were given the contract, while the other two consortia were given two contracts each, making a total of five AGRs. APC started work at Dungeness in 1966 and soon found they were unable to cope with the job. By 1969 the consortium collapsed and BNDC reluctantly agreed to finish the work. The aftermath of the government policy of encouraging competition between consortia with different designs (five AGRs built, to three separate designs) has been overrunning of the completion dates and escalation in costs. Rush, MacKerron and Surrey (1977) even go so far as to say that the existence of the three massive consortia and their need for work provided the deciding impulse behind the government decision to start a second nuclear programme at a time of no perceptible threat to coal or oil supplies. The chaotic state of the nuclear industry at this time prompted the government to set up a Working Party to inquire into the choice of thermal reactor systems. The report, the Vinter Report, remains unpublished but was apparently concerned more with reorganization of the industry than the details of reactor systems. The SCST, in their hearings on nuclear power policy in 1972–3, tried to discover more details about this report but were always referred back to the department or the minister. Reform of the industry was in the air, with the amalgamation of BNDC and TNPG into one company managed by Sir Arnold Weinstock being strongly advocated. At the SCST hearings, Sir Arnold refused to comment on the proportion of shares GEC would require in any new company, and stated that he thought the existence of a healthy nuclear industry would be to the ultimate benefit of GEC. Shortly afterwards, in March 1973, the National Nuclear Corporation was formed by merging TNPG and BNDC under Sir Arnold Weinstock's management. GEC held 50 per cent of the shares, UKAEA 15 per cent and British Nuclear Associates (BNA) 35 per cent. BNA was a consortium of companies with engineering and electrical interests: Babcock and Wilcox, Clarke Chapman, Head, Wrightson & Co., McAlpine, Strachan and Henshaw, Taylor Woodrow and Whessoe. Later in 1973 the Nuclear Power Company Ltd (NPC) was set up as a wholly owned subsidiary of NNC to design and build reactors; however, no orders were forthcoming. The GEC shareholding in NNC was reduced to 30 per cent in 1976, UKAEA increasing its holding to 35 per cent, as recommended by the SCST in its report of June 1973 on nuclear power policy (HC350, Session 1972/73, para. 26). The reason for the transfer was to protect NNC from any instability caused if the main commercial shareholder decided to withdraw; a farsighted recommendation in the light of the events of early 1978.

By 1976 the government decision to order the Steam Generating Heavy Water Reactor (SGHWR) for the third round of nuclear power plants was under review, and the SCST was again in session. Lord Aldington, the NNC chairman (and GEC chairman), told the committee that the system of supervisory management by GEC was working satisfactorily, but that he could not see it extending indefinitely given the lack of reactor orders. The matter of reactor choice for the third round of power plants came to a head in 1978, with Tony Benn deciding on the British-designed AGR rather than the PWR which Sir Arnold Weinstock had advocated. As a result of this decision, Sir Arnold decided to end the GEC management contract with the nuclear industry and D.En. is to reorganize the management structure. It is possible that the National Enterprise Board may be brought in to provide financial backing. Several of the companies with smaller shareholdings in NNC have been discontented with GEC management, notably Babcock and Wilcox and

Clarke Chapman who favoured the AGR but were overruled by GEC. Babcock and Wilcox and Clarke Chapman are now merging their power station interests to form one powerful boilermaking company, which should have a stronger influence on nuclear decision-making than the smaller BNA members.

Sir Arnold Weinstock and GEC originally helped the government out by taking over the APC Dungeness contract, and Sir Arnold was then seen by the Conservative government as the saviour of the nuclear industry. However, his relations with the Labour government and Tony Benn in particular have been less than smooth, and the projected changes in NNC management were not unexpected. GEC, with their record of arms sales to South Africa and involvement with various repressive regimes, were perhaps not likely to share the same aims as a Labour government. Sir Arnold has been quoted as saying of GEC that: 'The justification of our existence is to satisfy the needs of consumers' (CIS, 1972, p. 34). His influential position in the engineering industry has been criticized as having been arrived at undemocratically, and CIS accused the GEC of creating 'social and human carnage' (CIS, 1972, p. 33) because Sir Arnold's decision-making was based solely on the need to maximize profit. Of course, GEC's reason for entering the nuclear industry in the first place was that it appeared profitable, and the demise of GEC followed by the projected NNC reorganization may lead to a more competent nuclear industry not biased in favour of one large shareholder. Advice to the government from the nuclear industry tends to be unanimous, and with such large amounts of money to be invested there is a need for alternative views of the choices involved in reactor programmes and other nuclear-policy matters. The Nuclear Power Advisory Board (NPAB), set up in 1973 by the government 'to provide continuing and concerted advice on all strategic aspects of civil nuclear energy policy' (Cmnd 5731, 1974, p. 1), is composed of leading members of the nuclear industry and chaired by the Secretary of State for Energy. It has only reported once, in 1974, on the choice of thermal reactor systems, and could not even reach agreement then. Its membership at that time consisted of the chairmen of the UKAEA, CEGB, NNC, Electricity Council and SSEB, two academics and members of the UKAEA and BNFL. It was unlikely to be able to provide a neutral view of the industry's problems, and after its initial report met only once between 1974 and 1976. This hardly augured well for the continuing role in policy-making specified in its terms of reference.

The SCST recommended that it should be strengthened and given an independent chairman, so that the advice given to the government would be '. . . coherent, consistent and free of preconceived attitudes' (HC89, Session 1976/77, para. 63). Since that SCST report of December 1976, most advice to the government has emanated from the usual range of sectional interests, particularly in late 1977 when the choice of reactor type for the third nuclear programme was being discussed. Tony Benn has remarked several times on the strength of the nuclear lobby, most recently in Parliament when announcing the choice of the AGR for the third nuclear programme: 'This argument has involved a greater use of pressure on me than I have seen in almost any other issue that I have had anything to do with and it has included a systematic attack upon British technology' (*Hansard*, 6 February 1978, col. 1398).

The Nuclear Installations Inspectorate (NII) exists to provide a neutral view of safety issues, but is often criticized on the grounds of its close working involvement with the nuclear industry. The NII was created in 1960 by the Nuclear Installations (Licensing and Insurance) Act 1959, and is responsible for the safety of commercial nuclear power stations and research reactors. The NII was removed from D.En. in 1975 and transferred to the Health and Safety Executive (HSE), which at least symbolized its independence of the nuclear industry and the decision-makers. The present Chief Inspector of Nuclear Installations is Ronald Gausden, an engineer who worked at AERE Harwell and for the UKAEA at Windscale before joining the NII in 1960, becoming Chief Inspector in 1976. The previous Chief Inspector, E. C. Williams, had a scientific Civil Service background and had not worked in the nuclear industry before joining the NII. The SCST discussed the functioning of the NII within the HSE in 1976, and were told that the HSE had taken over the Secretary of State's formal responsibility for taking decisions about licensing nuclear installations and other safety matters. The Secretary of State now did not interfere unless it was to give a direction on a particular matter. The deputy director-general of the HSE is also the director of nuclear safety, and three members of the Executive are formally responsible for nuclear matters. J. H. Locke, the HSE's director-general, commented to the SCST that the NII had added to its appearance of independence by moving to the HSE. The official aim of nuclear safety policy '. . . is to eliminate the possibility and potential consequences of accidents as far as is reasonably practicable' (D.En. Fact Sheet 5, March 1977, p. 7). The word 'reasonable' does not necessarily imply that all parties concerned in the nuclear industry agree with the safety standards and radiation exposure levels adhered to by the NII. International limits for radiation exposure are set by the International Commission for Radiological Protection (ICRP), a self-appointed body accountable only to the International Congress of Radiologists and chosen by them on the basis of individual scientific reputation. The ICRP assessments are endorsed in the UK by the Medical Research Council (MRC) and the National Radiological Protection Board (NRPB).

The NRPB was set up in October 1970, taking over the functions of the Radioactive Substances Advisory Committee (which had been in existence since 1948) and the MRC's Radiological Protection Service. The Board is administratively answerable to the Secretary of State for Health and Social Security. The Flowers Report on Nuclear Power and the Environment criticized the identification of the Board with the UKAEA, due to staff movement from the UKAEA to the Board and the Board's base at Harwell. The report stressed that the Board should be a completely independent entity, and that it should become more of a focal point in the organization of radiological protection. Until late 1977, it did not have the formal duty of endorsing ICRP standards, but this has now been transferred from the MRC. The Flowers Report asked for high-level changes in the NRPB: 'We are clear that the changes we recommend in NRPB responsibilities are sufficiently far-reaching as to call for its reconstitution at Board level and for a review of the organization and expertise of the executive body. We would again stress the importance we attach to NRPB independence; specifically, its independence from the AEA' (Cmnd 6618, 1976, para. 224). The only Board changes made since the publication of the report have been the appointments of Sir Frederick Dainton, the chairman of the University Grants Committee, and Raymond Beverton, the biologist and environmentalist. The UKAEA member on the Board, A. M. Allen, has been reappointed for a year, and the Board has increased in size from seven to nine with the two new appointments, which slightly diminishes the influence of the four medical radiologists already on the Board. These changes hardly seem an adequate reconstitution, as required by the Flowers Report. At present, the NRPB tends not to encourage public discussion of the social acceptability of the risks inherent in nuclear power production, and adheres zealously to the ICRP standards even though these are less strict than those of the USA, for example. There is little explanation of the value judgments involved in weighing up the scientific and social facets of the problem. 'The NRPB's assertion that radiation doses to the individual below a certain low level and doses beyond a certain period in the future should be ignored (even in calculating risks let alone assessing their significance) is an attitude to be expected from the nuclear industry, not from a body which is supposed to be expert, open and independent' (Wynne, 1978, p. 209).

Much criticism of the nuclear industry and its predilection for secrecy was vented at the Windscale inquiry into the need for a reprocessing plant, but the report came out strongly in favour of building the plant and keeping the nuclear industry alive and able to expand if necessary. The report apparently vindicated the long-held attitudes of the nuclear industry, in spite of its criticism of some safety and security criteria.

The nuclear industry, in common with all the other sectional interests in the energy industry, tries to push forward its own claims in parallel with its definitions of the national interest and flexibility of policy. The 'national interest' is never explicitly defined by any of the industries which refer to it in conjunction with their own aims; it appears to be perceived as an overall economic aim with which any particular energy industry will concur provided it entails the constant growth and health of that industry. It is a reflection of the commercial aims of the nationalized energy industries, and is normally seen in rather a narrow context relating directly to the interests of a specific industry. The UKAEA have always been strongly in favour of keeping a sound basis for the expansion of the nuclear plant construction industry with the probability of building a series of fast breeder reactors at some time in the future. The Nuclear Power Company, in a very muted paper to the National Energy Conference, stressed the place of '. . . a limited programme of thermal reactors, and . . . the capability to exercise the fast breeder option . . .' (D.En. Energy Paper No. 13, vol. 2, 1976, p. 60) in keeping energy options open, and thus the need to maintain a domestic nuclear industry. At the same conference Lord Aldington, the NNC chairman, also stressed the need for developing an experienced nuclear design and construction team, and stated: 'I do not think that if you look at the facts of today, there are any facts which indicate that in the end nuclear power will be expensive' (D.En. Energy Paper No. 13, vol. 1, 1976, p. 28). This opinion, and the oft-expressed need to maintain a viable nuclear industry, are still highly controversial points. An economist has recently put forward the view that there are no falling costs in nuclear technology, and tried to challenge the arguments of the nuclear establishment: 'The key syndrome of the nuclear industry is that the risks are worthwhile and acceptable because there is a trade-off between the admitted risks and the established benefits. If however it were established that there are no benefits, which I strongly suspect is the case, then the ground rules for the debate are changed. If there are no benefits then why take undeniable risks?' (Sweet, 1978, p. 38).

There is no shortage of economic arguments for and against various nuclear power strategies, often the solutions being governed by the differences in initial assumptions. The Flowers Report had some sympathy with the nuclear industry, saying that: 'It seems that nuclear power has in some ways become the whipping-boy for technological development as a whole' (Cmnd 6618, 1976, para. 499), but it did have severe reservations about the increasing use of nuclear power, and was particularly concerned about the fast breeder. 'Our consideration of these matters, however, has led us to the view that we should not rely for energy supply on a process that produces such a hazardous substance as plutonium, unless there is no reasonable alternative' (Cmnd 6618, 1976, para. 507). Thus the debate continues, with the UKAEA putting in writing its commitment ' . . . to explain fully and in public not only the advantages of nuclear power but also the problems and implications of a large nuclear programme' (UKAEA, 1977, p. 6). The Flowers Report has certainly had the effect of slowing down the rate of development of the fast breeder programme. The prestige attached to the RCEP meant that its conclusions could not be completely ignored, and during the Windscale inquiry the government accepted the need for a further inquiry into fast breeder development. As a result of the proceedings at Windscale, several reports have been published suggesting alterations in the inquiry mechanism, ranging from the use of the Planning Inquiry Commission (PIC) to two tier systems with preliminary information-gathering exercises before an adversarial inquiry. There has been no decision taken concerning the date or form of the inquiry, and it may well be 1980 before it takes place. Meanwhile, the UKAEA is also having a difficult passage with its applications for planning permission to do test drillings in the radioactive waste disposal programme. In three out of four cases, the initial application has been turned down, and appeals will be necessary, giving more opportunity for the steadily growing band of anti-nuclear campaigners to gain publicity. The complexity of the entire debate, as typified by the Windscale inquiry and its poor coverage in the media, is gradually being resolved into a series of local issues, more difficult for the nuclear establishment to contest. The form of the fast breeder inquiry will partly define the opportunity and effectiveness of public participation; it will undoubtedly be a slow process, as there is no planning mechanism in existence at present which can cope with debate on future lifestyles. It is fortunate that the government has the will to undertake debates of this nature, as the nuclear establishment in industry and the Civil Service is powerful and naturally takes a narrower view of the problems associated with nuclear power.

BRITISH NATIONAL OIL CORPORATION AND THE OIL INDUSTRY

The legal niceties of exploration on and under the sea bed have been discussed internationally since the end of the Second World War. The Truman Proclamation of 1945 by the USA, whereby they laid claim to their Continental Shelf, led up to the 1958 Geneva Continental Shelf Convention passed at the first UN Law of the Sea Conference. This established the principle of equi-distance between coastal states as a boundary for exploration and exploitation rights, and clearly favoured countries with long coastlines. In 1964 the British Parliament passed the Continental Shelf Act which provided a framework in domestic law for the granting of exploration and exploitation licences. The first significant discovery of gas beneath the North Sea was made in 1959, while oil prospecting began to look more encouraging by 1962. Thus the first round of licensing was held in 1964, with the North Sea divided into equal blocks of about 100 square miles. Policy for license allocation at that time, and for the following three rounds, was based on the need to encourage rapid exploration and production; the requirement that profits should be taxable in the UK; equitable treatment for British companies in the country of origin of foreign companies; the ability of the applicant to conduct the work; and the present position of the applicant with respect to the development of continental shelf resources and the fuel economy. The most important of these points was the urgency of exploitation.

Because of the need for speed, the successful applicants in the first round were not necessarily the highest bidders, but those with the most intensive work programmes. Block rentals were low, and there was some reliance on foreign, particularly American, companies for their expertise and ability. The second licensing round of 1965 took place under a Labour government, which decided to consider the contribution applicants had made to the balance of payments, and arrangements which could be made to encourage participation by public enterprise, as well as the five original points. This round of licensing was not carried out on an entirely competitive basis, and in 1970 the third round of licenses was allocated by administrative discretion. Round four, 1971–2, was as important in area as the first round, and in this case some blocks were auctioned. The first gas was brought ashore from the North Sea basins in 1967 and the first oil in June 1975.

Between the fourth round of licensing in 1971–2 and the fifth round in 1977 the oil crisis occurred and prompted a reconsideration of British policy for offshore oil and gas. The first Labour government of 1974 was elected with a clause in its manifesto stating that it was determined to ensure full public ownership of North Sea oil and gas resources and keep the distribution of resources under full government control with majority public participation. The government produced a White Paper in July 1974, *United Kingdom Offshore Oil and Gas Policy* (Cmnd 5696, 1974), which initiated the idea of a British National Oil Corporation (BNOC) through which the government would exercise its participation rights in the licences. In order to increase the government revenue from the continental shelf, an additional tax on the oil companies' profits was proposed. All future licences were to be issued with the condition of state majority participation in any fields discovered, and talks were to begin on the subject of state participation in existing licences. Various changes in corporation tax were proposed to ensure that the state derived a fair return from the oil resources, and arrangements were set in hand to transfer some funds to Scotland and Wales. The use of oil revenue in the regions was mentioned in another White Paper, *The Challenge of North Sea Oil* (Cmnd 7143, 1978) which reiterated the government's intention of channelling funds through the Scottish, Irish and Welsh Development Agencies. The existing framework of investment incentives was to be retained, rather than any new agencies being set up to deal with the short term oil revenues.

The fifth round of licensing was completed in February 1978, and BNOC had a 51 per cent interest in all licences granted (except those in which British Gas was involved), and is to be an operator in six blocks. Tony Benn announced a decision to award a further nine blocks to BNOC and one to BGC in Parliament on 5 April 1978, and also gave notice that the sixth licensing round would consist of about forty blocks. This was consistent with government policy in licensing fewer blocks but at more regular intervals than in the past, as explained in the 1978 Brown Book.

BNOC and the National Oil Account (NOA) finally came into being on 1 January 1976 as a result of the Petroleum and Submarine Pipelines Act 1975. BNOC's revenues are automatically paid into the NOA which also meets BNOC's expenditure needs. BNOC differs from other nationalized corporations because of its close contact with the government: '. . . it is both a commercial enterprise operating in competition with other oil companies and an instrument of government policy and adviser to the government on oil policy' (Steel and Stanyer, 1977, p. 394). A unique feature of the BNOC board is that a statutory requirement exists for two civil servants to be appointed as non-voting members. These are ex-officio positions, held by the D.En. deputy secretary responsible for all the oil and gas divisions (J. G. Liverman), and the head of the Treasury industry sector, deputy secretary F. Jones. The D.En. member ensures that BNOC takes into account the government's overall energy policy when making decisions, and the Treasury member represents their interest in the NOA and keeps BNOC informed of the government's wider economic strategy. Apparently this innovation of having civil servants on the board of a nationalized industry has caused some concern in Whitehall, as it changes the previous roles and responsibilities of civil servants with respect to the nationalized industries.

After a year in business, BNOC had acquired equity interests in one gasfield in production and five oilfields under development; it had also taken over the oil interests of the NCB and Burmah Oil. Government policy is to secure a 51 per cent state holding through BNOC in all existing commercial oilfields. This is to be done through negotiation, but in the fifth round of licensing in 1977 BNOC was a co-licensee in all blocks from the outset. The chairman of BNOC since its inception has been Lord Kearton, a member of the Energy Commission who is also a part-time member of the CEGB and UKAEA and was chairman of Courtaulds from 1964–75. Its deputy chairman until late 1977 was Lord Balogh, also Tony Benn's oil adviser; he had to resign his post on reaching the statutory finishing age of 72, but immediately became a consultant to BNOC, with much the same influence as he previously held. Lord Croham (formerly Sir Douglas Allen, head of the Home Civil Service until 1977) was appointed as a part-time deputy chairman in September 1978, nearly a year after Lord Balogh's resignation. Lord Kearton himself was due to retire at the end of 1978, but it has proved difficult to find a suitable candidate for the post of chairman, which Lord Kearton combined with the role of chief executive. Political uncertainty as to the future of BNOC and the relatively low salary being offered are the main reasons why no appointment has yet been made. Lord Kearton would prefer an internal appointment, but ministers would like someone from the oil industry. Other board members include Sir Denis Rooke, BGC chairman; two bankers; Gavin Laird, the trade union representative from the AUEW; and a public relations consultant who previously worked for British Steel and Gulf Oil.

There is a great deal more contact between government and the oil industry than in the cases of the other energy industries. There is a Minister of State, Dr J. Dickson Mabon, who has special responsibility for offshore oil and gas, and six divisions of D.En. are devoted to oil or gas. The Offshore Supplies Office (OSO), which exists to increase UK industrial participation in North Sea development, is taking an unprecedented role as an initiator of contracts and a source of information in its own field. There is, of course, a BNOC representative on WGES. The precise role of BNOC is still hotly debated, and its financial priorities not yet settled, although Lord Kearton said in early 1978 that BNOC had sent details of their financial objectives to Tony Benn for his approval.

Criticism of BNOC comes both from the political left, who see Benn as being unduly deferential to the multinationals, and BNOC as being under-capitalized to do its job of ensuring full public participation in the blocks licensed during the first four rounds, and from the right who see it as a massive extension of state activity in a previously competitive area. BNOC feel that they have been hard-pressed initially to cope with their rapid growth, but Lord Kearton told the Select Committee on Nationalized Industries in 1978 that BNOC could foresee a time when it was left alone to develop the North Sea because of falling profitability. The corporation was therefore working on a ten to fifteen year plan to recruit and train people to operate in the North Sea as an insurance against the time when the multinationals pull out. He felt that the attraction of the North Sea for the multinationals had been profitability, and that as the work became more complicated and the Americans became more concerned with increasing their domestic oil supplies, the worse half of the oil recovery work in the North Sea could be left to BNOC. The oil companies have never been happy with the role of BNOC, mainly because they see it as being both state oil company and government watchdog, but their greater worry concerns the lack of incentive to explore the second generation of oilfields. The chairman of Occidental felt that further incentives from the government would be needed to keep the multinationals interested in the North Sea, saying on the question of excessive profits that: 'If an overall view was to be taken of the industry this would totally deflate many of the profiteering claims that have been heard' (Cook, 1978d). BNOC's position has been strengthened recently by a new oil find in one of its own blocks east of Dundee, and it is slowly beginning to recruit experienced workers from the multinationals.

The government has gradually been taking oil and gas revenues and depletion rates under control. BNOC is assuming 51 per cent participation in an increasing number of fields, and the government is able to delay to a certain extent depletion from finds made at various stages of the licensing rounds. It seems now that BNOC at least has an assured future even under a Conservative government, as although their original policy was to destroy the corporation, their latest statement of intention leaves BNOC purely as an operating company with no regulatory functions for North Sea development. These functions would be hived off to a separate agency, and BNOC would then have to act as a normal commercial company, which means it would be liable for petroleum revenue tax, from which it is now exempt.

The BNOC attitude to national energy policy tends to be coloured by its chairman's strong views on nuclear power; he is, after all, a UKAEA member. He has frequently advocated the claims of the fast breeder reactor as an essential for ensuring adequate energy supplies for Britain, even when speaking on behalf of BNOC, as at the National Energy Conference; his main points were the importance of the North Sea to the balance of payments, the need to keep the coal industry viable and the urgency of a decision to embark on a commercial fast breeder reactor programme. The BNOC paper endorsed these points and also defended the continuing degree of involvement of multinational corporations in the North Sea.

The multinationals had realized the possibilities of the North Sea well before the British government, and in the rush to define the national boundaries which led to the Continental Shelf Act of 1964, '. . . the British were allocated only thirty-five per cent of the North Sea, when they might, according to most legal authorities, have obtained a much larger area by taking the issue to the International Court at The Hague' (Sampson, 1976, p. 193). The generous initial licensing arrangements encouraged the American-controlled multinationals, and by 1973 the most successful fields were held by Exxon, Texaco, Mobil, Socal, Gulf and Total, although BP controlled 20 per cent and Shell 15 per cent of North Sea oil. The 1973 report of the Public Accounts Committee (HC122, Session 1972/73) on North Sea Oil and Gas confirmed that Britain was receiving a smaller share of oil revenues than other countries, and the incoming Labour government proceeded to change the tax structure and licensing regulations, as well as setting up BNOC. At that time 48 per cent of BP shares were owned by the government, although this situation changed as a result of the Bank of England's rescue of Burmah oil. The government reduced its BP holdings from 48 per cent to 31 per cent in 1977, and stated its intention to acquire the Bank of England's holdings of 20 per cent gained as a result of the Burmah financing arrangements. The government's intention was to: '. . . maintain its relationship with BP in a way which does not breach the traditional practice of non-intervention in the administration of the company as a commercial concern' (British Petroleum, 1978, p. 3). Apart from the government's BP holding, its negotiations for majority state participation with companies holding interests in commercial fields licensed during the first to fourth rounds are under way, the actual negotiations being conducted by D.En. and BNOC.

The recent international activities of BP have caused some concern in government circles. The Labour Party's 1978 conference called for the government to acquire the remaining 49 per cent of BP shares in order to increase accountability; although this is unlikely, the government's shareholding may be transferred from the Treasury to D.En. BP was involved in several international share deals during 1978, including one in which they bought part of the West German energy concern Veba (with its interests in the nuclear field – see Figure 6) and it is felt that the two government directors on the BP board wield too little power. The involvement of BP in Rhodesian sanctions-busting has also emphasized their relative independence of government policy. A committee of ministers is to examine the various options for change in BP, which will probably include encouraging the state appointed directors to use their powers more frequently. At present the state appointees are Lord Greenhill, ex-head of the Diplomatic Service, who is on the point of retiring, and Tom Jackson, General Secretary of the Union of Post Office Workers.

The wider interests of the oil companies are dealt with by the United Kingdom Offshore Operators' Association (UKOOA), which is the pressure group handling the companies' interests in broad aspects of energy policy and in all matters which affect them as a whole rather than as individual operators. It came into being in June 1973, and was a new organization created from the North Sea (UK) Operators Committee. The UKOOA had 39 members in 1976, all of which were oil companies active as operators in UK waters, and acts as a forum for discussion of common technical and administrative problems. Many of the UKOOA members have predominantly foreign interests, due to the multinational nature of the oil industry and the rapid development of the North Sea; this means that the UKOOA cannot always speak for every member under all conditions. The UKOOA concentrated solely on offshore energy in their paper to the National Energy Conference, although, of course, welcoming a stable, long term UK energy policy. Their main worry was the increasing interest taken by the government in North Sea affairs, as their spokesman said:

> Members of my Association are concerned over the apparent shift of emphasis in Government policy from stimulus and encouragement to tightly regulated control as reflected in recent legislation. In order to enable the industry to find and develop further petroleum reserves, . . . the Government . . . should establish conditions which are conducive to high risk commercial enterprise coupled with technical innovation and ingenuity.   (D.En. Energy Paper No. 13, vol. 1, p. 30)

This insular outlook on energy policy, apparently common in the oil industry, was reinforced at the National Energy Conference by the only multinational company to be represented, BP. Their chief executive spoke almost entirely on the importance of oil to the country, neglecting energy policy in any broader context.

Although the UKOOA do not have a seat on the Energy Commission, they did comment on the first Energy Commission paper, the Working Document on Energy Policy. Their main point was that the continued presence of the companies could only be assured as long as terms that provided for profitable exploration were in existence. They also felt that a more comprehensive presentation of the reserves was necessary in order to give an adequate basis for further discussion, and pointed out that further exploration would be carried out in increasingly hostile conditions, where the ratio of successful to unsuccessful wells would decrease. The UKOOA attempted to ward off the threat of BNOC by recommending that: '. . . licensing, as in the past, should continue to be open to the entire oil industry willing and competent to participate'. They then tried to reassure the commission by stating: 'Exploration activities, undertaken by the entire industry, need not lead to production earlier than the national interest requires' (Energy Commission Paper ENCOM (77)8, 1977, para. 3.4). The UKOOA were clearly disgruntled at the provision of a seat on the Energy Commission for a representative of the Petroleum Industries Advisory Committee rather than the UKOOA.

The Petroleum Industries Advisory Committee (PIAC) is a body consisting of the chief executives of the oil companies which have both refining and marketing interests in the United Kingdom. It was set up in December 1947 at the request of the then Ministry of Fuel and Power, its terms of reference being: 'To supply information to the Government and to cooperate with the Government in safeguarding the national interest in all questions relating to the supply, refining and distribution of oil in the United Kingdom' (D.En. Energy Paper No. 13, vol. 1, 1976, p. 12). The PIAC's main committee — the industry's chief executives — exists to maintain close contact between the industry and the government, and the chairman, Dr A. W. Pearce, is a member of the Energy Commission. Pearce is also chairman of Esso and has been a member of ACEC since 1974. The PIAC welcomed the evolution of an energy policy at the National Energy Conference, with the proviso that too rigid a strategy should be avoided because of the difficulties in forecasting total demand and the contributions of the various fuels. They linked the idea of economic growth with the oil industry's role in meeting energy requirements, and argued that the industry should be encouraged to operate on a sound financial basis in order to deal adequately with future supply and demand problems.

There are, of course, many problems associated with the integration of offshore resources into British energy policy, some stemming from the nature of the resources themselves. Even the amount of reserves available is an extremely contentious subject,

Professor Peter Odell (a consultant to D.En.) and Sir Denis Rooke being far more optimistic about the amount of oil and gas which could be produced than others in the energy industry. Britain's membership of the European Economic Community (EEC) has also caused conflict over British oil supplies to the EEC in times of crisis, over the amount of North Sea oil which should be refined in Britain, and over the subsidy scheme which helps British oil-rig manufacturers compete with foreign companies. Relationships with the multinational companies are not always smooth, especially following the new regulations laid down by the 1974 Labour government and the setting up of BNOC. There is still a lobby in favour of harsher regulation of the companies to obtain greater revenues for Britain, and Odell is in favour of creating conditions whereby the companies are forced to produce as much oil as possible in the national interest (ITV, 23 January 1978, *Personal Report*). The use of the oil revenues is still being debated, and the strong Scottish lobby has not been appeased by the resources allocated to the Scottish Development Agency to promote the Scottish economy, or the siting of the BNOC headquarters in Glasgow. (In fact, Aberdeen would have been a more logical choice as the centre of industrial activity, Glasgow being more of a political base.) Part of the Scottish National Party's rise in recent years has been due to their insistence on using the revenues from 'Scotland's oil' for solely Scottish purposes, rather than seeing it disappear into a national fund and only receiving a certain allocation at a later stage. The Cabinet originally intended to create a special oil fund to administer the North Sea revenues, but decided against this and only went as far as stating their intention to publish a series of reports showing progress with the objectives set out in the White Paper *The Challenge of North Sea Oil*. The government concluded that a separate fund '. . . would either be largely cosmetic or have the effect of undesirably separating the decisions that will have to be taken' (Cmnd 7143, 1978, para. 59). The Scottish National Party (SNP) naturally preferred a separate oil fund as the amount allocated to Scotland would then be clearly defined, but the government countered this by saying that their reports (the first to be published in summer 1979) would review in particular the benefits for Scotland, Wales, Northern Ireland and other assisted areas in the UK. The deputy leader of the SNP stated that his party's policy was to keep a check on the oil revenue now being diverted to London, so that allowance for this could be claimed in negotiation for independence when the time came. He added that 'In an independent

Scotland most of the money would be used as part of an industrial strategy designed to rebuild the Scottish economy' (Kerr, 1978b). In spite of the SNP's promotion of the idea that a London government was 'stealing Scottish oil', the SNP have not fared well in recent by-elections, and their MPs have now turned to criticizing the small amount of specifically Scottish contracts in the offshore supplies industry. In a May 1978 parliamentary debate on the 'mismanagement of Scotland's oil resources', the subject chosen by the SNP, the Minister of State for the Scottish Office replied to criticism, saying that the government had seen that the Scottish economy got the maximum benefit from oil-based industry. The reduction in support for the SNP will no doubt be seen by the government as confirmation that they were correct in their decision not to set up a separate oil fund or special agency for administering the revenue, as suggested by the Church of Scotland. The lengthy parliamentary debate on the Scottish Devolution Bill may have appeased Scottish fears that their interests were being ignored by Westminster, although the SNP is still far from satisfied with the present administration of oil revenues.

Offshore research is pursued through a variety of agencies, one of the most important being the Offshore Energy Technology Board (OETB) chaired by the D.En. Chief Scientist. The Board was established in May 1975, taking over the functions previously carried out by the Ship and Marine Technology Requirements Board and the Chemicals and Minerals Requirements Board. The OETB advises D.En. on research objectives and priorities in support of the department's offshore policies. Its membership consists of government and industry representatives, and a few academic appointments. The D.En. is represented by J. P. Gibson (OSO) and G. F. Kear (under-secretary, petroleum production division); there are also MOD, DI and DT members, and representatives of BGC, UKOOA, AERE Harwell, BP and Shell. The OETB has produced a strategy for research (D.En. Energy Paper No. 8, 1976) and liaises with D.En. through the Offshore Technology Unit which provides the secretariat. The Board has a programme committee to coordinate projects, and keeps close links with the Marine Technology Support Unit (MATSU) which is based at Harwell. The OETB delegates much of its project management work to MATSU. Several other agencies are involved in offshore-related research: also based at Harwell is the United Kingdom Offshore Steels Research Project (UKOSRP) which is concerned with fatigue in structural steels of the type used in production platforms. The National Maritime Institute (NMI) has a wide range of projects including nine within the Offshore Structures Fluid Loading Advisory Group (OSFLAG). The NMI was set up in July 1976 by DI to take over the marine and engineering aerodynamics work previously undertaken by the National Physical Laboratory (NPL); it is now sponsored by the D.En. through its OETB. Research on one particular aspect of gas production, the viability of a gas-gathering system in the northern basin of the North Sea, is carried out by Gas Gathering Pipelines (North Sea) Ltd (GGP), a study company set up by BGC and BNOC. This followed from a report by the consulting engineers Williams Merz to D.En. which was an overview of the area. GGP reported on the prospects for recovering the gas associated with the Northern Basin oil in July 1978. They recommended that there was no case for a gas-gathering system based on a new pipeline, but in spite of this, D.En. has reached an agreement with Shell/Esso concerning the building of a small gas-gathering system for the Brent and some nearby fields. It appears that a political decision has been taken to avoid the flaring of gas wherever possible, but the final outcome depends on the reactions of other countries with interests in gas gathering, particularly Norway. GGP has now effectively ceased to exist.

The oil industry is the one sector of the British energy industry which has to work hand in hand with the purely commercial companies, ranging from the giant multinationals to the smallest offshore operators. A unique corporation, BNOC, has been set up to deal with and regulate offshore production. It is unusual because of the civil servants on its board, and this may be a foretaste of the eventual restructuring of other nationalized industries. The nuclear industry also has certain idiosyncrasies, for instance the supposedly commercial company BNFL which is in fact totally state owned, and the one third state holding in the reactor building company, but this is something of a hangover from the days of the military nuclear programme. BNOC is a very young venture, and its success or failure will probably only be assessable as the oil and gas reserves begin to run down near the end of the century. BNOC comes under heavy criticism both for being too commercially minded and acting like a multinational and for being a public body over-concerned with regulation rather than production. Indeed, its nature may be altered with a change of government, and the degree of devolution of power agreed with Scotland will affect the use made of the oil revenues. Although the Conservative Party appear to have rejected the idea of scrapping BNOC altogether, it is a strong possibility that they would remove the advisory and regulatory functions, as they see them, if returned to power.

The Conservative energy spokesman, Tom King, in a parliamentary debate on 14 April 1978, accused BNOC of completely lacking commercial discipline, and it would appear that some changes in BNOC's structure are certain under a Conservative government. The publication of financial objectives for BNOC will put its activities on a firmer and more public basis; it appears that strong powers were taken by the British government just in time to give it some control over the production and depletion of the nation's own resources. The Brown Book (D.En., *Development of the Oil and Gas Resources of the United Kingdom 1977*) strikes an optimistic note as it states that the UK is now well on course to self-sufficiency in oil by 1980. Here as in the rest of the energy industry technical and political decisions are inseparably confused and compounded by inevitable disagreements among experts.

RESEARCH BODIES

British academic research is coordinated by the Advisory Board for the Research Councils (ABRC), a body consisting of higher civil servants and representatives of the research councils, which exists to advise the Department of Education and Science on the allocation of the research budget. The ABRC has been chaired since 1973 by Sir Fred Stewart, Professor of Geology at Edinburgh University, who was previously chairman of the Natural Environment Research Council. The ABRC advises on the balance of research between the various councils, on international cooperation, and liaises between the councils and the users of research. Although energy research had been taking place before the 1973 oil crisis, this provided the impetus for the setting up of the ABRC Committee on Energy Research in December 1973, with the following terms of reference: 'To provide a focus for consideration of energy research relevant to the production and use of energy in the United Kingdom, which the scientific community in the universities and Research Councils could undertake; and to report to the Advisory Board for the Research Councils as appropriate' (ABRC, 1974, p. 2). The Committee was chaired by the ABRC chairman and included the Social Science Research Council, Science Research Council and Natural Environment Research Council chairmen, civil servants from D.En., DI, DOE and the Cabinet Office, and the chairman of the University Grants Committee. The task of the Committee of Energy Research was to ascertain if '. . . the energy research effort sponsored or carried out by the Research Councils was of the right size and kind' (ABRC, 1974, p. 1). To this end they produced a report in September 1974 outlining the councils' energy-related work and reviewing the interests of other organizations. The report (ABRC, 1974) did not make recommendations but simply summarized the state of the art; however, it did appear to help the councils in their efforts to review research in the light of the energy crisis.

The Science Research Council (SRC) set up its own Energy Round Table in December 1973 to examine its support of energy research; membership consisted of representatives of relevant SRC committees, industry and government departments. The overall remit of the SRC is to support post-graduate education and research and development in science and technology, with no specific guidelines as to areas of research; thus the SRC's policy on research support reflects both the national interest and the academic and industrial expertise of its members. The SRC chairman since October 1976 has been Professor Geoffrey Allen, Professor of Chemical Technology at Imperial College of Science and Technology. The SRC itself is a large body of academics, industrialists and civil servants, and it is split into various boards and committees for ease of allocation of research funds. When the Energy Round Table was set up in 1973, most energy research was supported by either the Science or Engineering Boards and their committees, to which applications were made for research funds by academic institutions. After the Round Table's first review of energy research in 1974, an Energy Proposals Committee was set up in 1975 to report direct to SRC, to be '. . . responsible for support through grants in the technico-economic policy area of the energy field and for evolving policy towards SRC support of energy related research' (HC 568, Session 1976/77, p. 20). This committee was chaired by Dr Peter Chester of the CEGB's Central Electricity Research Laboratories at Leatherhead (also chairman of the Round Table), and was necessary because the size of the Round Table, at twenty-six members, was too cumbersome for the discussion of individual grant applications. The committee has ten members, including Dr N. J. Cunningham (D.En. Senior Economic Adviser), Dr J. Butterworth (ETSU), a representative of the British Steel Corporation and six academics. By March 1977 the committee's current grants totalled £208,000; the total of SRC current grants at the same date was £67.5 million, of which £5 million was allocated by other SRC subject committees for research aiding the better production and use of energy. In their second review of energy research, the Round Table recommended that the Energy Proposals Committee be allowed to continue to fund energy research, and also that a support unit should be established. Thus the Energy Research Support Unit (ERSU) was set up at the Rutherford Laboratory to back up the work of the committee and the Round Table. The unit offers technical support to academic researchers. Although energy-related research takes only a small part of the SRC budget, the existence of the Energy Proposals Committee and the Energy Round Table signify its importance in national terms.

The Social Science Research Council (SSRC) also became interested in energy problems around the time of the oil crisis. The SSRC held a meeting to discuss the development of energy research in September 1974, under the auspices of its newly established Energy Panel, and as a result of this several research topics were suggested as suitable for academic research. In October 1975 the North Sea Oil Panel was set up to place contracts for research into the '. . . political developments, immigrant groups and their impact on native populations, planning systems and their capacity to cope with major change, working relationships and environments within the oil and related industries' (HC481, Session 1976/77, p. 11); five contracts were awarded during 1976/77 and £90,000 was allocated to the panel for 1975–7. During 1976/77 an Energy Advisory Panel was set up by SSRC to review the social science contribution in the energy field, and in 1977 a report on *Energy Topics in the Social Sciences* (SSRC, 1977) was produced by a working group chaired by Michael Posner of Pembroke College, Cambridge. The group consisted of eight academics, representatives of the NCB and the UKAEA, and T. A. Kennedy, under-secretary of the Economics and Statistics Division of the D.En. Their report was prepared for the Research Initiatives Board of SSRC, which exists to initiate research into topics receiving too little attention. The report concluded that: '. . . insufficient work is being done on energy topics at the moment; that the time is opportune to encourage more work; and that the Social Science Research Council have a role to play in the activity' (SSRC, 1977, p. 2). The report suggested research in five areas: the total market for energy, matters where interpretation of information is disputed, pure theory and analysis, international comparisons, and the impact of changes in the energy market on the structure of international economic and social relations. Particular topics for research were outlined, and a proposal was made for some sort of organizational device enabling the SSRC to consider grant applications in the energy field directly, rather than through existing related committees. The report listed ten energy projects already funded by the SSRC, but the SSRC budget is small compared with that of the SRC, so that although the suggested research initiative has been welcomed, the funds may not be adequate. The projected 1978/79 budget for the SRC is £139.2 million, compared with £14.6 million for the SSRC, and David Robinson, the SSRC chairman, feels that the hard-science councils need faster rates of growth than the SSRC. However, an Energy Panel was formed in 1978 and given an allocation of £750,000 to promote research in the energy field; in particular concerning how energy is used, economic aspects of supply technologies, world energy balances, decision-making and North Sea oil and gas. An assessment of the Windscale inquiry funded by the Energy Panel is already under way, and several seminars have been held to stimulate ideas for research topics. There is to be a 5 per cent cut in the SSRC's budget next year, but the arrival of Michael Posner as SSRC chairman in January 1979 should ensure that energy matters stay well to the forefront in SSRC thinking.

The Natural Environment Research Council (NERC) under the chairmanship of Professor J. W. L. Beament, head of the Department of Applied Biology at Cambridge, also makes a large contribution to energy research, often through its Institute of Geological Sciences (IGS) (the study of the geology of the Severn Barrage area, for example) and Institute of Oceanographic Sciences (IOS). The council feels that it can offer an impartial second opinion on environmental problems arising in the energy field, and that its '. . . prime responsibility, in the sphere of energy as in others, is to enable policy decisions to be based on the best available scientific evidence and judgment that fall within its competence' (HC567, Session 1976/77, p. 8). NERC energy research covers areas such as the discovery and evaluation of energy sources, the technical problems of energy source exploitation, the problems arising from energy use and other strategic research. The Medical Research Council (MRC) is also concerned with energy research in the areas of radiation protection and environmental and occupational hazards, and the Agricultural Research Council (ARC) because of its interest in energy efficiency. The work of all five research councils is overseen by the ABRC, which is fighting to be given a greater share of North Sea oil revenues to support research in readiness for the eventual depletion of the oilfields.

Another source of funds for energy research, at a more applied level than that supported by the research councils, is the National Research Development Corporation (NRDC). The NRDC is a government-supported supplier of capital to develop projects commercially in the national interest which otherwise would not find any backing. Its funds come from the Treasury, but at present no borrowing is necessary because the corporation's income has been exceeding its outgoings. The total expenditure by NRDC on energy-related projects was £350,000 in May 1976, but this is complemented by contributions from the firms engaged in the work, so that total support is greater than implied by the NRDC figure. The projects include work on a windmill for glasshouse heating, a low-head water turbine and fluidized combustion systems. NRDC has set up a company jointly with the NCB and BP – Combustion Systems Ltd – to develop and commercialize the various heat and power-generating processes stemming from fluidized combustion. The NRDC also has international connections, both with governmental agencies and commercially. The NRDC's work is overseen by the DI, and it has an important role in getting new ideas from academic and government laboratories taken up by industry. Manufacturers tend to be very conservative about taking risks with new ideas, as explained by the NRDC's engineering director, John Scholes: 'It is often a major problem to find a firm that is the slightest bit interested in taking up a new idea, even if we are prepared to put up substantial finance. Most companies have limited manpower and plant, and they prefer activities where a successful outcome is reasonably assured. They don't want to embark on a scheme that needs precious skilled manpower, with a higher risk, and taking longer' (Eiloart, 1978, p. 293). The NRDC role in energy research is to develop inventions which they feel to be in the national interest, and which are not receiving support from other sources; their close contacts with NCB, BGC, CEGB and so on facilitate their judgement of the commercial viability of potential projects.

There are a great number of other institutions carrying out energy-related research, ranging from government bodies to the private sector. All the nationalized energy industries have a research capacity, and several government departments have an interest in this field. The DI, through the National Physical Laboratory (NPL), Warren Spring Laboratory, and National Engineering Laboratory (NEL), and the

DOE through the Transport and Road Research Laboratory (TRRL) and the Building Research Establishment (BRE), are the main government departments outside D.En. to sponsor energy research. Work is also carried out by private industry without government sponsorship and by the academic world without research council funding; funds may come from industrial contracts or the nationalized energy industries. Contracts are farmed out and funded by all the bodies described above, and coordination is carried out through the research councils and the research divisions and committees of the government departments where relevant. The main coordinating mechanism is ACORD, with its representatives from private industry, nationalized energy industries and the SRC. Many other committees and working groups exist to assist the coordination and planning of energy R and D, but ACORD is the leading body in this field. Most of ACORD's members, or representatives of their organizations, sit on other research planning committees.

The chairman of ACORD, the D.En. Chief Scientist, also represents the UK on the International Energy Agency (IEA) Committee on R and D. This committee, with the aid of working groups for the areas of R and D it considers, nominates lead countries and organizations for each topic: the UK is the lead country for wavepower, coal technology and assessment studies for hydrogen. The IEA was formed in November 1974 in Paris by sixteen oil-consuming countries of the OECD, including the UK, as a response to the oil crisis. Preliminary moves to form the IEA began in February 1974 when a conference of industrial nations took place in Washington; one of the main aims of the IEA was to coordinate the responses of participating states to the world energy situation. Thus an oil-sharing agreement was made. France did not join the IEA, feeling that US power in the organization was too great and being unwilling to join in the oil-sharing agreement.

INTEREST AND CAUSE GROUPS

The range of groups and associations involved with energy matters is many and varied, and includes those entirely concerned with energy problems, the environmentalist groups, profession-based associations, site-based groups and those originally formed for other purposes but having various related concerns. There are also international associations which are interested in British energy matters and to add to the confusion many groups are formed only to tackle particular problems, and later may cease to exist or change their aims. There are also academic institutions which influence other groups and inject new ideas into debates, and their members may eventually come to take part in discussions or act in other roles. One example of this is the presence of A. J. Surrey of the Science Policy Research Unit, (SPRU), University of Sussex, at the SCST hearings, where he acted as a specialist adviser to the committee until June 1976. The Energy Research Group at the Cavendish Laboratory, Cambridge, have also contributed to the debate, and a paper they prepared for ACEC on energy supply prospects was published for the 1976 National Energy Conference (D.En. Energy Paper No. 12, 1976). Ideas emanating from academic bodies may be taken up by any of the interest or cause groups, or the government and energy producers. Interest groups may be defined as those people who come together out of a given common interest, examples in this area being the Institution of Electrical Engineers or the British Nuclear Forum. The interest group may become a pressure group if the need arises. For example, the British Nuclear Forum, the nuclear industry trade association, certainly had a view on the recent discussions concerning reactor choice for the third nuclear pro- gramme. However, the initial function of an interest group is the bringing together of people or organizations who have a common interest, most probably arising out of their work. Cause groups, on the other hand, are formed for specific purposes to campaign or act as a pressure group for particular causes or ideas, examples being Friends of the Earth, the environmentalist pressure group, and SCRAM, the Scottish Campaign to Resist the Atomic Menace. Although the energy-based groupings of the trade unions and the Confederation of British Industries could be considered under the heading of interest or cause groups, because of their basic political stance they will be included with the political groups. Clearly there are often no clear lines between political, pressure, interest and cause groups, and it is the function of the group rather than its categorization which is important.

In the van of the British environmentalist cause groups is Friends of the Earth Ltd (FOE) formed in 1970 and inspired by the original American group. Their aims are: 'To promote the conservation, restoration and rational use of the world's resources, including the recycling of materials, protection of endangered species and recognition of environmental considerations in energy policy.' During their short existence they have campaigned against non-returnable bottles, the Rio Tinto-Zinc copper mine in Snowdonia National Park and on various energy issues, most recently against the introduction of the pressurized water reactor to Britain and in favour of an inquiry into the expansion of Windscale. Their performance at the Windscale inquiry firmly established them as the most influential environmentalist group currently active, and brought them increased media exposure. FOE's best-known speaker is Dr Walter Patterson, a Canadian physicist who joined their staff in 1972. He has managed to become accepted as part of the energy establishment without losing the integrity demanded by the environmentalists, by seeming to base his arguments on the 'scientific factual' level rather than the 'emotional' plane so disliked by those within the energy-production industries. His image, 'protective coloration' as he puts it, enables his views to be heard by both sides in the energy debate. There are those who regard him as something of a subversive influence, for instance the Labour MP Ronald Brown, an electrical engineer and SCST member, during the Windscale debate accused him of spreading misleading information on the dangers of nuclear waste disposal. He went on: 'He has very little regard for the truth in terms of the total issue. . . . He is a fear salesman' (*Hansard*, vol. 946, No. 85, 22 March 1978, col. 1648). Research for FOE, which itself is a lobby group, is carried out by the charity Earth Resources Research (ERR). ERR was established in 1973 and is made up of several policy research units, one of which is the Energy Policy Unit. ERR is entirely dependent on charitable funds, and its director is Graham Searle. FOE's executive director until March 1979, Tom Burke, feels that it is difficult to claim successes for his organization because it has no power of its own; it exists to influence decision-makers. He says: 'Our role is initiatory. What we have done is combine information with a flair for getting attention – information that would otherwise get lost. Our work has been successful because we have been able to put the main outlines of an issue before the policy makers' (White, 1977, p. 553). Apart from its publicity and lobbying activities, FOE has over 150 local groups which often tackle local problems as well as supporting the initiatives taken by the full-time workers.

Several other environmentalist groups have taken part in the various recent debates on energy matters; one such is the Socialist Environment and Resources Association (SERA), which aims to encourage the Labour movement to '. . . give top priority to production for need and employment without waste, under healthy conditions' (Brown, Emerson and Stoneman, 1976, p. 160). SERA is an anti-nuclear group which gave evidence at the Windscale inquiry concerning the effect of nuclear and solar power programmes on employment prospects. It has strong connections with the Labour Party, with nearly twenty constituency parties, two national trade unions, two trades councils and over twenty MPs as members or affiliates. The Conservation Society (director Dr John Davoll) and the Society for Environmental Improvement (SEI) were also represented at Windscale. The Conservation Society was set up to convince the government that it should aim for a sustainable economy, rather than have continual expansion. The Committee for Environmental Conservation (CoEnCo) provides 'a forum for discussion of all aspects of environmental interest by the major voluntary conservation organizations in this country'; it also encourages concerted action by the voluntary groups. CoEnCo began to study energy in March 1973 and was concerned particularly with environmental problems arising from the exploitation of North Sea oil. In November 1973 a working party was formed with the Royal Society of Arts and the Institute of Fuel, which finally produced a report on Energy and the Environment. The chairman of CoEnCo is Lord Craighton, an ex-Minister of State at the Scottish Office, and its secretary is F. D. Webber, a retired diplomat. A founder member of CoEnCo helped to form the European Environmental Bureau (EEB), an international organization based in Brussels consisting of large non-governmental organizations from EEC member countries. Its objectives are the promotion of a sustainable lifestyle, the protection and conservation of the environment, dissemination of information and the making of recommendations concerning the environment to the appropriate authorities. UK members are CoEnCo, the Conservation Society, FOE, the Civic Trust, the Council for the Protection of Rural England, the Council for Nature, the TCPA and the IIED. The EEB has paid particular attention to energy problems, and discovered recently that EEC funds (and implicitly UK funds) were being used to finance the French fast breeder programme, prior to the UK public inquiry into the fast breeder. The Commission of the EEC have agreed to consult regularly with environmentalists on energy policy through the EEB, and the first meeting was expected to take place in late 1978.

The Oxford Political Ecology Research Group (PERG, coordinator Peter Taylor) has some expertise in the field of European anti-nuclear protest and has produced several papers calculating the effects of hypothetical accidents at nuclear power plants. The Open University Energy Research Group (ERG), initially directed by Dr Peter F. Chapman, has rapidly acquired a high reputation in the field of energy analysis and has produced several papers concerning CHP and the electricity supply industry. Chapman gave evidence at the Windscale inquiry as did the director of the International Institute for Environment and Development (IIED), Gerald Leach. The IIED is a non-profitmaking foundation working on international environmental issues, with an energy programme supported by the Ford Foundation. This programme is concerned with the implications of energy conservation policies and the use of renewable energy sources in Western Europe. A newly formed group is the unofficial all-party Parliamentary Liaison Group for Alternative Energy (PARLIAGE) which tries to influence MPs directly through lobbying. It was set up in 1978 to keep MPs informed of developments and new options in the alternative energy field, and consists of representatives of various environmental groups and sympathetic experts in the energy field.

The Town and Country Planning Association (TCPA) has recently become more involved with energy issues and their implications for planners and planning. The TCPA was founded in 1899 and since then has pressed for continuing improvements in the social and physical environment of the UK. Its director, David Hall, gave evidence at Windscale to the effect that the planning context of the proposal should be considered as well as the energy policy and proliferation arguments. A regular contributor to the TCPA journal has outlined the change in the planner's view of nuclear power, from the realization of a dream to a questioning of its necessity. He concludes that a world without nuclear power would imply changes in the concept of a standard of living, and that: 'As for planning, it can be said that it was never to its purpose to build the good city at lasting cost to the natural world. That such would be the case in a plutonium society there can hardly be any doubt. The challenge to planning, therefore, is to show that there are forms of human settlement that could sustain a non-plutonium society' (Ash, 1977, p. 298). The TCPA were one of the most influential groups, with FOE, in persuading the Secretary of State for the Environment, Peter Shore, to set up the Windscale inquiry. Another planners' organization, the Royal Town Planning Institute (RTPI), also takes an interest in energy matters, as does the Council for the Protection of Rural England (CPRE). There are also the smaller groups set up to pursue a particular goal, for example the Vale of Belvoir Protection Committee which is opposing the NCB developments in Leicestershire. Other environmental groups concerned with the energy debate are the Conservative and Liberal Ecology groups, the Green Alliance and Greenpeace. A group concerned with the more general effects of science and technology is the Council for Science and Society (CSS), a charity set up in 1973 to 'promote the study of, and research into, the social effects of science and technology, and to disseminate the results thereof to the public'. The CSS consists of 36 members, all eminent workers in science or other disciplines, appointed on a personal basis. It tends to be less overtly political than many other groups, concentrating mainly on long term problems of technology assessment, and is occasionally criticized by the more radical groups on these grounds. The British Society for Social Responsibility in Science (BSSRS) is also concerned with the effects of science and technology on society, but tends to concentrate on aspects of issues with more obvious short term political impact.

A prominent new organization concerned solely with energy matters is Energy 2000, set up in April 1977 to encompass the slightly differing views of all the anti-nuclear power groups. Its central point is that nuclear power is dangerous. Arthur Scargill, president of the Yorkshire Miners, is the chairman of Energy 2000, which counts among its membership representatives of the Labour, Liberal and Conservative parties, the Conservation Society, the Conservative Ecology group, some areas of the NUM, FOE and SCRAM (Scottish Campaign to Resist the Atomic Menace). It has branches in Scotland, Cornwall, South Wales and the Midlands, and has had a mass lobby of Parliament to promote non-nuclear energy strategies.

SCRAM is a national organization established in November 1975. Its objectives are:

1. To inform the public of the present and proposed nuclear developments and their social, political and environmental implications.
2. To oppose the further development of nuclear power in Scotland and elsewhere.
3. To press for a long term strategy based on conservation and on the use of renewable resources.

Apart from its acronymous meaning, 'scram' also means to shut down a nuclear reactor. The organization is based in Edinburgh and is non-party political. It has held several nuclear site occupations and national protests, the largest so far being the May 1978 rally at the Torness AGR site. It also has local groups throughout Scotland who campaign on local issues in a similar manner to the FOE local groups, and it produces a bi-monthly bulletin which occasionally displays the sense of humour so often lacking in the energy field. SCRAM was one of the many groups requesting a further public inquiry for the Torness site when the proposed reactor type was changed.

The Electrical Association for Women (EAW), director Ann McMullan, exists to inform women of the importance of electricity and further the development of the electrical society. It organizes information programmes, such as the 'Get Into Lane [Learning About Nuclear Energy]' scheme, in an effort to oppose what it sees as the over-emotive arguments of the anti-nuclear groups. It was a part organizer of the 'Energy Today and Tomorrow' conference of April 1978 in London, which was a discussion of energy policy mainly at the individual level of usage and conservation. The EAW is funded partly by the electricity industry and its director sees one of its tasks at present as ensuring '. . . that British women's groups as well as individuals are well enough informed about nuclear facts to enable them to understand the arguments rationally rather than to be swayed by them emotionally' (McMullan, 1977, p. 16). A similar organization concerned with the gas industry is the Women's Gas Federation and Young Homemakers. These organizations come somewhere between the consumer groups and the industry based groups, with information dissemination as their main aim.

Other energy-based groups are the Campaign Opposing Nuclear Dumping (COND), and the Network for Nuclear Concern (NNC) who gave evidence at the Windscale inquiry. There are many foreign groups interested in British energy policy, some of which take part in the debates and public protest — for example, the Movement Against Uranium Mining (Australia), National Energy Committee (Netherlands), Clamshell, Crabshell and Abalone Alliances (USA), and the Burgerinitiativen (W. Germany).

All the energy industries have their own house interest groups or societies, with the British Nuclear Forum (BNF) as the nuclear industry trade association, chaired by J. C. C. Stewart. Its views on the subject of reactor choice for the forthcoming nuclear programme and energy policy in general were put by Stewart at a BNF meeting in December 1977: 'Speaking for the BNF, we don't mind which we build. We would like to build both — but it is time the British public was given some realistic alternatives for the long term energy supplies of this country. That means the construction of a commercial fast breeder reactor as far as we are concerned' (Cook, 1977d). The Institution of Nuclear Engineers (INE) is also active in this field; it was established in 1959 to further the advancement of all types of peaceful nuclear technologies, and acts as a forum for discussion, by means of lectures, meetings and the publication of a journal. There are several other engineering institutions with an interest in energy and which have the opportunity of putting their views across to the government at various levels. The Institution of Electrical Engineers (IEE) was founded in 1871, with the object of promoting 'the general advancement of electrical science and engineering and their applications and to facilitate the exchange of ideas on those subjects amongst the members of the institution and otherwise'. The IEE has four divisions, one of which is concerned with power. The Institution of Gas Engineers (I.Gas E.) promotes the application of engineering science for the better utilization of gas, and the Institution of Mining Engineers (I.Min.E.) has similar aims with respect to coal and iron ore mining. Fifteen of the professional engineering institutions come together to form the Council of Engineering Institutions (CEI) which gives expression to the views of the profession as a whole and acts as a focus for joint action. It has 200,000 chartered engineer members.

Other relevant bodies include the Institute of Fuel (Inst.F.), which was founded to promote fuel technology and further the utilization of fuel of all kinds for the community at large, the Institute of Physics, the British Nuclear Energy Society (BNES), the District Heating Association, the Electrical Vehicle Association of Great Britain, the Society of Petroleum Engineers and the Institute of Petroleum. The Uranium Institute, formed in 1975, is a club of uranium producers existing to 'conduct research and do investigations concerning the world's requirements of uranium, the world's uranium resources and the productive capacity of uranium producers'. Its sixteen founder members, from Australia, Canada, France, South Africa and the UK accounted for 60 per cent of the western world's uranium production in 1975. Uranium consumers may become associate members of the institute, which intends to prepare an alternative set of statistics for uranium production, as it doubts the accuracy of those prepared by the IAEA. There are many more groups with a fairly direct interest in energy, some of which take part regularly in discussions at national level. Both the Electrical Research Association (ERA) and the UK section of the International Solar Energy Society (ISES) gave evidence to the SCST on Alternative Sources, while the Petroleum Industries Advisory Committee (PIAC), the Process Plant Association, the UK Offshore Operators Association (UKOOA), the Women's Solid Fuel Council and the Structural Insulation Association all spoke at the National Energy Conference in 1976. There are also, of course, all the academic institutions with research interests in the area and all the various bodies marginally concerned in the energy debate. The National Council for Civil Liberties (NCCL) and Justice – the British section of the International Commission of Jurists – both gave evidence at the Windscale inquiry and the National Energy Conference received contributions from the Child Poverty Action Group (CPAG) and Help the Aged, amongst others concerned with fuel costs. Since the 1973 oil crisis, many more groups have realized that their particular interests are affected in some way by energy policies, and further groups have been formed as a direct response to energy policy decisions. An instance of this occurred with the attempt to drill test boreholes in the Cheviot Hills to ascertain their suitability for radioactive waste disposal, which caused the formation of a group to oppose the granting of planning permission for drilling. The range of associations concerning themselves with energy matters is immense, each interest group selecting a particular problem relevant to their members. An example of this is the April 1978 conference 'Energy Today and Tomorrow' organized jointly by the National Federation of Women's Institutes, the National Union of Townswomen's Guilds, the Electrical Association for Women and the Women's Gas Federation and Young Homemakers. In addition to the mainly non-party political groups, there are also the party, trades union and employer associations concerned with energy, and the consumer groups such as the Consumers' Association, the National Federation of Consumer Groups, and the consumer or consultative councils for specific industries. The consumer groups are concerned mainly with energy pricing and payment policies, but have a relatively small voice in the energy debate, as the chairman of the National Consumer Council, Michael Young, pointed out at the National Energy Conference: 'Let me end, . . . by appealing to the industries so strongly represented here today not to reject every new idea from the consumer bodies as though it had come straight from Hell or Transport House . . .' (Energy Paper No. 13, vol. 1, p. 37). He went on to suggest that a consumer charter be embodied in British energy policy.

There are many more associations with a fringe involvement in energy policy, from the Royal Society for the Protection of Birds (RSPB) – concerned with the effect of the postulated Severn barrage on the bird population of the estuary – to the South-West Sports Council, concerned with the recreational implications of a barrage. Most groups take an informative or propagandist role on behalf of their members. In the case of those whose main concern is energy policy, they may venture to produce policy suggestions, for example *An Alternative Energy Strategy for the United Kingdom* (NCAT, 1977) produced by the National Centre for Alternative Technology. Other activities may include public debates or protests in the form of marches and occupations, and in this area conflicts between the various groups, and perhaps the government of the day, may arise. Nuclear power in particular has been the object of concerted protests in Europe, causing some concern to pro-nuclear associations such as UNIPEDE, the International Union of Producers and Distributors of Electrical Energy. At UNIPEDE's fifth symposium in 1977, a West German representative spoke on the activities and effects of pressure groups, implying that the radical political elements in the protesting groups could be differentiated from the civic action groups proper. His main emphasis was on the propagandist function of the electrical industry (in a similar manner to the information work carried out by the Electrical Association for Women), one of his points being that the efforts of the environmental associations in the public relations field often excelled those of the professionals within the industry. In common with many other pro-nuclear groups, a good grasp of factual information is seen to be the complete answer to most fears concerning nuclear power. A group formed in November 1977 has precisely this attitude, A Power for Good (APG) existing to 'counter the qualitatively persuasive but quantitatively unsupportable claims of the nuclear opposition' and to 'support nuclear power as an essential contribution to the future energy requirements both nationally and internationally'. APG is a non-profit-making organization, and was set up by people on the fringes of the nuclear industry. It will encourage its members to participate in nuclear debates at all levels, and make 'independent representations' at any future relevant public inquiries. APG is one of the founder members of the European Energy Association (EEA), an international pro-nuclear group formed in July 1978 to combat what they regard as unbalanced reporting on nuclear energy.

Each group and association, whatever its viewpoint, is likely to have an area in which it can bring some sort of pressure to bear on decision-makers, whether via public protests, writing to MPs or obtaining media exposure for problems. Some groups, especially the 'professional' bodies such as the engineers, have a higher status in government circles because of their direct involvement with the physical processes concerned; they are the experts, and as such are accorded increased attention. These institutions tend to share one failing of government, that of slowness in responding to changing circumstances, and this, combined with a natural inclination (and constitutional aim, often) of promoting a specific industrial interest, means that new ideas and new adaptations of old methods may not receive a thorough hearing by these bodies. It is extremely hard to define the success or failure of interest groups. Each has to be judged on the basis of its own aims, and the timescale of activity varies from the immediate (such as energy pricing changes), to the very long term (for example the attainment of a no-growth economy). To be effective and noticed at higher levels of government it is apparent that interest groups need to develop the image of being reasonable, which may imply not straying too far from present government policy. The presence of a counter-argument may give the impression that the argument is being taken seriously, whereas in fact decision-making may pay no heed to it whatsoever; this point can only be judged with reference to longer term outcomes of policy, and indeed may never be apparent. It is a rare group which can point to a policy decision achieved solely through their own endeavours. The interest groups form a vital part of the energy debate as the promotion of their vast range of interests is the only widespread method at present available of ensuring any sort of public participation. The main public gain from their activities is wide publicity for energy matters and the acceptance of energy policy as an important but everyday topic of discussion; perhaps the ultimate sign of public interest in energy matters was the inclusion of a reference to the 1978 Women's Institute Energy Conference in *The Archers*!

EUROPE

British relations with the European Economic Community (EEC) have been as uneven in the field of energy policy as in other foreign policy areas. Even before the EEC came into existence in 1958 Britain and the rest of Europe disagreed over the allocation of coal supplies which had been thrown into disarray by the Second World War.

Immediately after the war, a time when 90 per cent of primary energy supplied in Europe came from coal, the European Coal Organization (ECO) was formed, at the instigation of the USA, to organize coal supplies. In 1947 this was taken under the wing of a United Nations body, the Economic Commission for Europe (ECE), and further progress towards European cooperation took place in 1948 with the formation of the Organization for European Economic Cooperation (OEEC). The OEEC incorporated a permanent commission concerned with European energy resources, and in 1952 yet another body, the European Coal and Steel Community (ECSC) was established to stabilize coal and steel prices and oversee supplies. Initially the UK refused to join the ECSC, considering that it was 'utterly undemocratic and responsible to nobody' (Lucas, 1977, p. 4) but later became an associate member. The UK also refused to take part in the preliminary European approach to nuclear energy, which began in 1956 and culminated with the setting up of the European Atomic Energy Community (EURATOM) in 1958, the same year in which the EEC came into being. The UK, of course, was not a founder-member of the EEC.

The European Commission, the EEC equivalent of the Civil Service, has a role in policy-making as well as administration. Since the inception of EURATOM it has been strongly in favour of a large nuclear power programme for Europe, originally inspired by the collection of nuclear scientists brought together to staff EURATOM. After EURATOM's relative failure, in part due to Britain's lack of support, a pro-nuclear pressure group remained within the Commission and has exerted its influence over EEC energy policy ever since. Lucas (1977) suggests that the oil crisis of 1974 helped the Commission by enabling it to show its initiative in solving the problem of resource shortage by suggesting a large nuclear programme. This instinct for self-preservation on the part of the Commission, together with its inclination to view a common energy policy as a means of promoting European unity, meant that nuclear power became the backbone of the post-oil crisis EEC energy policy. Lucas sees nuclear power as being easy for administrators to manage because there are no multinational corporations as in the oil industry; for the Commission there is also the advantage that if a member state builds too much nuclear capacity, it has to stand the losses itself and the Commission's reputation remains unimpaired. Until recently, there has been little sign of any debate within the Directorate-General for Energy on energy priorities; in fact: 'The only constraint on the advocacy of poor technical solutions for political reasons is the long term requirement to maintain the credibility of the Directorate-General for Energy. This is not, perhaps, a strong constraint' (Lucas, 1977, p. 100).

Since the UK joined the EEC in January 1973, Community energy policy has continued in its course of setting general objectives but being powerless to enforce them. Lucas suggests that part of the explanation for the lack of progress stems from the opposing planning traditions of Europe, particularly France, and the UK. French methods have always included indicative planning, with planners given some power to wield, but the British tradition is one of pragmatism and gradual policy development. This is exemplified by Tony Benn's frequent rejection of targets for the energy sector. Benn was president of the EEC Energy Council from January to June 1977, and tried unavailingly to promote his ideas on open government at council level. He summed up his term of office as follows:

> The UK presidency of the Energy Council has not brought dramatic progress in the formulation of a Community energy policy, and we did not expect it to do so. However, I believe that it has been marked by strong Ministerial – political – control over energy affairs which is essential. We have promoted greater informality and closer Ministerial links and, I hope, a greater sense of realism in our approach to a subject which must be seen increasingly in a wider international framework.   (D.En., *United Kingdom and Community Energy Policy*, 1977, p. 3)

Later in the year, Benn spoke in a House of Commons debate to the effect that the Community handling of energy matters required changes in three areas if it was to be acceptable to the UK. He felt that ministers should meet in open session, that the Commission should report to ministers on its activities as well as laying documents before them, and that Parliament should be allowed to examine Community proposals in detail. He went on to emphasize that our energy policy decisions would continue to be made within the UK rather than by the Commission and although this position won parliamentary support in general, it may hark back to the days of Benn's strong opposition to British entry into the EEC. This insistence on going our own way has met with some resistance from the Commission, most recently concerning the UK decision to expand refining capacity so that two-thirds of its North Sea oil output could be refined in the UK. This was originally felt by the Commission to be incompatible with the Treaty of Rome, due to the total European overcapacity in refining, but the Commission finally decided not to oppose UK plans. A similar argument took place over the amount of oil the UK would need to stockpile as an emergency reserve for the rest of the EEC; the EEC insisted that the oil was stockpiled rather than left in the ground and wanted a guarantee from the UK that it would supply all other EEC countries in the event of an emergency. However, Benn refused to give any guarantees on the grounds that it might result in reduced supplies being available to the UK, and a D.En. spokesman was reported as saying: 'If this, as it appears, is a wheeze to get hold of part of the North Sea oil we shall have very grave doubts about it. It is, in any case, ridiculous that Britain should be required to finance oil reserves in such an expensive way when we have so much in the ground' (Palmer, 1977b).

It is hardly surprising that UK reserves of oil and gas have caused policy disagreement within the EEC, mainly due to the imbalance between our energy reserves and those of the other EEC countries. Another point of contention at the December 1977 meeting of the Energy Council was EEC policy on coal supplies, the UK view being in favour of an increased coal burn throughout EEC power stations in order to prevent the loss of coal-producing capacity. As it happened, the UK would have been a major beneficiary of the plan, being the biggest coal producer in the Community, and the plan was rejected because the coal importers felt their energy costs would increase if it was carried out. This caused Benn to say that 'The divergences in the energy policies of the Community member states are now so marked that it will be very difficult to proceed without more openness' (Palmer, 1977a). He went on to question the EEC decision to back the rapid development of the fast breeder reactor, which the Commission felt was essential to reduce Community dependence on outside sources of energy; the council did revise their estimates of future energy trends downwards during the December meeting, although the Commission still appeared to see a high future demand for nuclear electricity.

In order to open up the European debate on nuclear power the EEC held two public hearings on the subject in December 1977 and January 1978. The hearings were conducted by Guido Brunner, the EEC Energy Commissioner, a West German lawyer and diplomat (though born in Madrid) who served at the UN in New York for eight years. He became a member of the Commission in 1974, and is responsible for energy, research, science and education. After the first hearing, during which Walter Patterson criticized the EEC, saying: 'The Commission's brief is clearly to build nuclear cathedrals for the glorification of the Community' (Kenward, 1977c), Brunner said that the Commission would evaluate what they had heard and incorporate any convincing arguments into their policy. In spite of the preponderance of anti-nuclear opinion at the first hearing, Brunner claimed at the second hearing that some agreement had emerged on the need for a nuclear programme. This statement was rejected by the environmentalists and the second session seemed only to highlight the differences between the pro- and anti-nuclear groups. In general, Commission policy has always retained the aim of making energy a uniting force in Europe, as the Director-General for Energy stated during the oil crisis:

> Energy policy and policies to deal with the repercussions of the energy crisis have become central to Community solidarity and to progress over the whole spectrum of policy. Without some progress towards a Community energy policy, progress in the foreign policy and the economic, monetary, social and regional fields, which involves real compromises of national interest as part of a total package, is now hard to envisage.   (Spaak, 1974, p. 11)

This general strategy of unification through harmonization of policies does not appear to be working any better now than before the energy crisis of 1974. Some member states choose to seek the support of the USA rather than to present a united front to the rest of the world, and others such as the UK strive to maintain their right to decide on their own energy policy. Only in the area of research is there any high level of cooperation, and even this may be marred by political wrangling – witness the two-year argument over the siting of the JET fusion research project. Lucas argues that the nature of the energy problem, with its limited or decreasing resources, makes the formulation of a common policy difficult, and concludes that a Community Energy Agency would be of some use in funding research, particularly on energy conservation and alternative sources. He would not give the agency any interventionist powers, so that it is difficult to see how this would assist in harmonizing the differing national policies, apart from emphasizing that nuclear power need not necessarily be the sole solution to future demand problems.

Community energy policy appears to be at the mercy of the various national energy policies, but the same could be said with respect to Community policies in other fields, notably agriculture. It may be towards the end of the century, when the UK oil and gas boom has passed and perhaps the nuclear debate has become less heated, before there is any prospect of a truly European energy policy. Meanwhile, Brunner continues to expound the now famous energy policy of keeping all the options open, and each of the EEC countries continue to pursue control of their own interests rather than to agree to a common compromise on policy. Lucas summarizes the effect on international relations as follows: 'The Community has not agreed enough within itself to define a common attitude to energy policy; consequently the Community presence at international conferences and its participation in international agreements can only be a charade; the Community represents no point of view' (Lucas, 1977, p. 77). A hopeful sign from the Commission is their willingness to open up the debate, both in terms of wider participation and the acknowledgment of the existence of a variety of possible strategies. The present UK position on European energy policy remains one of cautious cooperation where possible while retaining the right to make our own policy on matters such as nuclear power and depletion of oil reserves.

POLITICAL GROUPS

Each parliamentary party has a structure of committees and advisory groups which exist to ensure that the view of the constituency MP is taken into account by ministers and the Cabinet when formulating policy. The exact structure and influence of the groups varies from party to party, but they have roughly similar aims. The smaller parties, of course, have less need of such an organized structure since the opportunities for personal contacts with the leadership are greater. None of the groups have any specific powers within the parties, and interest in the subject is the sole membership criterion. When the subject tallies with a departmental responsibility, it is expected that the minister concerned will take an interest in the proceedings; on the other hand, ministers may use the committees for discussions prior to legislation or policy decisions.

The chairman of the Parliamentary Labour Party (PLP) energy group is Peter Hardy, MP for the Rother Valley. Hardy was a

Yorkshire schoolteacher before being elected in 1970, and had served for ten years (including a year as chairman) on the Wath-upon-Dearne UDC. He was also president of the local Labour Party. In addition to chairing the energy group he is also vice-chairman of the forestry group, interests which appear to stem from his hobby of watching wildlife (he has published a book on badgers). At present he is also Parliamentary Private Secretary to the Foreign Secretary. The vice-chairman of the energy group is Arthur Palmer, a Bristol MP since 1964 and the chairman of the SCST. Palmer is an electrical engineer who has always taken a great interest in scientific and technical matters, and has been on the SCST since its inception, apart from the break from 1970 to 1974 when the Conservatives were in power. Labour Party interest in energy matters has not always been particularly intense, often relying on the long experience of members such as Palmer who have made it their particular subject. Energy has begun to command greater attention now because of the publicity attached to the nuclear debate and the Windscale inquiry in particular, and MPs such as Leo Abse have taken a strong line on specific nuclear questions. Energy debates in the House of Commons were often relegated to a late hour and thus had relatively low attendances, but the debate on the Windscale expansion was held at a reasonable hour and well attended, with many MPs wishing to speak. The effect of the PLP energy group discussions on Tony Benn and Labour energy policy are imponderable; divergencies of opinion mainly concern the amount of nuclear capacity required and the place of renewable resources in the overall strategy.

A Labour Party body with slightly more influence than the subject group is the National Executive Committee (NEC). The NEC submitted a paper to the National Energy Conference of 1976 stating its policy on energy, and although the plans for each specific fuel were roughly similar to those of the D.En., the proposed planning framework and aims were rather different. The NEC suggested that the Secretary of State for Energy should be given specific powers of direction over the nationalized energy industries, and that their statutes should be brought into line with overall energy policy. Their long term planning objectives would have to be approved by the Secretary of State, and their statutory financial obligations should be changed, again to fit in with overall policy. The first objective of the NEC's energy policy was to ensure that everyone could afford adequate heat and light at home. Industrial energy needs came in second place. Tony Benn has since suggested this as the first priority of

British energy policy, and alterations have been made in the relationship between the nationalized energy industries and the minister. The NEC may have more influence over a minister than the subject group because of its standing within the party as a whole; however, it is still possible for ministers, even Prime Ministers, to ignore its policies. Harold Wilson neglected the NEC when he was Prime Minister: 'His tactic for dealing with the NEC was simply not to turn up at its meetings and ignoring any decisions it took with which he disagreed' (Haines, 1977, p. 13). Thus even when policies are clearly stated ministers may choose to overlook them when the occasion demands. Once again, this is an example of a body with no direct power and little influence.

Outside the PLP and the NEC opinion is often difficult to gauge, but at the 1977 Labour Party Conference the trades union representatives were nearly unanimous in their opposition to a resolution calling a halt to nuclear developments at Windscale. Trades unionists criticized anti-nuclear groups as proponents of hysterical and inaccurate propaganda, called them ill-informed publicity seekers and condemned conservationists as middle-class loonies. Tony Benn wound up the energy debate with some typical remarks on the importance of the public expression of views on the nuclear issue and the problems involved in the growth of nuclear power. Thus all sides merely restated their positions, and the influence on policy was probably negligible. If there is no popular pressure from within a parliamentary party for action in a particular area, then the subject groups simply function as discussion groups with only weak general influence over policy direction. The situation is the same for the party in the country as a whole; popular pressure needs to be extremely well defined to change policy. Often a good point may be made by an individual MP asking a series of questions in Parliament about a single issue; for example, Trevor Skeet, Conservative MP for Bedford, has concentrated on sulphur dioxide emission from power stations and other industrial sources and brought the matter to public notice.

The Conservative Party Committee on Energy is chaired by Tom King, their front-bench Energy spokesman. King has been MP for Bridgwater since 1970 and was Minister for Industrial Development in 1972–4. He was Opposition front-bench spokesman for industry before moving to Energy. The second energy spokesman is Hamish Gray, MP for Ross and Cromarty. The energy committee has two vice-chairmen, Trevor Skeet and John Hannam. Skeet, MP for

Bedford, is a barrister who has also been secretary of the All-Party Committee on Airships since 1971, amongst various other committee activities, whilst Hannam, MP for Exeter, was a motel developer before entering Parliament where he is an active sportsman and Commodore of the House of Commons Yacht Club. One of the two joint secretaries of the energy committee is Nigel Forman, who is rapidly becoming more well known in the energy field than either of the party spokesmen. He became MP for Sutton and Carshalton in March 1976. After studying at Oxford and Harvard, he worked for the CBI and was Information Officer at the University of Sussex. He then moved to the Conservative Research Department, where he stayed from 1971 until 1976, finally becoming assistant director. He joined the SCST in July 1976, and in 1977 produced a book entitled *Towards a More Conservative Energy Policy* which outlined his view of '. . . a more conservative energy policy which could be adopted by the next Conservative government' (Forman, N., 1977, p. 7). Present Conservative policy is based on the use of the market and the price mechanism to ensure adequate continuous supplies of energy. John Biffen, then the Conservative energy spokesman, outlined his party's ideas at the 1976 National Energy Conference:

> . . . we should be commercial in our treatment of energy. Price and profit should remain indispensable in the guides they give to society about the use and conservation of so basic a commodity as energy. . . . The most successful planning framework for the energy industries and the community generally is one in which the politician sets out general commercial and social obligations which must be observed by the energy producing and consuming industries. He should then desist from . . . political intervention. (D.En. Energy Paper No. 13, vol. 1, 1976, p. 15)

Conservative activity of late has centred on their continuing opposition to the expansion of BNOC and its stake in the oil industry, although it would appear that they do not now intend to dismantle the corporation if they regain power.

The Liberal spokesman for energy is David Penhaligon, MP for Truro. Liberal energy statements tend to concentrate on the effect of policies on people, both directly as consumers and in the long term, as exemplified by the Liberal speech at the National Energy Conference: '. . . the primary objective of our energy policy now . . . should be very much to that of saving the fossil fuel resources as far as possible for the use by our children and grandchildren . . .' (D.En. Energy Paper No. 13, vol. 1, 1976, p. 51). Their written conference submission dealt with electric heating in council houses. The 1977 Liberal Party national conference adopted a radical non-nuclear motion, which opposed the construction of any further power stations or reprocessing facilities, suggested no fossil fuel power stations were necessary for ten years and called for more research into alternative sources. The debate was split between the usual two camps supplying technical and more broadly based environmental arguments, with the case for limited development of nuclear power being put by Lord Avebury, president of the Conservation Society. He felt that the motion was in direct contradiction to party policy and attacked what he described as the ridiculous technological nonsenses in some anti-nuclear speeches. The Liberal presence in Parliament made itself felt when they refused to back the Bill seeking to reorganize the electricity supply industry, along lines similar to those proposed in the Plowden Report, in March 1978. David Penhaligon objected to the part of the Bill abolishing the regional electricity boards and merging them into a central authority, which he described as 'bureaucracy gone mad' (Hoggart, 1978). The Liberal veto had the effect of forcing Benn to change the proposed Bill into a White Paper (Cmnd 7134, 1978). The Scottish National Party (SNP) spokesman on energy is Gordon Wilson, MP for Dundee East. He is the deputy leader of the SNP and is also responsible for devolution and oil matters. All SNP proposals on energy have concerned the use of North Sea oil, which they naturally see as Scotland's oil. They have suggested that a special fund should be set up to distribute the revenue from the oil, but this has been rejected by the government in favour of special reports on the use of the revenue. In an independent Scotland, the SNP plan to use the oil revenue as part of an industrial strategy designed to rebuild the Scottish economy. Other SNP ideas on energy policy have not been well publicized, in spite of the fact that wave and wind energy would be strong possibilities in Scotland, and one of the AGRs in the third reactor programme is to be sited at Torness, East Lothian. An Ecology Party now exists in the UK, in the wake of the success of the 'green parties' in Europe, and it intends to contest at least ten seats in the next general election. Its chairman is Jonathan Tyler of Birmingham and its policies are based on increased community responsibility for the environment and self-imposed constraints on resource consumption.

The amount of influence on government energy policy exerted by either subject groups or party committees, both of parties in and out of government, is very limited. The policy of a newly elected government is highly constrained by the outcome of previous decisions and the nature of planning in the energy field with its long lead times. Thus immediate back-bench and party influence can only make itself felt through changing the general framework in which decisions are taken; for example the back-bench pressure exerted on the Secretary of State for the Environment, Peter Shore, in early 1978 asking for a debate in the House of Commons on the Windscale inquiry report. In this case the pressure was successful and a broad spectrum of opinions was heard. The main function of party pressure at the moment seems to be one of ensuring information on energy matters reaches a wider public than in previous years. There will always be instances of direct influence on policy – as in the Liberal veto of the proposed reorganization of the electricity supply industry – where a government has only a small majority, but over a longer time-scale this influence may be imperceptible. Party interest in the subject groups may be slight, not only for energy but for most topics. Richard Crossman commented on this apparent lack of commitment when he was Secretary of State for Social Services, and often called to Labour Party group meetings where the attendance was in single figures: 'The PLP is the most non-participating party in the world. It could have enormous influence but it is so browned off now that it has lost the will to try' (Crossman, 1977, p. 349). There is a great deal of scope for the individual MP with a good grasp of the problems of energy policy, both technological and social, to influence policy-makers by working on select committees (Arthur Palmer) or coming up with well reasoned and original policies (Nigel Forman). As energy matters receive more publicity it is to be expected that more MPs will involve themselves in the details of the problems, which must be all to the good as far as the relevance of debates and the questioning of ministers is concerned.

The main trade union group which is able to bring pressure to bear on government policy is the TUC Fuel and Power Industries Committee. The Trades Union Congress (TUC) itself is a voluntary association of trade unions, founded in 1868, which meets annually. The Fuel and Power Industries Committee has representatives of all the energy-producing sectors and formulates TUC policy on energy matters. As Joe Gormley of the NUM said of the committee: ' . . . we all get involved in discussions about energy policies as we see them for Britain, and not just peculiarly for our own industries'

(D.En. Energy Paper No. 14, 1976, p. 12). Seven members of the committee sit on the Energy Commission: the chairman Frank Chapple, general secretary of the Electrical, Electronic, Telecommunications and Plumbing Union (EETPU); the secretary, D. E. Lea; F. A. Baker, national industrial officer of the National Union of General and Municipal Workers (GMWU); Reg Birch, executive councilman of the Amalgamated Union of Engineering Workers (AUEW); G. A. Drain, general secretary of the National Association of Local Government Officers (NALGO); Joe Gormley, president of the National Union of Mineworkers (NUM); and C. H. Urwin, deputy general secretary of the Transport and General Workers Union (TGWU). The 1976 National Energy Conference produced several union views of energy policy, most of them making the point that future employment could be most effectively ensured by an expansion of the electricity supply industry by means of increased coal and nuclear generation. All the unions wanted more representation at board level in the nationalized energy industries, including NNC and BNOC. This point was made most strongly by Jack Jones of the TGWU:

> Frankly, an energy policy cannot be imposed. In the past, the civil servants and professional experts thought they had a monopoly of expertise in this field. Some may still think so. In my view, they need to be disabused of this idea. If an energy policy is to be effective, working men and women must be involved in energy policy-making, and their unions generally. There is a strong case for the trade union movement to be fully involved in the policy-making process in each and every one of the public and private concerns in the energy field. This should mean involvement from the start in the corporate planning process.   (D.En. Energy Paper No. 13, vol. 1, 1976, p. 25)

The unions were also nearly unanimous in recommending some sort of central body to discuss and advise on energy; the TUC Fuel and Power Industries Committee suggested a National Fuel and Power Board, the AUEW an Energy Council and the TGWU an Energy Planning Authority. Union concern at this stage centred round future employment prospects rather than the environmental or other social effects of particular policies, and although each paper had its emphases in slightly different areas, the only different note was struck by the AUEW-Technical, Administrative and Supervisory Section

(AUEW-TASS). This body produced a paper entitled 'The Layman's Guide to the requirement for Energy' (D.En. Energy Paper No. 13, vol. 1, 1976, pp. 114–16) which covered everything from Einstein's Theory of Relativity to estimates of world energy reserves.

By the middle of the following year, at the TUC conference of September 1977, trade union opinion had veered away from the purely employment-orientated line on energy policy towards views encompassing the social effects of policy decisions. The conference passed a motion seeking a balanced development of energy resources and expressing concern at the rate of consumption. It set out several decisions which needed to be taken on conservation and R and D, and suggested an expanded and socially acceptable nuclear programme including the construction of a demonstration fast breeder reactor. The TUC statement for the first Energy Commission meeting of November 1977 stated that it would be prudent to plan for as high a growth rate in gross domestic product as possible, and equated this with high energy demand. Thus most of the trade union movement at present promotes the growth of nuclear power generation and an increase in economic growth rates. A few unions, or parts of unions, such as Arthur Scargill's Yorkshire miners have come out against the expansion of nuclear power, and some union groups have produced alternative strategies relevant to their employment prospects. The Energy Group of the Conference of Socialist Economists, in cooperation with AUEW-TASS, have suggested diversification in the power plant manufacturing industry instead of redundancies and closures. They want nationalization and workers' control of the industry, and indicate the possibilities of plant manufacture of energy-generating equipment in areas such as nuclear, wind and wave power. They sum up: 'A socialist economy would provide a long-term plan for energy based upon social needs not private interests. One of its objectives would be to preserve rather than squander scarce reserves of fossil fuel . . . instead of riding the nuclear tiger, socialism would exploit the clean, everlasting resources of sun, wind, waves and tide' (AUEW-TASS, 1977, p. 21). Another union plan for diversification, that produced by the Lucas Aerospace Combine Shop Stewards Committee, contains a design for a heat pump which the Burnley plant management have been persuaded to back after a long drawn out struggle. The Combine Committee plans have only been backed by the TGWU and AUEW-TASS, other unions ignoring them or being hostile, so that the present TUC strategy of supporting the increased use of electricity looks unlikely to change in the near future. The minutes of the first Energy Commission meeting reported Joe Gormley, of the NUM, as saying that he would put the objectives of a sensible national energy policy in the following order: '. . . first, the guarantee of future supply for industry and the public; second, conservation; and third, pricing'. He said the way to ensure that everyone could afford adequate heat and light was to get the wages position right (Energy Commission, *Minutes of First Meeting 28 November 1977*, 1978, p. 3). The rather sparse minutes showed very little participation in the discussion by the TUC Fuel and Power Industries Committee representatives; whether they retain their strong line on employment via growth and increased energy usage remains to be seen. The TUC certainly has the ability to influence short term policy-making through the actions of the members and consultations with government, and the possibility of direct action by, for example, power workers in the future may lead to the alteration of medium term plans to ensure continuity of supply in all contingencies. Although the TUC Fuel and Power Industries Committee apparently discusses policy strategies as it sees them for Britain rather than merely in a union context, its proposals are still sectional to the extent that it considers people as workers first, rather than people as consumers having to live with the environmental outcome of whatever policies are adopted. Union policies are gradually making their mark in the field of worker participation in management; a clause in the draft bill to reorganize the electricity supply industry requires that the new Electricity Corporation should 'promote industrial democracy in a strong and organic form' (D.En. Press Notice Ref. No. 105, 1978, p. 4).

In the long term, naturally, the TUC will probably pursue the energy policy most likely to keep its members in full employment. Majority union opinion now holds that high employment, high economic growth rates, high energy use and thus electricity generation go together, so the TUC view at present is logically based on the expansion of coal and nuclear generation. However, this view may change, if new technologies or small scale manufacturing, for instance, begin to infiltrate into industry. If the TUC do alter their stated energy policy, then they have the industrial muscle power to ensure that changes occur, at least in the short term. There is some dissension within the union movement on energy policy already, and as Walter Patterson of FOE said at the National Energy Conference:

In general, I think we should be moving in the direction of more and smaller energy supply technologies, decentralized, emphasizing heat rather than electricity; and I would like to suggest to my Trade Union friends that it is my impression that we would be able to provide far more long-term skilled jobs with such an approach than we will be able to provide by increasing emphasis on centralized nuclear electricity.   (D.En. Energy Paper No. 13, vol. 1, 1976, p. 23)

The employers' organization, the Confederation of British Industry (CBI), has three representatives on the Energy Commission. The CBI states that it is 'the acknowledged representative of the management element of industry and commerce for the UK', and exists to promote and safeguard the interests of British business. The CBI has an Energy Policy Committee, and the three members of this who sit on the Energy Commission are the chairman, E. C. Sayers (chairman of Duport Ltd), T. Carlile (managing director of Babcock and Wilcox Ltd) and R. L. E. Lawrence (vice-chairman of the British Rail Board and a board member of the National Freight Corporation). At the 1976 National Energy Conference the CBI felt that they had no effective means of bringing industrial consumers' opinions to bear in the early stages of energy policy-making. There were the various trades associations and employers' federations, as well as the CBI's Industrial Coal Consumers' Sub-Committee (set up at the request of the government and the NCB) and the Joint Energy Policy Discussion Group between D.En. and the CBI, but the CBI felt the need for some sort of national energy forum. Basically the CBI required greater consumer consultation, as expressed by their representative S. Gibbs: 'The industrial consumer's needs are simple, and their scale is reasonably predictable if he and his forecasts are brought fully into an overall energy plan' (D.En. Energy Paper No. 13, vol. 1, 1976, p. 49). By 1977 and the first meeting of the Energy Commission the CBI representatives were concentrating their efforts on pointing out the need for early decisions in the energy supply industries, particularly a planned development of the nuclear industry. The CBI were against abrupt changes in energy forecasts and technologies, and supported both the government's working document and the TUC's paper.

The influence of private industry on government thinking on energy policy is more imponderable than that of the TUC. One of the objectives of energy policy is to be able to supply the needs of industry, thus in this field the CBI is basically a consumers' organization writ large. There is an increasing overlap between state-owned and private industry caused by the activities of the National Enterprise Board (NEB), but the NEB invests in consuming industries, though often large-scale consumers. Private industry's biggest influence on government policy is its mere existence, and its requirement for energy to fuel the economy. The CBI take a fairly sectional view of energy policy, looking to it for the assurance of continuing supplies on the correct scale and for freedom of choice for the consumer.

MUTUAL RELATIONSHIPS

It is clearly very difficult to describe the ever changing and close-knit web of relationships between the government, the energy supply organizations and the other related bodies. However, an attempt has been made in each of the above sections of this chapter to outline the official and unofficial connections between the myriad of organizations comprising the energy industry. Relationships would be relatively simple if the officials of one body did not frequently sit on other committees or perform different roles, and it is easier (but possibly misleading) to judge relative weight of opinion by the outcome of decisions rather than assumptions about the roles played by various individuals. Representatives of different bodies may be brought together in conflict, as at the seminal Windscale inquiry, or in circumstances requiring cooperation such as tripartite discussions. The role of an organization changes with its sphere of activity, and its aims may vary for reasons ranging from legislation to a change in the chairmanship. Individual opinion can alter the course of policy and the effects may not be realized until long after the individual concerned has ceased to be a policy-maker.

Changes have certainly taken place in official relationships between the energy supply and consuming bodies over the years since D.En. was formed and the National Energy Conference took place. There now exists a body, the Energy Commission, with representation at the highest levels of all the organizations concerned: all, that is, except the civil servants of D.En. The WGES has opened its workings slightly to the public in that it published a paper for the initial Energy Commission meeting, and it appears that this body is one of the twin hubs around which policy is developed. It has both board-level members from the supply industries and higher civil servant members from D.En. The membership is at the level where economic planning is formulated and put into action, and it is interesting to note that there is no trade union representation. The collection of nationalized energy industry chairmen, union leaders and consumer representatives pulled together to form the Energy Commission appears to be too broad-based and unwieldy a body to be able to study and decide upon highly technical matters in particular. It is noticeable that there is no expert opinion available on the Energy Commission from people working in the field and most of the papers so far presented have been written by organizations with representatives on the Commission, a rather incestuous arrangement.

The second hub of the policy-making machine, ACORD, has a slightly broader-based membership than WGES, but at the same high organizational level although on the research side. Only one man sits on both ACORD and WGES: R. W. Orson of the Electricity Council. ACORD's role is to advise on research, and although research has to lead in the development of energy sources, it is likely that WGES has greater control over policy-making because its members are orientated purely towards their own problems perceived by their own representatives. The civil servants have a close relationship with the particular industry which is their responsibility, and again there is no outside, neutral voice of criticism or source of ideas.

Possibly the structure of the high-level government policy-making bodies may undergo some change in the near future, as a result of Tony Benn's continued openness in D.En. and the public and party pressures for greater availability of information and control over decision-making. It may be that the fringe organizations will become part of the energy establishment at approximately the same time, but further fringe groups will no doubt form to fill new roles proffered by future policy decisions. Even the trade union movement may broaden its outlook away from purely employment-based policies, as it will surely need to do if and when its representatives reach the boards of the nationalized industries. On the other hand, this might be treated by their membership as a watering down of union objectives, so that perhaps structural change in employment prospects is a more likely cause of changes in trade union energy policy. It is probable that industrial democracy and change in the type of employment available will affect the unions in different ways over a varying timescale; thus the reasons for any change in their policy will be difficult to detect.

The causal effect of a change of circumstances depends on the original opinions of the union membership, and these differ, although only slightly at present, in the case of energy policy.

The government is still considering changes in its official relationships with all the nationalized industries, but the conclusion appears to be forming that as the problems of each industry are quite different, so ought the working relationship to be. This is a time of considerable flux in the mutual relations of the energy industry, and also a time when several important policy decisions are being discussed. It is possible that the scale of policy-making has precipitated some of the changes required in the industry as a whole. To understand fully the workings of the energy industry it is necessary to consider the major policy issues and options, and how these have a bearing on the shape of the organizations involved. The structure of the relevant bodies and their relationships have already been considered and the next chapter looks at the object of their interactions – policy itself.

7 Major Policy Issues

The major energy policy issues of today are all affected by decisions taken in the past: policy for the newer energy technologies such as nuclear power is affected by the presence of the results of capital investment in fossil fuel generation; much-needed changes in the balance between fuels used in industry may be inhibited by the inertia of present working methods; and research and development decisions affect options many years into the future. The high cost of capital investment in power production and the long lead times associated with most developments intensify the policy-making problems, and additionally there is the uncertainty caused by varying estimates of resource reserves to contend with.

Over the years, governments have issued a series of Green Papers, White Papers and consultative documents identifying problem areas in energy (or, as it used to be known, fuel) policy. The major issues were usually set out in terms of the main fuels in use at the time. Before the Second World War the British economy was fuelled mainly by coal and although the coal industry had its ups and downs, in keeping with the economic state of the country, fuel policies offered fewer options than they do today. Consumption estimates, resource estimates and the use of the various systems of power production are all under discussion at the moment, and it is not only the options for each issue which cause disagreement, but the very existence and importance of certain issues. The definition of issues and options is the starting point for assumptions in policy-making, and each organization in the energy industry may accept a different set of issues as being relevant.

It is necessary, then, to outline the issues as defined by the various bodies of the energy industry and to discover how their definitions have changed over the period of time. Most of the government policy statements and reports on energy policy include a list of objectives which the government or committee feel that a national energy policy should fulfil. Over the years since the first post-war policy document in 1946, the Simon Report, certain issues have been at the forefront of policy objectives only to disappear in the intervening period between reports or White Papers. Energy conservation is a case in point, being given a high degree of importance in the immediate postwar years of relative fuel shortage, and then losing pride of place in the 1960s as imported oil lessened worries about supplies and resources. At that time, fuel was seen basically as an industrial feedstock, and the introduction of more sophisticated statistical analyses of the fuel-supply situation with the 1967 White Paper underlined the government's objective of providing adequate fuel for economic growth at competitive prices. After the 1973 oil crisis, conservation returned to the fore in energy policy objectives, and was included in the 'traditional' objectives of energy policy in the 1978 Green Paper, under the heading resource costs. An alternative formulation of objectives in the Green Paper saw the return of social policy to the list, in the shape of ensuring that everyone could afford adequate heat and light at home. Apart from the 1977 Energy Policy Review, this subject had not entered the list since 1946, where the first objective had been to ensure good standards of heating in the house. Some factors in energy-policy formulation have stayed constant: the recognition of the uncertainties implicit in trying to plan in a field where resources are often uncertain and lead times long is a recurring theme, as is the response of keeping options open as long as possible. Unfortunately this has occasionally resulted in policies as vague as the objectives they seek to meet, but the most recent policy statements have emphasized points for decision whilst still retaining an awareness of the need for flexibility. It is clear that subjects included in the various government papers reflect the position of the country with regard to its energy supplies at the time they are produced. This natural concern with the contemporary scene may lead to wrong decisions, or at least options being closed, only to be reopened later at possibly greater cost. The enthusiasm for alternative sources of energy has increased since the oil crisis, but in the 1960s they had hardly rated a mention, and were dismissed, although at least considered, in the 1952 Ridley Report. Some problems appear to persist over the years in spite of all attempts to produce solutions, two of these being tariff policy and the coordination and planning of the nationalized energy industries. Apart from uncertainties inherent in energy policy concerning resources, there are also political considerations, both national and international, to be taken into account. Political objectives may override the best laid energy policies, thus policy needs to be robust enough to be above party political matters. Tony Benn seems to be trying for a consensus on energy policy, to ensure some continuity for planning purposes.

The preceding chapter mentioned points of importance to many of the quasi- and non-governmental bodies involved with energy policy, but did not concern itself with overall strategies. The following sections comprise a guide to the main policy issues as defined by the government in their pronouncements on energy policy since the Second World War, when matters became complicated by the advent of new technologies and the growth in consumption of fuels other than coal. This is followed by a guide to the few overall energy strategies which have been produced by non-government groups. The majority of energy-producing industries try to pursue their own interests within the overall government policy as they see it, whilst the associated bodies, such as research committees or pressure groups, also tend to single out their own particular interests and causes in energy debates. The bulk of overall energy policy formulation has so far been undertaken by governments, with greater resources than all of the smaller groups which are now attempting to produce alternative strategies. Energy policy-making being the uncertain business that it is, previous government attempts at outlining strategies have often dated rapidly, but most have a few suggestions which stand the test of time.

THE SIMON REPORT, 1946

The Fuel and Power Advisory Council was set up after the Second World War to advise the minister on matters of his choosing. Their first reference was: 'To consider and advise on the use of fuels and the provision of heat services in domestic and similar premises, in the interests of the occupants and of the nation, with special regard to the efficient use of fuel resources and to the prevention of atmospheric pollution' (Cmd 6762, p. ii, 1946), and the council, chaired by Sir Ernest Simon, produced a report in March 1946 (Simon Report, Cmd 6762, 1946). The problem of domestic heating efficiency was urgent because of the instigation of the newly elected Labour government's massive home-building programme.

The council began by stating their view of the main objectives of a national fuel policy:

(a) To ensure good standards of heating in the house.
(b) Low cost and more convenience for the householder.
(c) National fuel economy.
(d) Smoke abatement.

The council then considered heating in small dwellings, finding the open coal fire inefficient and dirty. They recommended that smokeless solid fuel should be substituted for bituminous coal and that minimum standards should be established for heating appliances. They also looked at district and central heating, saying that central heating should become accepted as the normal form of heating blocks of flats and large houses. They made no recommendation on district heating, mainly because of the difficulty of introducing it into this country, and advocated no decision until a further report had been produced.

The council then considered the various fuels in use at the time and concluded that '. . . even in thinly populated rural areas, the ultimate objective should be to lay electricity to every house, so long as this does not throw excessive burdens on the consumers of electricity elsewhere' (Cmd 6762, p. 15, 1946). They did not feel it necessary to extend the gas supply to all areas, but one council member, Viscount Ridley (who was to chair the next fuel policy inquiry), produced a memorandum of reservations on the report in which he stated that electricity should be provided for all rural areas regardless of expense. He suggested that the cost should be spread over the whole community. This is one of the first illustrations of a contentious point in energy policy: the problem of who pays the costs of investment in, say, electrification or research – investment which is necessary or desirable for the efficient running of an industry but which may only bring results in the future. Costs may be passed directly to the consumer, or the taxpayer or government subsidies may be used to ease the burden. This problem is bound up with the view of nationalized industries as fully commercial bodies which should be able to cover their own costs; this, of course, is a short term view in fields where investment must be made many years ahead of predicted returns, for example nuclear power generation. There is no single solution to the problem of deferred returns, each industry being in a slightly different situation, but governments in general have not faced the question at all, tending to muddle through in one direction or another depending on the party in power. Writing off capital debt, government subsidies and increased prices have all been seen as tools to help out the energy industries with long term investment problems.

The Simon Report also considered the long running saga of gas and electricity pricing, coming down in favour of free competition between the two provided that prices were appropriately related to costs. They felt that prices should be a direct reflection of the costs of production and distribution, stating: 'Cost is in the long run the most accurate, and indeed the only practicable, index of the resources needed to supply any particular commodity or service' (Cmd 6762, 1946, p. 20). They also drew attention to the virtual monopoly held by the electricity suppliers for lighting, saying that this should not be used to charge unfairly high prices. The council came out strongly in favour of government staffed information centres to provide consumers (or housewives, as they were then known) with advice on the efficient use of appliances, and a national smoke abatement programme. They did, however, take some note of the social problems of changing from open coal-fire heating: 'It is the traditional way of heating rooms; it gives a very pleasant warmth; it forms a social centre and adds to the pleasure of an evening's talk; it can be used to destroy refuse. Indeed, the open coal fire is a national institution' (Cmd 6762, 1946, p. 5). Again, this is an example of a prevalent problem in energy policy, the question of enforced or free choice of fuel for the consumer.

Possibly because it was limited by its terms of reference to domestic fuel policy, the Simon Report showed an awareness of the implicit social problems unusual in government considerations of energy policy. Although its recommendations were limited to a narrow policy area, they were well reasoned, and the strong emphasis on smoke-abatement measures set the whole campaign in motion. One of the few omissions was the neglect of a proposal for district heating, which could have been useful in view of the large amount of house building which had just commenced.

THE RIDLEY REPORT, 1952

A Committee on National Fuel Policy was appointed by the Minister of Fuel and Power in July 1951 with the following terms of reference:

In view of the growing demands for all forms of fuel and power arising from full employment and the rearmament programme, to consider whether any further steps can be taken to promote the best use of our fuel and power resources, having regard to present and prospective requirements and in the light of technical developments.   (Cmd 8647, 1952, p. iii)

The committee, under Viscount Ridley and including Professor W. A. Hawthorne, now chairman of ACEC, produced a report in September 1952 concerning *National Policy for the use of Fuel and Power Resources* (Cmd 8647, 1952) which was much broader in scope than the Simon Report. It began, as was the custom, by stating what the committee assumed to be the aims of a national policy to promote the best use of fuel and power. These were as follows:

1. To meet in full the demands of the community for the different fuel and power services, when these services are sold at prices which closely correspond to the relevant costs of production and distribution.
2. To provide for export fuels on such a scale and of such types as can be sold abroad with most gain for the country.
3. To promote the maximum economic efficiency in each use of each fuel.
4. To encourage the use for particular services of the fuel which gives the best returns on the resources consumed.   (Cmd 8647, 1952, p. 1)

These aims were not discussed in the report but taken as given, and the committee went on to look at the present state of shortages in fuel supplies and future prospects. They did not see room for much increase in imported oil supplies, because of the strategic risk of relying on imported fuel and the cost in dollars or other foreign currency, but there was a proviso: 'However, much will depend upon developments in the world oil market; we cannot foresee what these will be, and much more – or less – oil may be used than we assume . . .' (Cmd 8647, 1952, para. 32). In fact the cheapness of imported oil stimulated an increase in demand of the order of three times the committee's estimated consumption in the following ten years. They also considered energy sources other than coal and oil, including water (i.e. hydro-electric power), peat, wind, tidal, solar, waves, geothermal and nuclear, but all except the hydro-electric schemes were dismissed as being unlikely to yield any significant return within the next few years.

The committee made several recommendations along the lines of the Simon Report concerning domestic fuel efficiency and increases in the government information service to both domestic and industrial consumers. Conservation, in terms of fuel efficiency, was seen to be unattractive to industrialists who preferred to use their resources to increase output directly, because coal was undervalued with respect to other resources and taxation made fuel efficiency unappealing economically although still viable in terms of coal economy. Today's conservation measures face similar problems, particularly in the area of capital spending on conservation measures. District heating was again damned with faint praise:

> Despite its attractions as a fuel saver, we are informed that the wide adoption of district heating in this country for domestic purposes is not economic, because of the increase it occasions in power stations' plant cost for a given electricity output, the very high costs of connection either to existing houses or to new low density housing estates, and the difficulties of coping with non-simultaneous demands for power and heat.   (Cmd 8647, 1952, para. 201)

The main point of the report was that fuel shortages could be eased by using available fuel more efficiently, and most of its recommendations concerned various means to that end. The tariff debate was in full flow again, and the committee suggested a Tariffs Advisory Committee of independent experts who would advise the minister. They felt that the fuel industries should remain competitive and separate, but did see them as parts of a whole: 'We look upon the nationalized gas and electricity industries as in a sense branches of one undertaking, within which, however, competition is a valuable aid to efficiency' (Cmd 8647, 1952, para. 287). In order to coordinate planning in the fuel industries, the committee suggested the establishment of a Joint Fuel and Power Planning Board, composed of representatives of government and the nationalized fuel boards. They did not envisage the Minister of Fuel and Power as being chairman of the Planning Board. One of the overall, and timeless, conclusions of the report was that '. . . the need for increased fuel efficiency and the duty of conserving our fuel resources will remain permanently' (Cmd 8647, 1952, para. 293). Although this report was concerned with fuel policy at a much broader level than the Simon Report, many of the problems remained the same: means of control and coordination of the fuel industries, consumer choice, tariff policy and incentives for efficient fuel use. Although this report was the last in the era of great dependence on coal rather than oil, many of the questions it raised carried over into the years of cheap oil, and its emphasis on conservation and efficiency is as relevant now as it was then. Its recommendations on advice to consumers, domestic and industrial, have only been recently put into effect primarily as a result of the oil crisis.

FUEL POLICY, 1965

Thirteen years passed before another government cared to try its hand at producing a national fuel policy. By 1965, coal demand had passed its peak, although the troubles of the coal industry were mitigated by the increase in overall fuel consumption. The demand for oil was increasing steadily, and electricity consumption grew at 8 per cent per annum between 1950 and 1964; gas demand also increased, but not as rapidly. A review of the energy industry was one of the matters put in hand by the newly elected Labour government, under Harold Wilson, and their White Paper (Cmnd 2798, 1965) *Fuel Policy* was produced almost exactly a year after they took office. Its objective was to describe the principles on which a coordinated national fuel policy should be based, and the machinery available to the government for the maintenance of such a policy.

The initial overview of the situation showed that although a change in consumption patterns of coal and oil was taking place, fuel policy was still being formulated on the same premise as had been relevant since the Simon Report, that our large scale home-produced fuel resource was coal. 'There would be a further powerful stimulus to the growth of the gas industry if the search for petroleum in the British part of the Continental Shelf were to result in a substantial find of gas' (Cmnd 2798, 1965, para. 25). Thus energy policy issues were still on the brink of the drastic changes in circumstance which were to come. The government of the day had a broader view of the place of fuel policy in the national economy than some of its predecessors: 'The overriding objective is that the fuel sector should make its full contribution to the strengthening of the economy and the balance of payments' (Cmnd 2798, 1965, para. 35). The White Paper set out five objectives with this aim in mind:

(a) Adequate and continuous supplies of fuel of suitable quality should be available to sustain the desired rate of growth of the economy.
(b) The price of fuel should play its part in making the UK economy competitive with other countries, especially in Western Europe.
(c) Fuel industries should be technically progressive and viable.
(d) Imports of fuel, especially oil which will increase in quantity quickly, should be in their least costly form.
(e) Consumer freedom of choice should be seen as an essential guide to planning, as well as being desirable in itself, provided that prices reflect relevant costs.

In the thirteen years since the Ridley Report, the import of fuel had replaced exports as a subject of concern, and the emphasis on fuel efficiency as such had disappeared from the list of objectives altogether. The primary aim of providing supplies of fuel for consumers remained the same, but the White Paper connected this with the need for continued economic growth, and this theme dominated the whole White Paper. It set fuel policy in the context of national economic policy for the first time, and saw fuel policy as serving the needs of the overall economy rather than being unilaterally determined by resource levels.

The White Paper looked at each fuel separately, and decided to retain the protection given to the coal industry by its preferential treatment at power stations and the import ban on foreign coal. Nearly half the industry's capital debt of £960 million was written off, and it was decided to close the loss-making pits, to try and make the industry viable as a whole. The White Paper foresaw a rapid growth in oil consumption, and felt that this could not be constrained without impeding the development of the economy. In order to reduce the effects of relying on imported oil, it suggested that adequate oil stocks should be maintained and that the oil companies be encouraged to diversify their sources of supply. The exploration of the North Sea was also to be pursued. Nuclear generation had been established as a reliable source of power by 1965, and the White Paper advocated a flexible programme of expansion, to be kept under review. It did not see the import of uranium fuel as an obstacle, as the amount required was relatively small. The White Paper recommended closer coordination between the coal and electricity industries, and admitted that a certain amount of government interference took place in the running of the gas and electricity industries. The electricity industry had to suffer the costs of building nuclear power stations before they were strictly competitive, and bringing electrification to rural areas, while the gas industry had been set lower financial objectives. The overall conclusion on fuel policy was that it should not be rigid, and should be kept under review because of unforeseeable technological changes.

One interesting point brought up in the paper is its comparison of the relationship between economic activity and energy consumption. It was felt that the figures were difficult to interpret because a number of different factors contributed to the relationship: comparisons between different countries were unclear because of the differences between their energy consumption patterns and economic structures. The government felt that: 'The most difficult single problem in fuel policy is the health and size of the coal industry' (Cmnd 2798, 1965, para. 38). They also reflected the growing realization of the interaction between environmental effects and fuel policy: '. . . it must not be overlooked that the preservation of amenity imposes extra costs on the electricity industry and hinders the task of meeting the expanding demand' (Cmnd 2798, 1965, para. 97). Problems of coordination between industries existed as they had in the days of the Ridley Report, and differences in treatment of the gas and electricity industries still remained. The machinery of policy-making had advanced somewhat in the intervening years, producing an Energy Advisory Council, set up by the Minister of Power in January 1965, with the following terms of reference: 'to consider and advise the Minister of Power about the energy situation and outlook and the plans and policies of the fuel and power industries in relation to national objectives for economic growth' (Cmnd 2798, 1965, para. 13). The council was comprised of the heads of the nationalized fuel industries, the heads of the trade unions and representatives of government departments. Thus the council's membership had two important differences from today's Energy Commission: the presence of government departments and the absence of consumer bodies. The council discussed estimates, considered long term policy including the White Paper, and assessed the revised second nuclear programme. The presence of government departmental representatives may have made the council a more useful body than today's Energy Commission. Another policy-making body was the Coordinating Committee, which consisted of the Minister of Power as chairman, with the chairmen of the coal, electricity and gas industries. This committee discussed the development of national fuel policy.

The White Paper's version of the future was of a more viable coal industry, increased use of imported oil mitigated by measures such as the expansion of the British refining industry, and greater government control and coordination of the gas and electricity industries. Although the government appeared to be aware that change could overtake their policy at any time, they felt that: 'The national interests which fuel policy must seek to serve, and certain basic characteristics of the various fuel industries, change slowly if at all' (Cmnd 2798, 1965, para. 97). Thus they subordinated the demands of fuel policy to those of national economic policy, and objectives concerned more with fuel resources than their economic consequences disappeared. Neither fuel efficiency nor information to consumers are prominent in the White Paper, although environmental considerations make a first, small, impact. The objectives of the new fuel policy were summed up as follows: 'Fuel policy, therefore, must be flexible enough to move with the trend of events, and must maintain all possible room for manoeuvre by refraining from making, earlier than is demonstrably necessary, major changes which it may be impracticable to reverse' (Cmnd 2798, 1965, para. 36). This statement reflects some of the few constant factors in fuel policy-making: calls for flexibility, unhurried decision-making and appreciation of the uncertainty of the situation at any time. As it happened, a dramatic change in circumstances occurred almost simultaneouly with the publication of the White Paper – the first discovery of natural gas reserves in the UK sector of the North Sea basin.

There are few sources which illustrate the inner workings of the government of this era when considering fuel policy. The Minister of Power from October 1964 until April 1966 was Fred Lee, a trade union MP. The Crossman *Diaries* show how political pressures can influence decisions on the matter which the government itself considered to be the overriding problem of fuel policy – the state of the coal industry. They also show the effect of Civil Service departmental opinion on a minister, as reflected by the diarist, in June 1965:

[Fred Lee's] main concern seemed to be that we should on no account give any kind of tapering subsidies to help declining coalfields such as those in Scotland and South Wales. It's extraordinary how a Department can get a Minister down. It would have been difficult to conceive nine months ago that Mr. Lee would have been opposed to any help for the coalminers and blind to the fact that tapering subsidies are politically essential.   (Crossman, 1975, p. 258)

Later the Cabinet decided to give subsidies, which Crossman saw as the Cabinet saving Lee from his department. The saga of coal prices rumbled on throughout 1965, with Lee asking for a rise in March and having it postponed because of the municipal elections. He tried again in June and was refused because of the incomes policy. In August it was decided to wait until September to decide, as the TUC meeting was in September. In September, at a special Cabinet meeting, '. . . the idea of increasing coal prices now, over which we had split at the previous Cabinet meeting, was simply pushed to one side as something inconceivable before the TUC met and the prices and incomes policy was announced. Poor Fred Lee was left speechless, with the vast Coal Board losses piling up' (Crossman, 1975, p. 316). Thus in spite of the long term importance to the economy of a viable coal industry and the basic agreement of the government on the necessary measures, these were not taken at the correct time because of short term political considerations. It is also interesting to note the minister's change in attitude to the miners apparently caused by his new-found departmental responsibilities. Lee's tough methods of dealing with the miners did not stop Crossman describing him as '. . . an obviously inadequate Minister of Power' (Crossman, 1975, p. 495), and he was replaced by the then 38-year-old Richard Marsh in April 1966, immediately after Labour's election victory. Harold Wilson described Marsh as '. . . one of our best Parliamentary Secretaries . . .' (Wilson, 1974, p. 285) but Crossman felt otherwise, thinking him '. . . brash, erratic and unnecessarily rude . . .' (Crossman, 1976, p. 111).

Marsh suffered political pressure on his policies in a similar manner to Lee when he asked for an electricity price rise in March 1967 and was refused because GLC election day was imminent. Prices were then raised against his will in July 1967, as the Treasury and the Department of Economic Affairs (DEA) were both in favour. The DEA were against raising gas prices, which prompted Crossman to comment: 'The fact is we've been panicked as badly on these nationalized industry prices as we have been on pit closures . . .' (Crossman, 1976, p. 446). Marsh also had the inevitable disagreements with the Civil Service, for instance the confusion over power-station construction in March 1967, when he asked for a coal-fire and a nuclear station but the DEA were against the former.

> [The Cabinet Committee] had finally decided that we simply didn't know enough to make a decision and had instructed the officials to come back with absolutely clear facts and figures about both the nature of the power stations and about the state of the electricity supply in the 1970s. Now, three weeks later, the officials had come up with a completely different view and, even more sinister, with quite different figures. Three weeks ago it was suggested we didn't need the new coal-firing station. Now we are given figures that demonstrate we need both.   (Crossman, 1976, pp. 268–9)

This is interesting in view of the emphasis placed by the Ministry of Power on their new methods of analysis in the November 1967 White Paper on fuel policy.

FUEL POLICY, 1967

Although much had happened beyond the bounds of government in the two years between the White Papers (the discovery of natural gas reserves and the increase in nuclear power generation were most prominent), within the policy-making arena old problems recurred. *Fuel Policy* (Cmnd 3438, 1967) was published simultaneously with a White Paper on *Railway Policy*, and 'What had happened in both cases was that the officials of all the Departments concerned had agreed on the texts, the Ministers had been told that the officials had agreed on the texts and the Ministers were therefore bound by the official agreement. Therefore the White Papers were written totally by officials, and no Minister had taken any active part in their drafting' (Crossman, 1976, p. 523). The introduction to the White Paper made it clear that the Government's policy objectives had not altered, but that a review was necessary '. . . to re-assess the balance between the available primary fuels (coal, oil, nuclear power and natural gas), and to set the framework for the most beneficial development of our energy supplies' (Cmnd 3438, 1967, para. 1). Although the paper is entitled *Fuel Policy* it is the first government paper which makes frequent mention of energy supplies as such, perhaps as a consequence of the influence of worldwide environmental activity. It must also be born in mind that although the natural gas reserves had been discovered, North Sea oil was not to make its first appearance until 1969.

The government saw the future in the shape of a four-fuel economy, and stated that its main aim was to supply energy requirements in the way which yielded the greatest benefit to the country. The White Paper provided no explicit list of objectives, since these were unchanged from the 1965 paper, but it did add a few extra considerations to be taken into account, such as security of supply (prompted by the first Middle East war), the efficient use of resources (making a return from the Ridley Report of 1952) and the economic, social and human consequences of changes in the supply pattern. An important departure for the White Paper was the amount of forecasting which had taken place to produce the future demand estimates, prompted by the increasing cost and long lead times of capital investment in the energy industries. An appendix to the White Paper described the new methods of statistical and economic analysis which had been introduced,'. . . designed to examine the implications of a wide range of assumptions about future trends in the fuel industries and in the economy' (Cmnd 3438, 1967, p. 56). In fact, very little detail was provided. Nuclear power, which the White Paper heralded as having come of age as a potential major source of energy, was referred to as follows: 'Separate work on nuclear power costs . . . made it possible to dispense with alternative assumptions as to how much nuclear power there would be by 1975, and to work on the basis that the existing programmes would be fulfilled' (Cmnd 3438, 1967, p. 61).

The appendix on nuclear power costs (Cmnd 3438, 1967, pp. 78–81) went out of its way to make the strongest assumptions for the case against cheap nuclear generation at that time, but still came up with a clear advantage for nuclear power. Some of their assumptions have not proved to be correct, for example the economics of repeat AGR orders, but the appendix did explain the methodology in some detail. However, this work could hardly be seen to render other cost assumptions untenable. Even though the department's statisticians were not granted the benefit of hindsight, a more flexible approach to nuclear power costing might have allowed for some leeway in the nuclear programme, which turned out to be disastrously behind schedule and costly in the case of the AGRs. In the case of the other energy sources, the small range of cases selected for study (the process of and reasons for selection were not divulged), militates against any meaningful results being obtained, even taking into consideration the unexpected arrival of resources such as North Sea oil. It is, to put it mildly, unfortunate that what appears to be the first serious exercise in forecasting undertaken by the department's newly formed Energy Model Group began with such limited aims. These aims have carried over into present-day forecasting techniques, which are internally consistent methodologically but do not include assumptions on a wide enough base to provide a range of alternative policy options. The limitation on possible routes of policy-making laid down by the results of this type of analysis shows the importance of the original assumptions, which are often least open to change. The driving force behind the introduction of the new methodology may have been Michael Posner, who was director of economics at the Ministry of Power in 1966–7 before moving on to be economic adviser to the Treasury.

The White Paper analysed the fuel industries individually: the size of the natural gas reserves was still unknown, but it was calculated that it was worthwhile to convert the town gas distribution system to enable natural gas to be used. In the longer term, gas depletion was to be rapid in spite of the shortening in the life of the gasfields which would result. The government felt that the benefits to the economy would outweigh the resource considerations. Future electricity generation was expected to be mainly nuclear, on the strength of three eulogistic paragraphs, 32–4, which hardly bear quoting now. One of the strong points of nuclear generation was stated to be that it caused no air pollution; however, radioactive waste material did not rate a mention. The White Paper tried to foresee the future of the world oil market, and appeared to blunder: 'On the evidence available, it seems likely that oil will remain competitive with coal, and that pressure to force up crude oil prices will be held in check by the danger of loss of markets' (Cmnd 3438, 1967, para. 53). However, in the wake of the 1973–4 oil crisis and the steep rise in prices came a stagnant period beginning around 1977, so that the prediction may not have been as much adrift as it originally seemed. The later discovery of oil in the UK section of the North Sea basin made the White Paper's oil policy redundant, but it also reinforced the aims of securing supplies and increasing refinery construction. Coal, as ever, was a major problem; the support given to the industry as a result of the 1965 White Paper had not resulted in any expansion of the market. The White Paper concluded that the industry's efficiency had to be increased and its costs reduced, meaning a concentration on the most economic coalfields and consequent decline in manpower. Further investment funds were to be provided by the government in order to continue the modernization programme. Not surprisingly, the continued closure of mines under a Labour government was the source of much protest from the miners and the miners' group of MPs.

The overall aim of this attempt at a fuel policy was summarized in the White Paper as having the basic objective of providing cheap energy, bearing in mind adequacy and security of supplies. Fuel conservation was not thought to be necessary except possibly in the case of natural gas: '. . . for the remainder there seems no reason why the possibility of exhaustion of reserves should be regarded as a constraint in determining the best way of meeting the nation's energy requirements' (Cmnd 3438, 1967, para. 77). In the chapter on the long term view of energy policy, there was some discussion of whether the forecasts provided by the Ministry of Power for fuel use in the mid-70s (total inland energy demand of 350 million tons of coal (equivalent) (mtce) in 1975), were desirable patterns. The White Paper concluded that it was in the national interest to accept the long term trends shown by the forecasts: rarely, if ever, are the forecasts of energy demand seen as undesirable. Had the government reacted to these – the first results of new analytical methods of forecasting – by discussing their implications rather than accepting them as near-inevitable, then the whole basis for the formulation of future energy policies would have been changed. Only one sectional interest, the miners, disagreed with any estimates made, and this was purely because of the unemployment which would clearly be the result of the policies. Possibly the overriding problems of the coal industry diverted the Cabinet from the less obviously important aspects of the White Paper.

The conclusion to the White Paper contained the usual references to the ideal of flexibility in policy-making, which had been a little muted throughout the paper by the appearance of so many apparently hard statistics on future production: 'The concentration in the White Paper on primary energy reflects its dominating importance for fuel policy as a result of recent developments. The magnitude of these developments highlights the need to think of fuel policy as an evolving subject, requiring constant review and susceptible to continuous adjustment' (Cmnd 3438, 1967, para. 136). Although the Energy Advisory Council still existed, and had been consulted before the production of the White Paper, there were few other references to consultation of any sort on future policy. The dissemination of information to consumers and the need for conservation of energy had been forgotten, along with any reference to renewable sources of energy. The White Paper presented a highly deterministic view of the government's relationships with the nationalized energy industries, written in a heady atmosphere caused by the availability of cheap nuclear power and natural gas. It is unfortunate that the extremely limited range of assumptions tested in this paper provided the base for future methodologies, and that forecasts tended to be treated as targets despite protestations to the contrary.

A few months after the publication of the White Paper in April 1968 Richard Marsh was replaced by Ray Gunter as Minister of Power. Gunter had previously been Minister of Labour, and Harold Wilson comments:

> I knew that Ray Gunter would be likely to take this change hard . . . But I wanted him for Power, where, with the strains on the mining industry and the need to get the post-nationalization steel industry firmly established, a high-level and experienced minister with strong union connections was required. . . . My one reservation was about fuel policy. Important negotiations were afoot on the allocation of North Sea gas and . . . oil franchises too. I was anxious for a fresh mind to look at these problems, given what I believed was the excessively oil-orientated prejudice of the Department. It had been thus, to my knowledge, for over a quarter of a century. The doubt lay in whether Ray Gunter would be ready to give his mind to the extremely intricate figurings involved in this process and in wider aspects of fuel policy and would be happy in his work. My anxieties were, before long, confirmed.   (Wilson, 1974, p. 660)

Crossman's view of the situation was, as usual, rather different: 'I've often heard [Wilson] talk about Gunter's outrageous leaks and how he was going to send for Gunter and really put him on the mat. I don't believe he ever sent for Gunter and when it came to the shuffle he didn't sack him but promoted him to the Ministry of Power' (Crossman, 1976, p. 783). It turned out that Gunter had indeed been sent for, and regarded his move from Labour to Power with great distaste. He eventually resigned from the Cabinet at the end of June 1968, only of couple of months after his move, and apparently tried to damage the government by making the most of the ensuing publicity.

His replacement in July 1968 was Roy Mason, Crossman seeing

this as putting a miner into the ministry to placate the miners. Once again departmental policy quickly appeared to cause a change of heart, this time at the end of July 1968 over the question of building Hartlepool nuclear power station in the middle of a coalfield (the reason being low running costs): 'I noticed that Roy Mason is already firmly against more coal-fired stations. It's astonishing how quickly these working-class boys get taken over by the civil servants' (Crossman, 1977, p. 162). What is surprising is the hold taken on the department by nuclear power between the 1965 and 1967 White Papers. In 1965 it was seen as having proved itself to be a reliable generator of power, and it was suggested that expansion of the nuclear industry might accelerate in the 1970s. By 1967 it had become part of the 'four-fuel economy' and it was expected that most future generating stations would be nuclear.

In October 1969 Roy Mason lost his post as Minister of Power when it was absorbed into the Ministry of Technology under Tony Benn. This move was suggested by members of Harold Wilson's political office, and was seen by the civil servants involved as a challenge. Wilson felt that 'It had several advantages. Atomic energy and electric power generation, together with the other fuel and power industries, were brought together under a single political direction; so was responsibility for electricity generation and for the heavy electrical plant industries' (Wilson, 1974, p. 893). This is one of the few references Wilson makes to energy policy as such in his entire record of government from 1964 until 1970. Even the 1967 White Paper, which caused so much trouble with the miners, is mentioned only in passing. Before the new Ministry of Technology had a chance to prove itself there was a change of government in June 1970, the Conservatives gaining power. Geoffrey Rippon became Minister of Technology for a few months and was then succeeded by John Davies in July. The ministry was taken into the Department of Trade and Industry in October 1970, still under Davies (who held the post for two years before giving way to Peter Walker in November 1972), still prior to the oil crisis but after the first four rounds of licensing for exploration rights in the North Sea. The Department of Energy was created at Christmas 1973, under Lord Carrington, to deal with the problems posed by the oil crisis and the miners' strike, but there were no energy policy papers published during the Conservative government's time in office. This was in spite of the remarkable changes in the situation which had taken place since 1967, with the prospect of the UK becoming nearly self-sufficient in energy. The major alteration which affected policy-making was the setting up of D.En., which although it contained much the same group of civil servants who had been shuffled around from ministry to ministry over the previous six years, did imply that energy policy was being seen as an entity for the first time.

UNITED KINGDOM OFFSHORE OIL AND GAS POLICY, 1974

The fifth postwar Labour government came to power in early 1974, and Eric Varley was appointed to D.En. in March. D.En. quickly produced a White Paper on *United Kingdom Offshore Oil and Gas Policy* (Cmnd 5696, 1974) in July 1974, which was a synthesis of an earlier Public Accounts Committee report on Continental Shelf policy. This short paper had as its objectives bringing the ownership and distribution of North Sea and Celtic Sea oil under government control, and conferring the maximum benefit of the resources on the community, particularly Scotland and the declining industrial areas. The most revolutionary move was the setting up of the British National Oil Corporation to exercise state participation rights.

This policy statement did not specifically take into account the remainder of UK energy policy, but was carried through soon after the election to show: '. . . the Government's determination to act, and act quickly, to ensure that the nation gets full benefit from the newly-discovered wealth' (Cmnd 5696, 1974, para. 22). The oil crisis had, however, caused much thought in D.En. about future policy, as was revealed to the public soon after Tony Benn became Secretary of State for Energy in June 1975. Benn's policy of openness in government resulted in a series of papers (the D.En. Energy Papers) being released to the public. They were background papers and did not necessarily represent government policy, but they did go into more detail on forecasting methods and research priorities. Throughout 1975 and 1976 various meetings and conferences took place between government, unions and the energy industry, and the government's view of energy research priorities, 'Energy Research and Development in the United Kingdom' (D.En. Energy Paper No. 11, 1976) was published in mid-1976. The result of all this discussion was the first D.En. statement on energy policy since 1967, the 'Energy Policy Review' (D.En. Energy Paper No. 22, 1977). This did not necessarily represent either the government's or D.En.'s view of future policy, but served as a basis for the energy debate then proceeding.

ENERGY POLICY REVIEW, 1977

The review was prepared by D.En. at the end of 1976 and, in his introduction, Tony Benn revived the notion of the consumer's need for adequate light and heat, and its place in energy policy. The Simon Report of 1946 had been the last policy statement to specifically include this point. In the ten years since the 1967 White Paper, not only UK resources but social circumstances had changed, and a new set of objectives was postulated. The traditional objective of energy policy was defined as '. . . to secure that the nation's energy needs are met at the lowest cost in real resources, consistently with achieving adequate security and continuity of supply, and consistently with social, environmental and other policy objectives' (D.En. Energy Paper No. 22, 1977, p. 11). This objective differed slightly from the 1965 version (objectives were not stated as such in 1967) in that economic growth and international competition were not specified. Also the objective now included the interrelationship with social and environmental policies. However, the basic aim of providing the cheapest possible secure continuous supplies of energy still stood. Benn's possible alternative formulation of objectives was to ensure that:

1. every one can afford adequate heat and light at home;
2. industry's needs for energy are fulfilled at a price which reflects full resource cost and has regard to the long-term availability of the various fuels;
3. these objectives are met on a long-term basis, taking account of risk; the depletion of our reserves of oil and gas is regulated; research and development in energy supply and use is adequately funded, and investment in energy industries to meet these objectives is properly planned;
4. freedom of the consumer to choose between fuels provided at a minimum price which reflects economic cost, should, where possible, be maintained and increased.   (D.En. Energy Paper No. 22, 1977, p. 1)

These new objectives reflected the growing influence of the

consumer movement on policy-making, as for once domestic needs came first on the list, before industrial needs. The introduction of resource costs and the increase of the timescale to include the long term also showed the effect of the environmental movement, heightened by the new-found but short-lived UK ownership of North Sea oil and gas. More emphasis was placed on energy research, and freedom of choice still remained in the objectives.

The bulk of the review considered each fuel and its future prospects. It showed a broader outlook on energy policy than any previous documents, including considerations of uncertainty, lead times, world supplies and, notably, conservation, making a re-appearance from the 1950s. However, the review did not reveal its forecasting methods, except to say that: 'The level and growth of economic activity are the major determinants of energy demand' (D.En. Energy Paper No. 22, 1977, p. 16). This was something of a reversal of the department's 1965 view of the uncertain relationship between economic activity and energy consumption, and shows the rise in departmental power of the Energy Model Group, now within the Economics and Statistics Division of D.En. It also reflects the general Civil Service acceptance of mathematical modelling as a useful technique and the introduction of new planning systems such as PESC in the Treasury. The total primary fuel demand was estimated by the review to be 380–450 mtce in 1985 and 500–650 mtce in 2000. These ranges were based on an assumption of 2 or 3 per cent annual economic growth.

The NCB, having been rejuvenated by the oil crisis, was expected to produce 135 million tons of coal by 1985, as had been agreed in the tripartite negotiations. This figure was seen as optimistic, given the difficulty in recruiting miners and the lack of significant increases in productivity. The main problem with natural gas was the depletion rate required, and also the size of the available resources; there was, in addition, the question of building a gas-gathering pipeline to collect the gas associated with the Northern Basin oil. It was predicted that most domestic oil needs would be provided by supplies from indigenous sources until the early 1990s, and for a period after that which would depend on the depletion rate adopted. Electricity demand had been depressed in the two or three years preceding the review, after several years of growing more rapidly than overall energy demand. This made future demand forecasts uncertain, but the electricity industry's and D.En.'s projected growth-rates coincided in the 2.3–3.4 per cent per annum band.

Before the drop in growth rate, the annual increase in electricity demand had been 4 or 5 per cent. The review stated that coal and oil generation of electricity would not be enough to provide the future requirements in the middle or upper parts of the estimated range, and that nuclear power was the only established source available to fill the greater part of the gap. Renewable resources rated a mention of one paragraph and an annex, and it was suggested that they might, in combination, provide no more than 40 mtce by the end of the century.

With the background prospect of scarcer and dearer energy supplies, the suggested long term strategy comprised:

1. proceeding with development of the coal industry;
2. ensuring reactor technology and manufacturing capacity available for a rapid build-up to take place in the 1990s if necessary;
3. taking into account the long term problems posed by the depletion of North Sea oil;
4. reviewing long term gas development strategy;
5. increasing efforts to secure cost–effective energy savings;
6. carrying out an adequate energy R and D programme, including in particular establishing the viability of renewable sources.

Conservation of resources appeared to be important when concerned with North Sea oil and gas, but of subsidiary importance in other circumstances. Cost–effective measures for energy savings were called for, but without any guidelines as to the suggested payback period, or the estimation of future resource costs (or resource replacement costs). Combined heat and power was also mentioned in passing, and once again a report was in preparation (as one had been in 1946). The review commented that with present prices CHP would not be economic in the UK except in particular circumstances, but that a doubling of fuel prices in real terms or a reduction in the test discount rate (TDR) would make it more attractive.

The review revealed that the Secretary of State proposed to set up an Energy Commission in order to discuss future policy, and it was to include representatives of the nationalized energy industries, the unions and consumer bodies, all of whom had taken part in the 1976 National Energy Conference. This body presumably replaced the similar Energy Advisory Council, which had disappeared in the period between the 1967 White Paper and the 1977 review. It was also stated that the formulation of future energy policy should take place with greater involvement of energy producers and consumers, and in the light of increased availability of information. The review closed with the now obligatory paragraph: 'Energy policy must be flexible, and any strategy adopted now must be kept under regular review and adjusted progressively in the light of developments' (D.En. Energy Paper No. 22, 1977, p. 31).

The review served the purpose of putting forward some of the issues on which decisions had to be taken, but carried on the 1967 tradition of producing only a small range of possible forecasts of future demand. There was no discussion of whether it would be advisable to aim for the lower or upper end of even the given forecasts; they were simply taken as the likely demand figures on an extrapolation of the existing uses of energy. Tony Benn's introduction included his view that: 'A consensus on the appropriate objectives for energy policy is a pre-requisite for settling an integrated energy policy' (D.En. Energy Paper No. 22, 1977, p. 1). However, the bulk of the review did not bear out this acceptance of uncertainty and need for discussion of aims.

WORKING DOCUMENT ON ENERGY POLICY, 1977

The next statement on energy policy to be produced was the D.En.'s *Working Document on Energy Policy* (Energy Commission Paper No. 1, 1977), produced for the first meeting of the Energy Commission in November 1977. During 1977 the SCST had produced its report on alternative sources of energy (and, in previous years, a series of reports on nuclear policy), and the matter of reactor choice for the third nuclear power programme was coming to a head. In addition, the Windscale inquiry into the expansion of the reprocessing plant had continued throughout the summer and on into early November. Thus energy policy had become the subject of a somewhat subdued public debate, in part due to encouragement from the Secretary of State.

The working document was intended as the basis of a Green Paper on energy policy which would be part of the development of the government's integrated energy policy. It began, as usual, with a statement of the traditional objectives of energy policy: 'that there should be adequate and secure energy supplies, that they should be efficiently used and that the two foregoing objectives should be achieved at the lowest practicable cost to the nation' (Energy Commission Paper No. 1, p. 3). It is noticeable that energy efficiency has returned to the list of objectives since the review earlier in the year, and that social and environmental considerations have disappeared. The alternative list of objectives were then quoted from the review, and the document stated that it was the duty of the government to decide on appropriate objectives.

The document devoted an entire chapter to conservation, which marked quite a dramatic change from the review's cursory treatment. It was estimated that a vigorous programme of government action could save 50 mtce per year by the end of the century. The review had stated: 'It is not practicable to make comprehensive and reasonably accurate estimates of the energy savings that could in principle be achieved within the limits of cost-effectiveness. Still less can we estimate the proportion of these potential savings that could be realised in practice with the help of Government action . . .' (D.En. Energy Paper No. 22, 1977, p. 32). Shortly after the publication of the working document, Tony Benn announced a programme of spending on conservation measures.

It was felt that the 135 million tons of coal output aimed at by 'Plan for Coal' might represent an upper limit, and the further target of 170 million tons in 2000 was seen as optimistic. The problem of oil depletion policy came to a choice between early production, a high peak followed by rapid falling away, or delayed production giving larger supplies when oil might be becoming expensive. The document was blunt about its knowledge of natural gas reserves: 'We do not know when gas will again need to be manufactured; on present assessment of known reserves, natural gas for the premium markets should be assured at least into the 1990s' (Energy Commission Paper No. 1, p. 34). This is a refreshing admission of uncertainty on the part of D.En., in an area where the estimates of reserves vary widely with the experts consulted. Electricity was seen to have a central role in the future energy economy, generated both by fossil fuel and nuclear stations and also renewable sources. Combined heat and power stations were still under consideration and were not seen as economic before the end of the century. The document showed some relenting of the D.En. review position on economic activity and energy demand: 'There is no firm relationship between the growth of GDP and SMD. The growth in electricity is determined not only by the overall growth in energy demand but also by the price of electricity relative to other fuels and the degree of possible substitution with them' (Energy Commission Paper No. 1, p. 36). SMD is the simultaneous maximum demand or peak demand on the CEGB system.

In fact the two cases of economic growth, average (just under 3 per cent per annum) and sluggish (slowing down to under 2 per cent per annum by the end of the century) were expected to produce growths per annum of just over 3 per cent and just over 2 per cent respectively in SMD; thus the relationship between the two still appeared to be fairly strong. Much of the chapter on nuclear power was devoted to environmental considerations, a far cry from the days of the 1967 White Paper. The central problem was seen to be the lack of orders for the nuclear industry, rather than any immediate need for decisions on the future extent of nuclear power. It was thought necessary to have fast reactor technology available in the future, whether or not it was ever used. Small sections of the chapter on research were devoted to each of the renewable sources, at last securing some sort of foothold in policy statements, but still seen as possibly producing only 30–40 mtce by 2000 and probably nearer 10 mtce or less.

The document indicated the government's intention of setting up a body to advise on the interaction between energy policy and the environment, which appeared in March 1978 as the Standing Commission on Energy and the Environment, chaired by Sir Brian Flowers, and responsible to the DOE.

Some of the assumptions of the forecasting model had been changed between the publication of the review and the working document, lowering the total primary fuel demand forecasts. Although the high and low range of economic growth remained about the same – between 3 and 2 per cent per annum – energy prices as a whole were estimated in the working document to at least double their present level in real terms by the end of the century. This compared with the assumption of either constant growth or doubling in prices by the end of the century in the review. Also conservation was given more weight in the working document. As a result of these changes, the working document figures for total primary fuel demand at higher and lower growth rates were 1985: 415–390 mtce; and 2000: 560–450 mtce. This compared with the review figures of 1985: 450–380 mtce; and 2000: 650–500 mtce. Thus there had been a clear decrease in predicted demand almost throughout the range and particularly at the high economic growth rate end. In fact, the lower growth assumption could be entirely supplied from our indigenous energy supplies which were estimated to total 475–515 mtce by 2000 (Energy Commission Paper No. 1, p. 56). There were several provisos attached to the estimated supply figure, including the facts that the coal and nuclear production figures were upper limits and might not be achieved, the uncertainty of the contribution from renewable resources and the effectiveness of conservation measures. On the other hand, even the figure of 2 per cent per annum economic growth as a 'low' figure did not seem to satisfy the D.En.: 'It should be emphasised that the lower growth case has been used as a means of generating a lower level of demand for energy. The economic and social implications of such a prolonged period of economic stagnation could well be unacceptable but to achieve the lower level of energy demand with a higher rate of economic activity could call for measures of energy economy going far beyond the levels obtainable through "conservation" as currently understood' (Energy Commission Paper No. 1, p. 72). Thus since 1967 there appears to have been little progress in broadening the scope of forecasting techniques to allow for the influence of new forms of energy usage and changes in the structure of the economy. The interesting experiment of forecasting in detail for a variety of scenarios, contained in the paper on R and D (D.En. Energy Paper No. 11, 1976, pp. 93–107), had apparently not been thought useful enough to be continued. The seven scenarios contained assumptions on economic growth varying from 4 to $\frac{1}{2}$ per cent per annum, and took into account energy prices and primary energy availability. Results were produced in the form of figures for total primary energy consumption and suggestions as to the expected impacts of the various technologies required. It is unfortunate that the working document contained only a choice of two forecasts, the lower one being referred to as not particularly credible in itself.

The document concluded that: 'On most views of the future the needs for coal, energy conservation and nuclear seem inescapable. Renewable resources could also make an increasing contribution' (Energy Commission Paper No. 1, p. 59). The proposed strategy was to proceed with the creation of further capacity in the coal industry, ensure access to the capability of expanding thermal nuclear power systems and using fast reactor technology, select appropriate depletion rates for oil and gas, pursue energy conservation and establish the viability of renewable resources. This strategy was almost identical to that suggested in the 1977 review, in spite of the fact that the energy demand figures had been decreased. This either shows the flexible quality of the adopted long term strategy, or warns of the inherent uncertainties in forecasting. Many of the decisions to be made during the execution of the long term strategy depend upon short-term problems being resolved soon, for instance the building of the gas-gathering pipeline and the viability of the power-plant industry. Since the Crossman *Diaries* and Harold Wilson's memoirs show political decision-making to be fraught with difficulties often factually irrelevant to the matter in hand, it is just as well that the long term strategy is flexible enough to cope with minor initial deviations. An expansion of the forecasting methods to include a wider ranger of possible patterns would be advantageous, and need not imply any judgement on the social consequences of the scenarios. It seems that some of the criticism of Energy Paper 11 has been taken to heart, as there is to be a sequel produced towards the end of 1978 which ACORD will discuss. The D.En. Chief Scientist has stated that: 'The range of futures covered in current work include a number which take account of the views expressed by groups who believe that substantial changes in the nature of our society and in the structure of our economy will be necessary in the future' (Energy Commission Paper No. 12, p. 4). This is a move towards increasing the number of possible scenarios and broadening the assumptions behind them. ACORD, the body which will receive the paper, is still made up of representatives of the nationalized energy industries and independents from the academic and industrial worlds. Their reaction to the new R and D paper will give a good indication of the reception alternative futures will receive from the energy establishment in general.

The working document concluded with a list of pressing decisions, and stated: 'Our energy policy cannot be static. We have to be alert to developments and possible developments over a wide area, in case we may need to change course' (Energy Commission Paper No. 1, p. 62). The document listed the areas of expected developments, such as world economic growth, population and wealth distribution, technological advances, changes in public attitudes and the changing relationship between economic growth and energy demand. The document was then presented to the Energy Commission for discussion and amendment in November 1977 before its appearance as a Green Paper in February 1978.

ENERGY POLICY, 1978

The Green Paper *Energy Policy, A Consultative Document* (Cmnd
7101, 1978) was the first official statement on energy policy since
1967. There were only a few relatively minor changes from the 1977
working document, and two of these were due to the government
policy announcements which had taken place between November
1977 and February 1978. The choice of reactor type had been decided
for the third nuclear power programme, and the energy conservation
measures had been introduced. An addition to the chapter on UK
prospects was a paragraph dealing with the manpower implications
of the proposed strategy, which presumably was a result of the union
representatives' remarks. The minutes of the Energy Commission
meeting refer to Frank Chapple of the EETPU and Joe Gormley of
the NUM as bringing up the matter. The extra paragraph (Cmnd
7101, 1978, para. 14.39) pointed out that a sufficient number of
skilled workers would be necessary to carry through the desired
energy strategy, and that some retraining and redeployment would
be required. Fast reactor policy as stated in the Green Paper showed a
softer line than that of the Energy Policy Review, which had taken
the position that it might be necessary to order a series of fast reactors
in the 1990s. The Green Paper merely noted that a decision on the fast
reactor would be made subject to the outcome of a public inquiry
which would not be limited to local planning matters. Access to the
technology was still thought to be necessary in order to keep the
option open.

The conclusion of the Green Paper remained largely unchanged,
and the basic strategy was identical to that put forward in the working
document. The object of publishing the Green Paper was to extend
the public debate on energy issues and achieve '. . . an improvement
in the quality of future decisions and, if possible, a substantial degree
of consensus on what those decisions should be' (Cmnd 7101, 1978,
para. 1.8). Tony Benn, in his foreword, stated that the strategy
contained in the paper would be kept under continuing review in the
Energy Commission and updated when appropriate, but did not
make any mention of a White Paper on energy policy. In fact the
paper states:

. . . there can be no question of constructing a blue-print which
pre-determines all the decisions required over the next 10 or 20
years. The aim must be rather to ensure that present decisions are

pointing us in the direction in which, having regard to all the uncertainties of the long term future, it seems desirable that we should for the present be moving.   (Cmnd 7101, 1978, para. 14.19)

It goes on to say that a change of course would be possible in the future, although not necessarily quickly.

It is unlikely that there will be an interlude of a decade before the next government statement on energy policy, but there may be an intermediate period while the results of the Windscale inquiry and the projected fast breeder reactor inquiry are digested. Meanwhile, D.En. continues to publish all the Energy Commission documents, thus giving a strong guideline on current government and energy industry thinking.

UNOFFICIAL ENERGY POLICIES

There are few cohesive unofficial energy policies for the UK; many advocates of specific forms of power generation push the claims of their particular interests, but rarely are they bound together to form a workable policy. The reasons for this dearth of ideas are mainly concerned with the resources of the academic institutions, interest groups and individuals involved, in terms of finance, time and research assistance. Also interest groups naturally concentrate their efforts around the activity which induced them to form a group in the first place, and only later branch out into the placing of that activity in a wider context. The Department of Energy, in its many guises, has been in the business of energy forecasting and planning for several decades, whereas energy research has only recently begun to gain acceptability in academic circles. Publicity for D.En.'s forecasts is automatic, whereas the results of the efforts of interest groups may not be easily available and thus have little influence. The Windscale inquiry helped to broadcast some alternative views of the future, but as most of this evidence was excluded from the report, it may have little long term effect. In the USA, more funding has been devoted to research into energy strategies, and there has been greater publicity for the various points of view. With the increase in openness of government instigated by Tony Benn, and the continuing energy debate, it is likely that a broader range of options will come under consideration in the near future. The amount of weight carried by unofficial views is entirely another matter, and one which is difficult to assess. Political expediency may well direct the actions of government policy-makers in a time of high unemployment and general economic restraint, so that any view of the future which could offer constructive ideas in these areas might be more acceptable to government and unions than those which concentrate solely on energy in the narrow sense. Neither the official nor most of the unofficial policies represent a holistic view of the future.

NATIONAL CENTRE FOR ALTERNATIVE TECHNOLOGY

The National Centre for Alternative Technology (NCAT) published its Alternative Energy Strategy for the United Kingdom in June 1977. It attempted to produce a strategy for the UK up to the year 2025 by setting a target for energy consumption in that year and then deciding on policy options which would achieve the aim. NCAT criticized the D.En. method of forecasting by extrapolation from past demands because: 'In this policy-making procedure the energy demand figure is sacrosanct and the fact that traditional fuel resources are limited only has the effect of requiring that new sources of energy be found and exploited in increasing amounts' (NCAT, 1977, p. 1). NCAT base their energy consumption target for 2025 on an estimation of how much energy income could be harvested, that is energy in such forms as sunshine, wind, waves, etc. It is also affected by decisions on depletion rates of the remaining fossil and nuclear fuels, and on an estimate of the energy needed to sustain an agreed quality of life for the population. Their target is to provide consumers in 2025 with as much useful energy as they used in 1975.

The report then details the amount of useful energy which could be provided in 2025 by various sources: solar, wind, wave, tidal, hydro, bio-fuels, heat pumps, coal, solar cells and geothermal. The estimates for wave and tidal energy contributions by 2000 are approximately the same as those of D.En., but they suggest that wind generation, with clusters of windmills sited offshore, could provide 39 mtce in 2000 compared with the D.En. figure of up to 8 mtce. They suggest the early introduction of heat pumps, as they '. . . would be compatible with most energy strategies, which are all likely to involve increased transmission of electrical energy for heating purposes' (NCAT, 1977, p. 14). However, other alternative views do not concur on this point, although the NCAT strategy would not always involve degrading firm electrical energy into heat. The report is strongly in favour of energy conservation techniques which would, if strongly applied, counteract the rise in useful energy consumption. The whole strategy is based on the premise that conservation measures will ensure that energy consumption in 2025 is similar to the 1975 level.

The report then turns to the problems of matching energy sources and end uses, noting that availability of storage affects the proportion of demand which can be supplied by each source, particularly in the case of renewable sources. NCAT states that without the use of renewable sources and vigorous conservation measures, the primary energy input needed to achieve their 2025 target in terms of quality of life would be similar to the D.En. estimate. Thus the strategy differs in its greater use of renewable sources, effectiveness of conservation, and the use of waste heat from electricity generation and industrial processes. It also places great emphasis on storage mechanisms to enable non-firm sources of power, such as wind and waves, to be used to their full potential. Storage is either in the form of large low-temperature stores — say water tanks shared between houses, possibly buried underground — or more compact high-temperature stores. NCAT notes that any energy strategy using large amounts of nuclear electricity would also need energy storage facilities. The NCAT strategy does not include nuclear power, and assumes that oil and gas supplies are dwindling by 2025. It does envisage retention of the national grid.

In its consideration of the economic implications of the suggested low growth scenario, NCAT accepts that if the present capital- and energy-intensive structure of industry persists through a period of changing energy supply patterns, then increased unemployment could well result. If the small scale energy sources such as solar and wind devices bring about a change in the industrial pattern, then more employment opportunities might arise. This question of the effect of the energy supply system on the industrial and social fabric is not discussed, and NCAT merely says that: '. . . there is little sign that the government sees the energy question as one which has implications for decisions affecting other sectors of the economy . . .' (NCAT, 1977, p. 26). It would have increased the utility of the report if NCAT's own assumptions about its agreed standard of quality of life in areas such as work, education, leisure, privacy, shelter, etc., had been made more explicit. The overall basis of the strategy is the rapid introduction of conservation measures coupled with the use of coal and renewable resources; no nuclear programme is involved.

OPEN UNIVERSITY ENERGY RESEARCH GROUP

The alternative energy supply policy of Dr Peter Chapman, ex-director of the Energy Research Group (ERG), was presented at the Windscale inquiry as evidence on behalf of FOE (ERG 019, 1977). Chapman first detailed his energy projections for the UK based on historical trends in useful energy demand, which took into account market saturation effects and moderate energy conservation techniques. He assumed no significant changes in lifestyle, but found that the demand for primary energy in the year 2025 did not increase substantially as the matching of energy supply and end-use was improved. The policy was set out to show that a large nuclear power component was unnecessary, and this was illustrated by breaking down the end-use energy into the categories of high and low temperature heat, work and electrical energy. These were further subdivided according to domestic, industrial or other uses. The primary fuels in 2025 then consisted of coal, oil, solar and a primary electricity supply of 154 mtce, which could either come entirely from waves, wind, hydro and tidal or include a moderate nuclear component. Chapman's figure of 218 million tons of coal per annum by 2025 looks a little optimistic at present but is clearly possible in terms of available resources. The oil component is 44 mtce, which is in line with D.En.'s estimates of a decline in production to about 90 mtce by 2000. The solar contribution of 38 mtce assumes that work on energy storage has advanced sufficiently by 2025 to make solar water heaters cost effective, requiring a reduction by about a factor of two in storage costs for low-grade heat. There is also a CHP contribution, mainly in the form of low-temperature heat but with some high-temperature heat for industrial use.

Chapman notes that the policy maintains a surplus of supply throughout the entire period until 2025 and does not stretch any energy source or energy conservation to its full capacity. He adds: 'By aiming for least cost (where such costs are known) it should create minimum social problems and by reducing the nuclear component it should reduce the potentially large environmental costs described in the Flowers report' (ERG 019, 1977, p. 39). One of the major problems of nuclear power stressed by the Flowers Report (Cmnd 6618, 1976) was the cost of radioactive waste management. Chapman's alternative policy rested on differing estimates of energy consumption in the future; his 454 mtce by 2025 compares with the D.En. low-growth figure of 450 mtce by 2000. D.En. forecasts do not go beyond 2000 at present. Behind the estimates lie the assumptions concerning energy demand, and here Chapman differs drastically from the D.En. forecasters. He takes into account the fact that the trend towards an increasing number of households cannot continue, and the near saturation levels of ownership of some appliances. 'Thus the historical growth in energy consumption, largely due to growth in home heating and personal transport, cannot be expected to continue' (ERG 019, 1977, p. 8). This reduction in the growth rate of car ownership also implies a reduction in the growth of road building, car manufacture and so on. Chapman goes on to point out that D.En. projections for energy demand are based on the presumption of the increasing use of electricity as a means of delivering fuel to consumers; this, of course, need not be the case. Chapman produced a further analysis of the possibilities of alternative energy sources in August 1977 (ERG 024, 1977) closely based on his Windscale evidence, but this view of the future has recently been challenged; Chapman is now doubtful of the usefulness of long term forecasting methods in general.

Chapman's policy is based on a refutation of the assumptions implied in the D.En. forecasts of energy demand. The evidence was given full public airing at the Windscale inquiry, but Justice Parker chose to treat it as irrelevant to the matter in hand. Thus the publicity for this alternative policy was short-lived. The criticisms of the methods adopted by D.En. may have some effect, as they are being repeated elsewhere. It is not the alternative policy itself which is important in this case but the weight of evidence backing it up. Again, little space is devoted to the social and economic implications of the policy, but this is not surprising as the evidence was directed towards a more specific end.

INTERNATIONAL INSTITUTE FOR ENVIORNMENT AND DEVELOPMENT

The International Institute for Environment and Development (IIED), based in London, is carrying out a programme of research into the implications of energy conservation policies and renewable sources in the UK and Western Europe. Gerald Leach of IIED outlined his critique of D.En.'s forecasting techniques at the Windscale inquiry (IIED, 1977), taking issue with their assumptions that energy growth must continue with economic growth and future growth trends will be exponential, as they have been in the past. The

report of the overall study was published in January 1979; Lean
(1978) suggested that it justified a modest nuclear programme and
showed no case for a fast breeder reactor. Leach has described the
results as showing that material growth could be maintained with no
increase in either electricity or energy demand; this results from
making only moderate assumptions concerning the introduction of
conservation measures, and studying energy demand sector by sector.
The two main points are that energy consumption targets should be
given for such things as electrical goods and cars, and that more
information on energy use should be available to consumers of all
kinds. Thus the weight of the study lies behind the avoidance of
unnecessary commitments in the near future, in particular to an early
start to a fast breeder reactor programme.

At present, there are few other alternative energy policies which
relate to the UK. NALGO has suggested the formation of a National
Energy Corporation to act as the overall policy-making body for the
energy supply industries, while the Communist Party would like to
see an Energy Authority bringing a greater degree of public control
to the energy production sector, including power-plant manufacturing and other related industries. Ryle (1977) has claimed that the
increased use of renewable sources is economically viable if greater
storage capacity is brought into the system. Lovins (1977) has
produced a comprehensive non-nuclear energy policy for the USA
with *Soft Energy Paths*, complete with calculations of the structure of
end-use energy patterns and how they could be supplied using soft
technologies which mainly rely on renewable resources. This strategy
may soon be adapted to the British case. Leach of the IIED pointed
out at the Windscale inquiry that 'The numbers of people considering
energy scenarios which assume vigorous policies for fuel conservation
and renewable sources are pitifully small, as are their supporting
facilities, compared to those working on conventional energy supply
technologies and programmes' (IIED, 1977, para. 11). The Windscale inquiry was the first chance given to the proponents of
alternative energy policies to expound their theories in an official
setting, but the view of Justice Parker was that: 'Forecasts of energy
demands which were advanced covered a very wide range as did
predictions as to how much demands could or should be met.
. . . Nevertheless it is clear that such evidence fell far short of what
I would require were it for me to make a definitive forecast. I have
not regarded it as any part of my task to attempt to do so' (Report
by the Hon. Mr Justice Parker, 1978, para. 8.37). Thus the matter

of energy forecasting methodology was found to lie outside the scope of the inquiry, and any criticisms of the merits of the methods used by D.En. and the other agencies engaged in this process were not discussed. Although Justice Parker felt that all forecasts were equally uncertain, a basic tenet of planning law is that challenges to government policy are beyond the scope of local inquiries, so that he was obliged to accept current D.En. forecasts rather than any others suggested. It appears that he took evidence covering a wide range of issues because he felt that: 'This report is, as I understand it, intended to form, as was the Inquiry, an element in a wide public debate on nuclear issues' (Report by the Hon. Mr Justice Parker, 1978, para. 2.1). Opposition to the long term official view of UK energy policy is small but growing. Differing ideas and analyses exist, but these are not often presented in a form which would provide a reasonable alternative to the D.En. view of the situation. It may be assumed that the projected fast breeder inquiry will provide a platform for alternative views of the future in a similar manner to that given by the Windscale inquiry; also, the facilities for funding opposition groups may have improved as a result of those lengthy deliberations. The major policy issue of the moment is not the choice between coal, nuclear, alternative sources or conservation, but the choice of a long term energy estimate on which to base policy-making. The fairly narrow view of the situation taken by D.En. precludes consideration of economic and social effects beyond those which could be expected given our present system of social institutions, and it is likely that future discussion will revolve around the type of society envisaged in the future rather than simply its energy consumption. Meanwhile, the main decisions to be taken shortly concern the fast breeder reactor, the gas-gathering pipeline, pricing policy, energy conservation and research and development of alternative sources.

The government's reply to the SCST reports on alternative sources came in June 1978 (Cmnd 7236, 1978), with the allocation of an extra £6 million to their research and development programme, bringing the total government commitment so far to £16 million. A Severn Barrage Committee was also created, to be chaired by the D.En. Chief Scientist, and given £1.5 million out of the £6 million for further studies on tidal power. Tony Benn was reported as saying that 'finding the right people to carry out alternative energy research caused more concern than finding money' (McLoughlin, 1978), and in a written answer to Parliament he stated that the government agreed with the SCST that '. . . work on the alternative sources should be pursued with urgency and determination . . . ' (*Hansard*, 6 June 1978, cols 2– 3, written answers). Thus the government appear to be firm in their support for alternative sources, and this is born out by the D.En. Chief Scientist in his paper to the Energy Commission on research and development (Energy Commission Paper No. 12, 1978), where he states that the apparently low funding of research into alternative sources reflects the state of research rather than the government's commitment. He also goes on to say that D.En. is now considering a broader range of future energy scenarios than it had previously used as a basis for forecasting, taking into account some of the ideas suggested by various concerned groups.

This broadening of thinking on the part of D.En. is to be welcomed, and it will be interesting to see if it is reflected in the next edition of the Green Paper on energy policy. Of course, the reason for changes in energy policy are not always based on the logic of energy requirements, as is shown by the Crossman *Diaries*. Even if, for example, a low economic growth scenario was settled on by D.En. as being the most likely of the alternative futures, the government would not necessarily agree that this should be taken as inevitable. Political rather than strictly envrionmental or energy resource arguments play a large part in the taking and timing of decisions. Even with policies where long lead times appear to be the overriding factors in decision-making, short term political considerations still play a vital part.

8 Policy Definition and Development

The first chapter of this book included the statement of a working definition of policy-making as the process of adjustment to future uncertainties.

Having looked at the institutions of the energy industry in some detail, it is now possible to see their interactions as part of a policy-making system; thus the various definitions of policy and policy-making must be considered at greater depth to produce a workable base on which to attach this institutional and personal framework. Townsend defined social policy as '. . . the underlying as well as the professed rationale by which social institutions and groups are used or brought into being to ensure social preservation or development' (Townsend, 1976, p. 6). He felt that control could range from the utterly conscious to the unspoken and unrecognized; thus policy in this case is seen as purposeful organized control. Friend saw policy as '. . . an expression of a stance in relation to a class of problem situations, formed by a set of actors with a legitimate concern in such situations' (Friend, 1977, p. 43). He went on to say that it could be interpreted as the response to a demand to reduce uncertainty about future actions. This definition includes the policy-makers, who are seen as actors with a legitimate concern. Thus Townsend emphasizes policy as underlying control, Friend sees it as a response to uncertainty, and Heclo and Wildavsky have a more pragmatic view: 'Policy is a series of ongoing understandings built up by political administrators over time, understandings left to run where practicable, repaired where necessary, and overturned when they are desperate' (Heclo and Wildavsky, 1974, p. 346). It appears that the definition of policy is to some extent a function of the particular policy-making situation under consideration; on the other hand, '. . . it is an analytic category, the contents of which are identified by the analyst rather than by the policy-maker or pieces of legislation or administration' (Helco, 1972, p. 85). This puts the onus of definition squarely on the analyst. He goes on to give his own view: 'A policy may be usefully considered as a course of action or inaction rather than specific decisions or actions' (Heclo, 1972, p. 85). The importance of time-scale is pointed out in this definition, as policy is seen to exist over a longer term than mere decisions. The other two frequent items which occur in definitions of policy are its purposiveness and the fact that it is a response to some kind of uncertainty.

Blume argues for a long term empirical consideration of changes in policy-making to show the evolution of theories, concepts, problems and orientations. He does see problems inherent in this approach:

> . . . which requires that conceptualizations, assumptions, 'theories' be extracted from policy statements, parliamentary papers, and so on. How is this to be done? How do we assess the changing scope of the debate surrounding a given social issue (i.e. how do we decide what is relevant, taken-for-granted, what disputed, at different points in time)?   (Blume, 1977, p. 260)

He gives no simple answers to this methodological problem, but in spite of the difficulties it would appear to have more usefulness as an approach than methods which simply study policy outcomes or the structural system producing the policy. Heclo feels that empirical studies should include the extent to which a government is a learning mechanism, as shown by the changes in their policies over time, but also comments that this type of analysis is only beginning as there is, as yet, no theoretical framework for the case studies.

To avoid a long and possibly sterile argument about the definition of policy-making, it is necessary to select some statement which will convey the essence of the subject, although a little more clearly than the working definition which concerned policy-making as a process and a response to uncertainty. The actors and their perception of the situation are clearly important and must be included, and thus a sense of purpose is also implied. Thus, with an expansion of the original definition, policy-making is a means of adjusting to perceived future uncertainty. A definition can only be as good or bad, or as useful, as the purpose to which it is put, so that it need not be seen as rigid or exclusive. Having defined the subject under discussion, it is necessary to look back at the energy industry and the official policy statements to see if any interactions or changes in time are perceptible. Klein (1974a) suggests a series of questions to ask in any policy-making situation, which are: to ascertain the actors involved, the extent of their commitment, which roles they are playing and how much information is available to them. He then suggests looking at the outcome of policy decisions and the definition of the issue.

The definition of the original issue and its perceived limits clearly plays an important part in policy-making, for if an issue is defined at the outset in such a way as to exclude particular perceptions or interpretations of it, then some possible courses of policy will be automatically ruled out without ever coming under consideration. Bachrach and Baratz saw issue definition as a function of power and influence within organizations where a mobilization of bias conspired to select certain safe issues for decision, ignoring other key issues where conflict might arise. They defined a non-decision-making situation as existing 'When the dominant values, the accepted rules of the game, the existing power relations among groups, and the instruments of force, single or in combination, effectively prevent certain grievances from developing into fully-fledged issues which call for decisions . . .' (Bachrach and Baratz, 1963, p. 641). This concept is useful in energy policy-making where certain issues are not seen as relevant by government officials. The slow development of alternative sources could be seen as a situation where the dominant values inherent in a high capital cost, centralized power supply and distribution network overruled any decision on the large-scale development of alternative sources which might threaten that network's existence. In the case of energy policy, the Civil Service have an inordinate influence over policy definition for several reasons: they take the major decisions on finance for new and continuing projects, they are permanent officials as opposed to politicians with ever-changing responsibilities and as a result of this a certain departmental culture exists which permeates all decisions and discussions. 'The distinctive attitudes of an agency can be seen as the product of accumulated experience and tradition, created by familiarity with a particular set of tasks and problems, and influenced perhaps by the personalities of leading administrators' (Self, 1972, p. 92). Self distinguishes between bureaucratic and technocratic agencies. Bureaucratic agencies are concerned mainly with the enforcement of given regulations with limited scope for discretion, while technocratic agencies perform more flexible services and use their professional or scientific expertise. The D.En. clearly comes into the latter category, which Self argues is '. . . more likely to have a distinctive or assertive view-point, particularly if it is manned by a strong professional group dedicated to a certain view of agency goals' (Self,

1972, p. 93). The professional elite in the case of D.En. may be the scientists of the department, who are frequently more influential than their numbers would indicate due to their membership of several committees in the government hierarchy. Mulkay (1976) has shown that a scientific elite exists in Britain which is engaged in regulating government and academic research relationships.

Henderson analysed the phenomena of departmental, or in this case, Civil Service, culture by looking at the administration of two public expenditure programmes, Concorde and the AGR. He concluded that four aspects of administrative conventions had deleterious effects on performance, and the first of these he labelled decorum. Decorum involved careful role definition for individuals and organizations, impersonality and administrative tidiness and resulted in a constriction of the flow of information and ideas in the decision process. Henderson felt that unbalanced incentives, caused by the need to conform to departmental standards rather than produce correct analyses, and the extent of anonymity within the organization, combined to weaken the responsibility of officials. Lastly, he felt that there was too great an emphasis on secrecy, which made the lessons of the past harder to learn and thus impeded future performance. His phrase, 'the unimportance of being right' (Henderson, 1977, p. 190), underlies his view of Civil Service culture which tends to produce impersonal, unimaginative decisions taken in an atmosphere of secrecy. The departmental culture will define perception of the decision-making situation as well as the mode of response, and Young suggests that the 'Behaviour of policy systems can be understood as a function of their image of the environment (or of their perceived environment)' (Young, K., 1977, p. 10). He goes on to say that value systems within a department are validated by reference to values held at a higher level within the department, thus reinforcing the departmental view of the world.

The prevailing value system of the department will determine the legitimacy of any issue brought to its attention. Solesbury (1976, p. 388) suggests that agencies are drawn to issues where their skills may best be employed, and that an issue must command attention before it involves a response. The response may then be to use a generalizing device, such as referral to a committee, where there are uncertainties; to suppress the issue; transform it; let it be overtaken by events; or take a decision, with varying levels of commitment to the outcome. Issues can be drawn to the attention of a department by pressure from non-governmental organizations, and Downs (1972) conceived an issue-attention cycle to describe the prominence of problems in the public eye. He felt that the ambiguity of most ecological or environmental problems ensured that they remained as issues long enough to force some action from the government. One key issue as seen by the British environmental groups in relation to energy policy is that of future lifestyle, which involves social and political considerations apparently perceived by the D.En. as beyond their jurisdiction. Thus the two parties to this discussion are not yet at the stage where they can mutually identify a common problem, and so far this has resulted in situations such as the Windscale inquiry, where Justice Parker admitted only the relevance of evidence as defined on the government representation of the issues. There was little else he could do, since to bring matters of lifestyle into the debate would have introduced more uncertainties than the procedure could cope with, and the type of decision required by the nature of the inquiry would have proved impossible. This simplification of decision-making and policy-making is a problem in itself, and is a result of the narrowing of horizons caused by departmental culture in action. The departmental method has repercussions in areas from policy-making to information gathering, since it acts to ensure the smooth functioning of the department as a whole. Townsend points out that:

> All organisations, and hierarchical organisations in particular, impose restrictions on the types of information which circulate internally as a basis for decision-making and externally as a basis for evaluating the work of the organisation. When the functions of administration and intelligence are served by the same department, the latter will tend to be distorted by the former.   (Townsend, 1976, p. 307)

This is particularly important for D.En., as it has the responsibility for both sponsoring and collecting information from the nationalized industries, and monitoring their performances.

Klein felt that because policy-making situations could be analysed in terms of expertise, content, ambiguity of information, difficulty of defining objectives and so on, there was a '. . . need to develop a way of conceptualizing policy-making as a sort of multi-dimensional chess' (Klein, 1974b, p. 235). He concluded that the explanatory power of the various theories of policy-making depended on the situation, and suggested that they need not be mutually exclusive. He was also in favour of looking empirically at particular situations, and felt this would help in the formation of an overall analytic framework as long as each case study was not taken out of context. Klein's ideas stemmed from Allison's (1969) argument that the choice of conceptual model by the analyst has significant consequences for the ideas contained in the explanation; that is, different models give different explanations. Allison suggested three models of governmental action, labelled rational choice, organizational process and bureaucratic politics. Model I, rational choice, sees government actions as trying to define a problem and the alternative solutions, and the strategic costs and benefits associated with each alternative. Model II, organizational process, asks which organizations in government act on a problem, and what standard operating procedures these organizations have for making information available at various decision points in government; it then goes on to consider what standard operating procedures are used to generate alternative solutions and implement courses of action. Model III, bureaucratic politics, looks at the existing government channels which act on a problem, which actors are involved and the pressures acting on those actors in their various roles. Allison concluded that models II and III were the most useful, and finally proposed a grand model including all three ideas, although he did not outline its implications (Allison, 1971, p. 257).

There are a wide variety of models of the decision-making process available, most of which can be extended to cover policy-making. The ruling class model works through class control of economic power and thus the government is seen as an instrument used by the ruling class to further its own ends. The ruling elite model postulates an unrepresentative elite drawn from the middle and upper classes which goes through the motions of the democratic process but which in fact manipulates the mechanism, although not necessarily always in its own interests. The pluralist model assumes that the powers of the state are shared with other, external groups. The government or bureaucracy simply act as disinterested umpires, but the outcome may be in the favour of powerful private interests at the expense of the less influential majority. The formal structural model implies that the most important part of the process is the taking of decisions by the formal office-holders as defined by law. The goal-seeking model assumes that the goals of the policy have overriding importance and that the most efficient means are found of pursuing them. The negotiated order model takes into account the interpersonal interactions of government, and implies a constant process of negotiation in search of compromise. The public control model involves the public as a whole, which sets the broad limits within which government decision-making operates. Public opinion acts through the mass media and creates a framework of attitudes, values and constraints. In contrast to all these very specific and tightly drawn models there is the concept of muddling through, as described by Lindblom. He felt that policy-making was '. . . a process of successive approximation to some desired objectives in which what is desired itself continues to change under reconsideration' (Lindblom, 1959, p. 86). Almost as a result of this definition, his model of the process involved administrators making a series of limited comparisons between small policy steps, none of which involved the thorough consideration of values implicit in either goals or policies. He felt that this realistically described the process of policy-making, and could be endlessly repeated with marginal adjustments to existing policies. It also implied that agreement on policy became the test of the policy's correctness or suitability; and it may be, as he says, that 'Democracies change their policies almost entirely through incremental adjustments. Policy does not move in leaps and bounds' (Lindblom, 1959, p. 84). However, certain decisions, especially in energy policy, do imply a policy movement which is more than just incremental. For example a decision to go ahead with the fast breeder reactor would, as seen by some of the environmentalist groups, involve a severe curtailment of civil liberties. Lindblom's model says little about how issues are selected for decision, or the process of comparison with previous policy, so although it apparently describes what happens in administration it is of little explanatory value.

Allison's three policy-making models – rational choice, organizational process, bureaucratic policies – can be seen as variations on the goal-seeking, formal structure and negotiated-order models respectively; these three, together with the ruling class, ruling elite and pluralist models are described in Open University (1972, D203, VIII). The public control model (Barber, 1976) assumes that the public is willing and able to take part in some form of opinion formation on an issue, and of course this is not always the case. Information is not always available to the public about an issue, and is invariably filtered by selection on the part of those giving out the information or those in control of the media. Certainly there are occasions when public opinion as perceived by those in power can perhaps influence the timing of a decision, or even the decision itself, but this perception of outside views does not necessarily, in fact cannot to a great extent in the British communications system, emanate from the public. Pressure from the media can be categorized simply as the means whereby the various interest groups put across their point of view; that is, the mechanism of the pluralist model. Thus the six models remain as simplified skeletons around which to hang the body of empirical data on policy-making, bearing in mind Klein's warning that models vary in their usefulness according to the situation.

O'Riordan put more stress on the individual than the process when he stated: '. . . in the final analysis the participants themselves will determine the success of environmental policy-making. The test of the adequacy of these measures will be only in their performance' (O'Riordan, 1976, p. 72). He concentrated on the individual within the decision environment which he defined as the set of rules, roles and procedures which guide behaviour. He felt that three sets of forces impinged on decision-making: the personality of the actors; the social, political and institutional environment in which they work; and the nature of the issues. In addition, he made the interesting point that: 'For environmental action groups to succeed, it seems that they will have to adopt the organisational structure, command of information, and leadership responsiveness of the well established lobbies. . . . Thus, in a curious way, pressure groups tend to resemble the very organisations they are designed to fight' (O'Riordan, 1976, pp. 61–2). Just as owners come to resemble their dogs, perhaps? This is simply an amplification of the point concerning departmental culture and the admission of evidence in relevant forms. To be able to communicate through departmental channels, pressure groups need to make themselves understood, that is to express their views in a way which is compatible with the experience of the department. Thus some opposition to the increase of nuclear power in Britain has moved to questioning the programme on economic grounds, rather than in terms of morality. Donnison, too, felt that individuals were important in the policy-making process as the origin of policy options. 'Well-tried formulae and new innovations are both alike generated within relevant professional, political and administrative groups' (Donnison, 1972, p. 103). He agreed with Lindblom that policy-makers did not always attempt to clarify goals and seek optimal solutions, but did say that 'Some policies cannot be tried out incrementally on the geographical and financial scales at which we are obliged to operate' (Donnison, 1972, p. 101). He concluded that governments needed social ideologies to enable them to guide and coordinate their work, but did not say how this expansion of departmental culture could be made more responsive to changes of opinion in the population as a whole.

Watt (1976) noted that the slow initial development of UK North Sea resources was due in part to the barriers to the provision of technical advice to the government and the poor communications channels within the administration, both of these being problems which Henderson had pointed out as relevant to the Concorde and AGR financial disasters, and both a function of the Civil Service way of working, which is not conducive to the assimilation of rapid change. Friend (1977) saw the perception of the future as involving uncertainties of three types: in the operating environment, in related areas of choice, and in policy values. Investigation and research could narrow down the uncertainty in the policy environment, and more coordination could reduce the problem in related areas, but his suggestion of value guidance to reduce uncertainty in policy values is unlikely to prove effective outside the policy-making organization. Groups in opposition to particular policies are unlikely to compromise on values, although the provision of greater information is likely to reduce uncertainty on both sides. Friend sees policy adaptation as the relaxation of stresses during a time of rapid change in attitudes and expectations, but it is exactly these small changes which are often anathema to interest groups. For instance, individual local issues such as opencast development plans illustrate the formation of current policy. If it is the case that policy-makers produce compromise policies after comparing a series of marginal adjustments to the existing state, then any pressure group desiring a complete change in policy is asking the impossible – the big bang solution rather than steady state theory.

The art of British pragmatic policy-making has been to arrive at a right answer by the wrong method or no method at all, but the introduction of model-making into the policy-making process may relax the stresses of the internal system. As with other technical aids to policy-making, the data produced by the model is only as good as the information and assumptions fed in at the beginning, so that departmental ethos will produce a model which gives results fitting into the department's policy time-scale and value system. Thus a good model is one which produces results correct in the terms of a stated value system rather than correct in any absolute sense. The model may be seen from outside the department or industry as simply condoning the extension of existing policies without any policy-makers having to resort to justifying their own value systems.

Particularly important in energy policy is the time-scale chosen for the operation of the model, as an inappropriate time-scale will preclude certain options. The D.En. model group aims '. . . to produce a computable model of the UK energy economy that balances supply and demand by fuel in each market in time. By time we mean future time and we expect the model to resolve the system for current or single year ahead problems, in the medium term (from now to 5 or 10 years ahead) as well as the long term (from now to 30 years ahead)' (Hutber, 1974, p. 4). Thus energy supply is seen in terms of conventional sources until the turn of the century, as the official policy statements do not see alternative sources making any significant contributions to the energy economy until that time. This supply and demand model has a rather conservative format, being based on the assumption that electricity demand 'grows over the years' (Hutber, 1974, p. 17). Presumably the model is not too inflexible to preclude the introduction of non-fuel consuming alternative sources of electricity, but it has to be borne in mind that 'Designing the future from systems-based predictions evinces the greatest danger stemming from the self-fulfilling prophecy' (Bailey, 1975, p. 67).

Policy decisions produced by the use of models may be consistent with the extrapolation of existing data, but they may not be suitable for future circumstances. Lindberg suggests that the policy response to the 1973 energy crisis was basically an uncoordinated reaction to events, coming as it did at the end of an era when policy-makers assumed their goal was to meet energy demand. He feels that energy producers

> . . . have developed natural symbiotic relationships with government officials . . . They have enjoyed privileged access to policy-making, directly by means of elaborate structures of cooptation and consultation, and indirectly by virtue of the fact that policy-makers have had a general propensity to identify the efforts of producers to increase supply with the national interest itself.   (Lindberg, 1977, p. 366)

This has produced an elite within the energy industry and government who can dominate the policy-making process, and who all have much the same ideology. He notes that 'Agencies assigned tasks of energy conservation are particularly isolated and politically vulnerable . . .' (Lindberg, 1977, p. 367). In spite of their lack of success, energy policies are very resistant to change, and methods of policy-making combining secrecy with scientific expertise exclude ideas from outside government and industry which would possibly provide more creative solutions to problems. In spite of the existence of a coherent elite group, Lindberg sees policy-making as fragmented because of the changing circumstances in which it is required to operate. The boundaries of energy policy have expanded to include most governmental organizations, making coordination difficult to achieve. Lindberg concludes that the decision environment of a growth-oriented society is dominated by a complex bureaucracy which reinforces the incremental approach to policy; a technocratic culture which perpetuates the idea of scientific expertise as the only basis of rational choice; and a class system in which the dominant industrializing classes wish to maintain the existing productive pattern. Thus Lindberg's analysis of the policy-making system combines parts of the ruling class, ruling elite and negotiated order models. Rather than settle for a complete Marxist view of the system, Lindberg feels that the industrializing or ruling classes exist in a pluralistic setting which is likely to prevent the development of any comprehensive energy policy, including one useful to the ruling elites and classes. Similarly Caldwell believes that 'An energy crisis has been built into the structure of modern industrial society' (Caldwell, 1976, p. 37), but sees no solution in a society committed to endless growth and universal abundance. He notes the lack of creative thinking in modern political institutions and feels that 'The proper context for a national policy for energy is the broader field of social and environmental policy with reference to the quality of life' (Caldwell, 1976, p. 43). The relevance of these ideas would be admitted only at a very general level in the D.En. value system; it is not the specified function of any government department to legislate directly on the quality of life. Caldwell foresees the only institutional changes to be reactive rather than the result of foresight, and doubts whether voluntary agreement on the priorities of energy use will be obtainable. Tony Benn, however, wishes to see a British energy policy evolve through discussion and participation, so that it will enjoy public confidence. In the past, discussion was less prevalent due to lack of concern as to alternative policies in an era of cheap energy, and to unavailability of information.

It is clear that the modelling of policy-making systems shares the same faults as the modelling of energy systems – the explanatory power and usefulness of the model depend to a great degree on the situation and the information available. It is necessary to begin policy analysis with some definitions or categories, simply to reduce the enormous amount of factual information to manageable proportions, but it is essential not to obscure the workings of the system by using an inappropriate model. In the following chapter one case study is taken and the various models are applied to it in order to ascertain their relevance and predictive ability, which may or may not be applicable to other policy-making situations. Some analysts point to the influence of the individual policy-maker, especially where several of them form the core of a technocratic elite, and it is clear that the energy industry has its share of powerful individuals. This is partially due to the institutional structure of the government and energy industries and their shared bodies, which requires a high degree of representation at board and higher civil servant level on committees and working groups. This nexus of individuals tends to share the same ideologies, being of roughly the same age, mainly male and having progressed in like manner upwards through the Civil Service or their chosen industry. The pattern in the lower levels of committees is the same, although less influential and with fewer people representing a multitude of institutions.

Government consideration of energy policy is at a particular disadvantage because of the difference in orders of magnitude between the average timespan of politicians in office and the scale of the policies they consider. There are few political prizes to be won as Secretary of State for Energy, and those that do accrue are mainly due to increasing employment or investment in a related field, rather than the intrinsic nature of policy decisions. The effect of a permanent body of civil servants with decided views on a subject can therefore be greater in energy than in other fields because they provide the continuity behind the policy decisions. This may have the effect of implying that there are no, or few, policy options in any given situation, which has been limited by their own previous decisions. A popular political consensus on the direction of energy policy would be useful, but to be effective would have to include the views of D.En., and their representatives are notable by their absence on many committees apparently devoted to open policy discussion. This is not to be over-critical of the D.En. Within the limits of the problems of energy policy as seen from inside the department, they have pursued a fairly conservative, effective policy for supplying the energy demanded in the country, although they can be accused of following fashions and performing as pragmatically as any other department.

The policy of open government does lend a new perspective to the energy debate, but because of the clash of value systems apparent between many of the interest groups on the one hand and the government and energy industries on the other, the debate is in danger of becoming sterile before it reaches any useful conclusion. The development of open government may be seen as an attempt to force a more pluralistic policy-making system into the closed world of the energy policy-makers, or possibly a device to exercise some control over the central elite.

One of the worst aspects of the performance of the policy-making system as it stands at present is its inability to comprehend and consider any long term changes in the institutional and social structure; this is all the more strange as changes such as structural unemployment are caused by technological progress of the sort envisaged by the policy-making elites. Apparently the consequences, in terms of institutional change over a lengthy time-scale, are beyond the wit of the policy-makers.

9 The Origins of Policy

It is clear from the abundance of theories concerning the policy-making process that there can never be a single simple answer to questions about where policy originated, how it developed or why one option was chosen rather than another. However, a close look at one particular British policy decision may help to narrow down the field of possible theories to those that are most useful.

The decision taken on the choice of reactor type for the third UK nuclear programme in January 1978 has a long history, beginning with an initial attempt by the Conservative government before Labour were returned to power in 1974. This decision was important for the future of the nuclear, electricity and power-plant maunfacturing industries, and formed part of a series of decisions on the building of nuclear power stations and allocation of funds for nuclear research which together made up the UK policy on nuclear power. Thus this decision on the new programme would not initiate new policy, but simply be an adjustment to existing policy. In July 1974 Eric Varley, then Secretary of State for Energy, announced that the SGHWR was to be adopted for the new reactor programme. He was advised by the NPAB in taking this decision, and by the NII as to the reactor's safety. After two years of inactivity, as the SCST put it: 'During the early summer of 1976 the Committee became aware of persistent rumours in the national Press and elsewhere that the Government were considering the cancellation of the SGHWR programme . . .' (HC89, Session 1976/77, para. 3). Answers to parliamentary questions in late June and early July 1976 confirmed that a review of reactor policy was to take place (at the instigation of Sir John Hill of the UKAEA), and at the end of July a one-year deferment of the proposed expenditure on the SGHWR was announced. The SCST duly decided to carry out an urgent inquiry into the SGHWR programme because of their anxiety about damage to the nuclear industry caused by any further delay of orders. The first witness, who gave evidence on 2 August 1976, was Tony Benn, Secretary of State for Energy, and he was followed in October 1976 by Sir Arthur

Hawkins and three representatives of the CEGB, Sir John Hill and Walter Marshall of the UKAEA, Lord Aldington of the NNC, Ned Franklin of the NPC, Frank Tombs and two representatives of the SSEB, three representatives of the Electrical Power Engineers' Association, J. H. Locke of the HSE and R. Gausden of the NII. Before the report was published, Benn had continued the policy review by accepting, in October 1976, a proposal from the NNC that an assessment should be made of the AGR, the PWR and SGHWR. A CPRS report on the power-plant industry was produced in November 1976, and the SCST report on the SGHWR programme (HC89, Session 1976/77) was produced on 22 December 1976. It recommended various costing and safety studies, but felt that the SGHWR should only be cancelled if it seemed certain to be more expensive than any other choice. The report criticized the confusion of responsibilities between the NPC and UKAEA, and the inactivity of the NPAB since 1974.

The review of the systems continued well away from the public eye until July 1977, when Benn, replying to questions in Parliament, said he was awaiting the NII and NNC reports before making a decision. Benn had just sacked his chief adviser, Walter Marshall of the UKAEA, apparently because of disagreement over the nuclear programme. By October of 1977 the whole matter was beginning to come to a head and receiving more coverage in the newspapers. At this point Benn had probably received the NNC report (to be published on 4 November 1977) and he began a series of interviews with leaders of the nuclear and electricity industries. On 20 October Glyn England of the CEGB proposed that the programme should be split between an AGR – with work commencing in 1980 – and a PWR to begin in 1982. The plan was described as a consensus between the nuclear and electricity industries, disliked by Benn who preferred an entirely British (AGR) programme. Five days later Cook (1977b) reported that the government were almost certain to accept the view of Sir Arnold Weinstock of GEC (and NPC) and build an American PWR in the new programme. Cook added that the CEGB and SSEB had been swayed by a strong lobbying campaign by GEC to include the PWR in their preferred programme, after they had originally been in favour of AGRs alone. A rebuff to this position came from Frank Tombs of the Electricity Council, theoretically the ruling body of the CEGB, on 1 November, when he made a speech at an IEE meeting to the effect that he disagreed with the compromise solution and supported the AGR.

The NNC report was published on 4 November and turned out to recommend the adoption of the PWR and the continuation of the AGR, the compromise solution favoured by the CEGB but still not supported by Benn. An outside influence on the debate was the quotation of an IAEA article in the NNC report which suggested that competition in nuclear export markets in the future would be severe, implying that the British manufacturers needed orders soon in order to remain in contention. During the following week, Benn met the nuclear and electricity industry chiefs and reiterated his support for the AGR, and received a petition from the NPC engineers advising him against this option. The first meeting of the Energy Commission took place on 28 November, and provided the first real public support for Benn's views – the Electricity Council again came out in favour of AGRs alone, and was backed by the rest of the commission, which of course had no CEGB representation. In the following week, Benn told the House of Commons that he was impatient to make an announcement on the nuclear programme. This was a rather embarrassing point in the debate, as news had been disclosed on 3 December of the damage to the SSEB's AGR at Hunterston, caused by a leakage of sea water into the reactor. On 9 December the NPC engineers publicized the fact that they had received no reply from Benn to their petition backing the twin AGR/PWR programme.

As Christmas drew nearer, it became clear that Benn was fighting on several fronts to preserve the option he favoured. Raphael (1977) eported that Benn was trying to remove Sir Jack Rampton from his post at the head of D.En., or create a post of second permanent secretary which would command more agreement for his views. He added that the CPRS under Sir Kenneth Berrill were backing Sir Arnold Weinstock, GEC and the PWR option. The Cabinet was re-ported to be split on the decision, and Raphael stated that the SSEB were supporting Benn, in contrast to their earlier AGR/PWR compromise position. The Treasury and D.En. were both said to favour the PWR partly because of its lower investment costs, but 'The campaign being exercised throughout Whitehall for the PWR is attributed by Mr. Benn's allies to the strength of the Weinstock lobby' (Raphael, 1977). Thus the debate was becoming more political than technical, with high stakes, especially if the Prime Minister were to overrule his Secretary of State and choose the PWR or the consensus option.

During the week before Christmas a Price Commission in-vestigation into the CEGB was published, focusing attention on the importance of electricity generating costs, one of the differences between the PWR and AGR (the PWR requires a lower capital outlay than the AGR, but its running costs are higher). On 22 December 1977 the Prime Minister received a letter from FOE of Britain and the USA warning him not to involve Britain in the US PWR industry. FOE pointed out that their views were strictly impartial as they felt the entire nuclear programme to be unnecessary, and recommended more attention to the safety issues. This was the first public intervention in the debate by an interest group.

After the Christmas break, battle resumed with accusations of misrepresentation flying between the various scheming bodies. The European branch of Westinghouse (the PWR designers) alleged in early January that the CEGB were overstating the performance capability of the AGR. Everett Long, the GEC executive who had originally persuaded Sir Arnold Weinstock to back the PWR, publicized his view that Britain would ultimately have to follow the rest of the world and use the PWR system. On 4 January 1978, the Electricity Council issued a statement denying reports of a rift between the CEGB and the council; council policy was to have a clear commitment to the AGR and develop the PWR as an insurance policy in case problems arose with the AGR. CEGB policy was only slightly different: they wanted construction of the AGR to begin in 1980, followed later by the PWR. Cook (1978c) reported that senior CEGB executives felt their views on the PWR were not being put forward strongly enough by the Electricity Council in the person of the newly knighted Sir Francis Tombs. At this time, Benn was still backing the AGR-only programme against most of his Cabinet colleagues, but with union support from the TUC Fuel and Power Industries Committee. By 7 January the SSEB was busily refuting rumours of catastrophe at Hunterston, and the Prime Minister was thought to be on the point of deciding on definite orders for both the PWR and the AGR. Rodgers (1978) wrote on 8 January that the CPRS report proposed a comprehensive switch to the PWR, and suggested ordering a series of reactors, more than the nuclear industry had ever asked for. Rodgers tried to outline the positions of the various factions in the argument, and picked out three groups: Sir Arnold Weinstock, some senior NNC executives and the CPRS favoured PWRs with possibly a couple of AGRs to keep the industry ticking over; the CEGB and the NNC who wanted to build both with no long term commitment to either; and Tony Benn and the Electricity Council who wanted the AGR built, and design work to

continue on the PWR. This latter option was strongly opposed by
D.En. The industrialists and the engineers were divided over the
options for the third attempt at a decision, causing one senior official
to say: 'I think we'll get it right the fourth time' (Rodgers, 1978).
Benn answered questions in the House of Commons again on 10
January, but would not be drawn on the coming decision; on 9
January a meeting of senior executives from the nuclear and
electricity industries had taken place to try and thrash out their
positions, before talking to Benn later in the week. Ned Franklin
(NPC) and Lord Aldington (NNC) met Benn on 10 January, then
Franklin visited Glyn England at the CEGB before his meeting with
Benn. Benn had also spoken to Sir John Hill of the UKAEA and Sir
Arnold Weinstock. The Prime Minister was thought to have given
Benn about a month to reach a consensus on the decision, as he was
going abroad until a Cabinet meeting at the end of January.
Callaghan was apparently still in favour of the mixed programme.

After a week of talks, Benn was still firm in his belief that the AGR
combined with a design contract for the PWR was the best option,
and by 13 January was being faced by threats from the PWR lobby in
the NNC that their design teams would break up if not given a firm
order. By 15 January it seemed that Benn had triumphed over the
opposition by persuading the CEGB to agree to his compromise, so
he now had the combined forces of the CEGB, the SSEB, the
Electricity Council and the TUC Fuel and Power Industries
Committee behind him. On 18 January, a senior Westinghouse
executive met Benn to discuss how large a commitment Britain
would have to make to the PWR for it to remain a real alternative
without signing a legally binding letter of intent to build one. Feeling
in the nuclear industry was still running against the AGR plus PWR
design study option, but apparently to no avail; a slight diversion
occurred on 22 January, when Lord Avebury spoke out about the
lack of publicity given to the AGR design in the debate, raising yet
again problems of the relative safety advantages of the two reactors.

Finally, on 25 January 1978, the decision was made public. Work
was to start in 1980 on two AGRs, one each for the CEGB and the
SSEB, and the NNC was to be commissioned to produce a British
design of the PWR in case one was needed later in the 1980s. The
CEGB and the Electricity Council both welcomed the decision,
which by no means ended the controversy because the announcement
did not make it clear whether permission to build a PWR in the 1980s
would be automatically forthcoming. In Parliament Benn had stated

that all future orders beyond the two AGRs would be a matter for decision at the appropriate time, and in a later press conference he apparently surprised many of his Whitehall and Cabinet colleagues by confirming that the only commitment was to the two AGRs. Thus after nineteen months of protracted negotiation and compromise, many meetings and advice from all sides, Benn was able to make the announcement of the decision he had originally supported – the all-British AGR option with the American PWR insurance policy.

The end result of this time-consuming exercise in policy-making was a definite shift in policy in that the SGHWR had been abandoned in favour of the AGR, but there was no real change in the rate of expansion of the nuclear programme (rather some delay because of the negotiations), and the reactor chosen was a British design, like the SGHWR. To follow Klein's (1974a) list of points to examine in the policy-making process, it is first necessary to ask who the main actors were and how deeply they were committed to their roles. The entire process revolved around Benn from the moment he received Sir John Hill's recommendation that a review was necessary. Benn was consistent in his view that a British design was preferable to an American design, and managed to keep the unions on his side throughout the discussions. Sir Francis Tombs, promoted from the SSEB to the Electricity Council, also supported him, and it was notable that the SSEB were not as opposed to the compromise as the CEGB were originally. The main opposition to Benn came from Sir Arnold Weinstock, who for many years had been in an extremely powerful position in the British nuclear industry. He appeared to feel that more profit could be made from backing the PWR, and was convinced of this by one of his executives. Sir Arnold had allies in high places, notably Sir Kenneth Berrill of the CPRS, but their report joined one of an increasing number of CPRS reports whose fate it was to be ignored. Within the D.En. and the Treasury the actors are unknown, but apparently were mainly in opposition to Benn, possibly because they were following the Treasury line or because the Permanent Under-Secretary, Sir Jack Rampton, was opposed to the compromise. The argument eventually boiled down to a fight over the loyalties of the CEGB, whose chairman, Glyn England, had only been appointed in May 1977. Sir Arthur Hawkins, a well known pro-nuclear enthusiast, might have been harder to convince had he still remained chariman.

A variety of information was available to the actors: a series of SCST reports on the pros and cons of various reactor systems; the

NNC assessment; the generating boards had their own opinions of the AGRs serviceability; the Weinstock/GEC/Westinghouse alliance was lobbying; and FOE sent their assessment of the situation. Much of the information, especially relating to safety, was extremely complex, making it impossible for the engineers to agree and changing the situation from one of technical to political decision-making. As to outcomes of the decision, had Callaghan eventually overruled Benn and forced him to resign this could have caused trouble within the TUC who had always supported Benn's stance. Benn may have realized that selecting the British option would increase the chance that Sir Arnold Weinstock would pull out of the nuclear industry altogether — in fact Sir Arnold had offered to do this in April 1977, but finally decided in February 1978 that GEC wished to withdraw from its management role in the NNC. Benn may have intended to restructure the industry anyway as there had been several criticisms of its management and organization. One consequence of a continuing non-decision would have been the further disruption of the power-plant manufacturing industry.

The lack of reported participation by interest groups throughout this debate was possibly due to the narrowness of the options available. There was no argument about the suitability of nuclear power for future electricity generation, merely a question over the cost, safety and progress of the various reactors. The issue was defined from the beginning as being technical, although during the course of autumn 1977 it resolved itself into a more political and nationalistic pattern, with the unions backing Benn and the AGR versus Sir Arnold Weinstock, GEC and various industry executives backing the PWR. There was little or no public participation in this debate, as most of it took place behind closed doors. The Energy Commission meeting came closest to achieving any sort of wider participation with its union and consumer representatives, and when the minutes of the meeting were eventually published in February 1978 they did indeed show the commission to be strongly in favour of the AGR.

There are a strange mixture of actors in this case study, including formal office-holders, private industrialists, nationalized industries, civil servants with strong opinions and assorted peripheral politicians and union officials. With such an agglomeration seeming to take a part in the policy-making, the pluralist model might at first be thought suitable, but this would imply a disinterested bureaucracy and a sharing of power, neither of which proved to be the case. The formal structural perspective is also slightly awry because although the Cabinet did take the final decision, it was more a case of rubber stamping a previously negotiated compromise settlement, even though most of the Cabinet members did hold a view on the issue. The goal-seeking model has a certain relevance, in that the object of the exercise was to keep the power-plant manufacturers and the nuclear industry viable while building a safe reactor with some possible export potential. There were doubtless further objectives, realized and unrealized, such as the removal of Benn's chief scientific adviser, the attempted removal of his departmental head and the restructuring of NNC. The goal-seeking model appears to be too simplistic to explain any of the convoluted discussions involved in this case. The ruling class model suffers from its own vagueness in that it has a low explanatory power. If its hypothesis that the government is simply an instrument of control is accepted, the actual means of control, the policy-making process, is still left unexplained. This is only slightly more unsatisfactory than the ruling elite model, which could, however, have a bearing on the AGR/PWR decision because of the presence of a scientific elite at a high level in government. The policy-making process was certainly almost closed to outsiders for this decision and the elite group of high level industrialists with scientific backgrounds were the main protagonists in the debate, but this model still gives no insight into the process itself.

The negotiated order perspective appears to be able to contain slightly more of the actual occurrences than any of the other models. The activity, as reported, consisted of a constant flow of opinion and discussion, with some parties moving slightly and then accusing others of misrepresentation or not appreciating the importance of certain points in the debate. The formal structure of the system certainly contributed to the organization of the discussions and thus the selection of participants was practically automatic, but the formal structure does not include the interplay between individuals in government and in the Treasury and D.En. Far from being a disinterested part of the background to the debate, the Civil Service were reported to be entrenched on one side of the argument. Ideologies also enter the process, with the left-wing socialism and nationalism of Benn on the one side and the multinational profit-making corporation on the other. The negotiated order perspective assumes that specialist knowledge is required to take part in the debate, which would explain the lack of outside participation, and also that parties, Parliament and interest groups have only a peripheral role: that is to exert pressure and determine the wider decision environment. The perspective includes civil servants as well as ministers in a policy-making role, and assumes the policy to be relevant to a wide area of government activity, thus bringing in other departments (the DI was heavily involved in this case).

Where this model fits less accurately with reality is in the part played by individuals, particularly Tony Benn. The crucial point of the entire nineteen months was his meeting with Glyn England of the CEGB during which he convinced England that a binding option to build a PWR was unnecessary. The other individual of overriding importance was Sir Arnold Weinstock, who appeared to initiate much of the campaign against the AGR (aided by the GEC executive who had originally convinced him of the worth of the PWR, to extend the emphasis on individuals a little further). Negotiation, compromise and endless discussions were certainly the cornerstones of the whole process, but the negotiated order perspective assumes that ministers have little day-to-day influence over policy, which is largely executed by officials. This is probably true for D.En. in the normal course of events, but this issue clearly divided the minister from his department, and the power of the individual overcame the usual departmental policy-making system. Heclo and Wildavsky's (1974) view of the Treasury was largely seen in a negotiated order perspective, and the Treasury was involved in the AGR/PWR decision because of the high capital costs of either option. The media, although reporting the continual flurry of talks, did not publicize the matter as a more popular subject in itself until the decision became public, when it became caught up with the general increase in publicity for energy matters caused by the Windscale inquiry. It appears that a negotiated order model, occasionally compromised by individual actions (perhaps ideologically based), fits best with the known occurrences and may begin to explain the unknowns in the system. It may not, of course, fit as well with any other piece of energy policy-making.

The extent to which changes in policy over a longer time-span can be interpreted using a policy-making model is also debatable; the operating environment for policy-making has altered since the 1946 Simon Report, but the general goal of British energy policy has always been to ensure that energy demand is supplied in full. During the years since the Simon Report, various ideas have risen and fallen in popularity: conservation, information, policy councils, CHP, financial targets, social effects of energy policy, and self-sufficiency, to name but a few. These ideas and their inclusion in policy documents tend to reflect, in a slightly out of phase fashion, the contemporary policy-making environment. Methods of working – forecasting, accounting – have changed and forced policy decisions to be made. In the context of the overall aim of extending supply to meet demand, a forecast of increasing demand requires a policy decision within a limited range of options. The negotiated order perspective can be of assistance in understanding the relationships between the energy industry, D.En., the Treasury and the government, but it is less useful in predicting the outcome when a new variable is introduced to the scene: for instance, the sudden rise in oil prices as a result of OPEC action in 1973. The negotiated order model tends to assume continuity of environment, and is not capable of coping with sudden change in any useful fashion. This, however, is probably a feature of all models of the policy-making process; the intervention of a new variable or the effect of a powerful individual is difficult to categorize.

Since D.En. policy is based to a great extent on forecasting future demand, policy changes in methods of forecasting are important. The assumptions made at the outset of model construction do alter as the decision environment changes, thus giving in recent years a tendency for demand forecasts for any particular year to decrease. Forecasting as a technique (unless the delphic method of prediction ranging over broad policy areas is used) involves extrapolating from the past into the future, and thus has an inbuilt conservatism; it cannot possibly predict dramatic changes, as the forecasts are based on aggregate data from previous years. The use of forecasting is a policy decision in itself, and its adoption in 1967 was a reflection of the general Civil Service attitude towards scientific management at that time. Prediction may be used as a weapon in the battle for increased expenditure with the Treasury, and specific departmental goals may not always tally with overall objectives of energy policy at any time; indeed, departmental goals of smooth internal functioning and living in harmony with the Treasury are likely to be uppermost in the minds of policy-makers. Using the negotiated order model, the importance of changes in policy may be subsumed to the effects these changes are likely to have in the internal structure of the departments involved. The effect of individual ministers may be felt most directly if they recommend change in the departmental formal structure, thus forcing new interactions to take place and removing old lines of communication. Heclo and Wildavsky noted that: 'Co-operation in the common society of officialdom is enhanced . . . by [civil servants'] working arrangements. The shadowy personal networks merge into more formal but still blurry structures' (Helco and Wildavsky, 1974, p. 85). The Permanent Secretary of the Treasury, Sir Douglas Wass, has stated that Heclo and Wildavsky (1974), Brittan (1969) and parts of the Crossman *Diaries* give a reasonable account of how higher civil servants spend their time. He said: 'I do not think I can recognize us from any of these works, but, as none of us has published a description of our daily lives as we see them, I cannot give better references' (Ritchie, 1978).

The negotiated order model is, then, a reasonable basis for analysis of the policy-making process, but it is only a basis. To this must be added the effect of individuals, often but not always in positions of power allocated by the formal structure, and the overriding limitations imposed by the various time-scales relevant to the permanent Civil Service, government ministers and energy policy. The nature of British political life means that the party in power is almost always looking over its shoulder to ascertain the political effects of any policy decisions. Moves that would be popular or strategic in the long term but unpopular in the short term have the least chance of winning favour in the Cabinet; thus enforced energy conservation measures are never likely to see the light of day even though the long term energy strategy would probably benefit from their introduction. Policy decisions of no particular benefit to powerful or vocal sections of the community may be ignored or lost in the flow of parliamentary business, the most recent example of this being the Bill to reorganize the electricity supply industry.

The only permanent figures to rival the Civil Service in energy policy are the nationalized energy industry executives, but because of their tenuous and changing relationship with the minister, they are not in such an ideal position to control the discussion of issues as the D.En. Sir Arthur Hawkins, on his retirement as chairman of the CEGB, gave vent to his feelings on Civil Service relationships with the nationalized industries:

A civil servant, particularly a senior one, has enormous power and relatively little accountability or responsibility. They are acquiring too much influence in areas for which they are neither trained nor fitted. Undoubtedly the greatest frustration I have encountered during my chairmanship has been in my dealings with the Civil Service. It has expanded alarmingly in recent years and increased its attempts to interfere in the Board's affairs. It has become an all-pervading organization of 'power without responsibility' – a dangerous development which threatens the foundations of our society.   (Cook, 1977a)

The nationalized energy industry chairman can alter the amount of influence exerted over their industries by the Civil Service by the expression of their public and private attitudes towards external control. Sir Denis Rooke of BGC is well known for his insistence that his corporation should be treated as nearly as possible like an independent private company. Here again individuals in positions of power defined by the formal structure can influence the issues raised in discussions. However, the formal structure of office is not always well defined (the responsibilities of the minister and civil servants with respect to the nationalized energy industries are notoriously vague) so that the constant process of negotiation and policy-making may alter actual relationships without changing the formal structures. The importance of individual influence is illustrated nicely by Tony Benn's sacking of his chief scientist, Walter Marshall, because of his apparent opposition to Benn's view on the third nuclear programme.

The D.En. has undergone several nominal changes since its birth as the Department of Mines, and there have been some structural changes involving the addition or removal of responsibilities. Its format at present reflects the general concern with energy as a subject worthy of policy-making in itself, rather than as an adjunct to industry or in the narrow sense of power supply. Change of divisional structure within D.En. appears to originate with the pressure of increasing work; the growth in the number of divisions related to oil and gas recovery began with the discovery of North Sea Oil, and the energy conservation programme announced in December 1977 was accompanied by the creation of a new Energy Conservation Division. Division of responsibilities within the Civil Service is part of the work of the ceaseless round of committees and meetings, and new ideas requiring policy decision – or reworkings and reformulations of old methods – are first discussed in committee and decisions made public only when a new internal structure is available to deal with the consequences.

There would be no point in policy-making without financial support from the Treasury, thus departmental relationships with the Treasury are vital to the workings of any department. The fact that energy policy-making may have changing consequences for expenditure over a longer range of time than the average departmental policy means that the Treasury must be strongly convinced of the necessity for initial expenditure before it is agreed. Research budgets are especially worrying for Treasury officials because of their propensity to increase endlessly with intangible results, so natural Treasury conservatism results in a straitjacket restricting expenditure to policies with known outcomes. Once a policy has gained a foothold in the yearly spending pattern it becomes difficult to remove, again not because it is intrinsically good or bad, effective or ineffective, but simply because it is there. The system of accountability of each department to Treasury officers means that all spending is controlled and new projects in particular are subjected to severe analysis. There appears to be a tendency to assume that policies previously put into practice must be useful, having been agreed at the outset, and thus spending on current policy can become excessive almost by default. This system is not responsive to the need for rapid increases (or decreases) in expenditure, and the new methods of control (PESC, PAR) seem to bureaucratize old procedures rather than impose tighter controls. Official routes of control seem to be honoured in the breach rather than the observance due to the close knit network of higher civil servants and their interchange between posts.

Ideas infiltrate only slowly into departments already preoccupied with ensuring present policies are carried through. A change of government can provide the impulse for policy changes, its ideas in turn originating from party or trade union research departments, party committees, sympathetic academics and select committees. The media play a large part in producing the political atmosphere in which the government makes policy decisions. If the media choose to interpret a possibly advantageous long term policy in the light of its possible short term disadvantages, then it is less likely to be agreed. The consequences of a policy decision are likely to differ between the various interest groups, a prime example of this being the local workers at Windscale who were in favour of expanding the reprocessing plant and the more nationally based environmental campaigners who were against expansion. The view taken by the media (or the total lack of publicity) can influence undecided public opinion, although not always in a predictable manner. Publicity of energy related matters at least encourages a general awareness of the problems involved, and discourages the most deeply committed from keeping the debate to themselves because of the difficulty of explaining complex concepts to the public. The effect of public interest and pressure groups on the policy-making process is often minimal in the short term, but the constant increase of external pressure may result in a widening of the debate on particular issues, although with the same ground rules as have been applied in the past. It is difficult to distinguish real progress in the introduction of new issues from the appearance of progress given by debates in the House of Commons, public inquiries and other areas outside the direct sway of the department. The pluralist model allocates too much responsibility to the effects of groups not having direct access to the department or higher ministerial levels. In so far as the general atmosphere for policy-making is set by external pressures it is correct, but only in the very long term will greater effects be felt. This is in part due to the age structure of the Civil Service; nearly all the higher civil servants (under secretary and above) in D.En. are in their mid-fifties, and thus have a similar experience of working life on which to base their future decisions. Another thirty years will elapse before the higher civil servants in the department have a background of increased environmental awareness. The age structure of the nationalized industries is similar, except that their executives have spent most of their working lives as engineers or accountants in the industry rather than as civil servants. This is an apparently small point but with far-reaching consequences. It means that both the formal and informal holders of power are working from the same set of values and concepts of reasonableness. Thus to put an argument in any other terms, to challenge the innate values of the system, is to invite disagreement and incomprehension. Chapman (1978) feels that the current energy debate is of doubtful value and that none of the major solutions so far proposed will provide an adequate energy policy for the future. He points out that most participants have jobs which require them to make judgements on the issues involved, therefore a questioning of the position appears to question the competence of the person involved. There are also institutional pressures at work which ensure success if the institutional line is followed, possibly to the detriment of common sense solutions. Finally he suggests that in public debates it is easy to predict disaster as the outcome of an opponent's policy and possibly come to believe this to be the case. He feels that this combination of personal commitments to forecasts, institutional goals and fear of unknown futures has contributed to the poor quality of the debate, but goes on to say that this is inevitable within the present institutional framework and made worse by the media who dramatize the conflict.

It is certainly the case that the process of conflict makes better television, for instance, than the actual points of conflict. 'Better', in this case, is used in the sense of increased audience ratings; there is an innate difficulty in explaining ideas, often within the time constraints of programming. Newspapers and radio may have either more space or time to allocate, but judgements of newsworthiness mean that the more esoteric points of energy policy do not always reach the front page of the *Sun* or the *Mirror* (or, for that matter, the 'quality' papers until very recently). Radio programmes have small audiences compared to television, and suffer from the same problem of having to play expert against expert in order to provide a range of views. The increasing attention given to energy problems has a snowball effect in that once the interest of the audience is aroused, it can then be said to have formed an opinion or at least have some knowledge of the matter and thus be more capable of criticizing further information and programmes. Television discussions suffer from the usual drawbacks of the medium, for example a group of miners standing in front of a pithead giving their opinion on some subject will be accorded less legitimacy by the audience than the pit manager speaking from behind an office desk. Interpretations of reality have as much relevance in the study of energy policy as they do in other branches of policy analysis, particularly now that the debate is moving away from polite studio confrontation towards public protest.

Policy appears to be produced through the workings of the Civil Service on the negotiated order model, with some inputs and external effects arising from individuals with prominent positions in the formal structure of the government and energy industry. Policy production takes place in an environment determined by the consequences of previous actions and by public opinion, initiated and reflected in the media. Underlying the policy-making process is the time-scale of events, the long term consequences of many energy policy decisions contrasting with short term political expediency. The functioning of the entire system is largely based on incrementalism in policy-making, the overall inertia of the system with its inbuilt restraint on changes in values and the introduction of new ideas making this the normal method of changing policies. As a learning system, the departmental structure is efficient in its control of public spending to the extent that a great deal of time is devoted to the vetting of expenditure programmes, but the superficial image of thoroughness can hide the larger programmes which are allowed to continue from year to year practically intact. Changes in government may force the department to implement policies which, from the previous experience of the civil servants, are known to be inefficient, but in the long term these decisions may be reversed. The learning process as applied to governments relates to the basic system of values used by those in power, as learning will be directed towards the better achievement of set goals. No amount of learning will be able to produce a 'better' policy in one value system if it is being determined by the tenets of a completely different system, and so wide are the divergences in thinking about energy policy at present that this problem is occurring, sometimes unnoticed. The argument is often not about the technicalities but about the reasons for their existence: this kind of debate is almost impossible to pursue within the confines of the policy-making system in its present form. One of the paradoxes of the energy debate is that for all its comparative openness, it still serves to underline the limitations on policy options offered within the departmental perspective. The D.En. Permanent Under Secretary of State, Sir Jack Rampton, was reported as saying at a conference on nuclear power: 'Keeping options open meant trying to look far enough ahead to see both likely demand and how to meet it. We did not have to keep all options open but enough to solve the expected problems' (D.En., Sunningdale Seminar on Nuclear Policy, 1977). This is an extremely rational, logical view of a complex situation, but it may not encompass enough future options to deal with the unexpected events which will invariably occur, as government policy statements always point out.

Models of the policy-making process do not illuminate the origins of policy as much as the progression of issues through the system, or the filtering out of unwanted ideas. However, they can formalize the vague, tenuous relationships obscured by the general (and official) secrecy surrounding the process of government, and this in turn assists in the analysis of the mass of apparently unrelated information concerning energy policy. Mere description of the process will not provoke any change, if changes are thought to be necessary, but it may enable influential actors to be identified and methods of working explained so that the introduction of new ideas into the system becomes less of a lottery.

10 The Future of Energy Policy

This review of the state of British energy policy has been completed at a time of increasingly intense activity in the energy field. The expansion of the Windscale reprocessing plant, the prospect of an inquiry into the need for a fast breeder programme, and the restructuring of the electricity supply industry are all symptoms of the new awareness of energy policy as an entity in itself, basic to the requirements of the economy rather than subordinated to sectional or political needs as was often the case in the past. The Department of Energy has only been in existence since Christmas 1973 and in spite of the professed wish of both main political parties to remove energy from the realms of inter-party conflict, many decisions still appear to be taken with more regard for short term political consequences than the long term future of energy supplies. Hence energy policy must always be considered in its overall political and social context in order to achieve any understanding of the reasoning behind the formulation of policies. The present energy debate has tended to concentrate on technical issues, about which there could be some factual agreement, while leaving the basic assumptions behind all points of view unsaid. This has encouraged needless polarization over technical issues. Differences in approach to problems of future lifestyles, from economic growth to civil liberties, are all reflected in the energy debate but cannot be fully discussed because of the limitations imposed by the initiators, the policy-makers.

Clearly, there is a real need for an arena in which more abstract questions involving the future can not only be discussed but be made to seem relevant to an increasing proportion of people. The consultative document on *Energy Policy* (Cmnd 7101, 1978) contains a wealth of information on sources of energy supply, but very little on the effects changes in energy policy will have on people at home or at work. This is hardly surprising considering the highly segmented structure of government departments, but it is unfortunate, as it excludes many people from the debate who would otherwise be interested in their futures and their children's futures. The information on alternative policies is in existence: all that is required is the use of a little more imagination in its dissemination. The popular appeal of environmental issues has been shown to exist by the success of Greenpeace in rousing feelings against seal culling. The energy debate must be conducted at all levels if any true consensus is to be reached and must include the real issues rather than be merely a vehicle for the repetition of the views of vested interests. The Energy Commission has so far failed to broaden the boundaries of the energy debate and its published papers have largely been of little importance. There is no mechanism for open discussion of problems relating to the long term, to intangible benefits such as the increase of human happiness and to future lifestyles. The various media are taking a growing interest in energy policy, but are inherently a one-way system of communication and the debate tends to remain at the expert level. Energy issues may well become more politically important as the employment implications of the various energy policies begin to emerge: thus energy policy will develop into a party political issue and popular interest will increase – to the possible detriment of any consensus policy.

The slow but sure process being undertaken to produce an energy policy is in contrast to the various attempts since the last war, most of which were eventually doomed to failure by force of circumstances and political pressures. The decline in heavy industry has made the political significance of energy policy more apparent, and made the taking of decisions purely in terms of energy considerations almost impossible. A comprehensive energy policy is under discussion, comprehensive in the sense that it regards energy as a whole, not simply a set of unrelated fuel sources, and is made more relevant to social and economic policies than has usually been the case. The oil crisis of 1973 and the growth of Britain as an oil and gas producer changed drastically the acceptance of an unchanging world position in energy supply. The inertia of past policies and the lesser importance of oil at the time meant that the 1956 Suez crisis, which resulted in disruption of oil supplies, did not cause a rethinking of energy policy except by a few farsighted individuals who were ignored by the policy-makers. The 1973 crisis reinforced the keystone of energy policy as defined by successive governments: that future uncertainties required robust policies.

The energy policy of today is a far cry from the agglomeration of decisions which used to pass for a policy, but it is not necessarily more successful. The judgement of successful policy used to be a great deal simpler. If policy is thought of as only relating to a narrow field, for example the basic question of meeting demand in full, then success is easy to estimate. The recent gradual change in the objectives of policy reflect the politicization of the subject and the growing awareness of longer term environmental effects produced by policy decisions. The criteria for judging the success of energy policy are not all clear today, and of course may change with time as perceptions of the national interest and the importance of facets of policy such as employment and pollution alter. Again, these points are hardly considered in the current debate. Perceptions of good or bad policy will naturally differ according to the viewpoint of the group or interest under consideration. All the nationalized energy industries profess to work in accordance with the national interest, but then disagree markedly amongst themselves on policy. Historical reasons for the ability or inability of certain industries to work together can be produced, and a background of conflict may decrease the chances of harmonious relations in the future. The suggestion of some form of national corporation involving all the energy producing industries has occasionally appeared in the past, and it would seem that too much time and effort is wasted by the nationalized energy industries on internecine argument. Pricing policy is the current stumbling block between BGC and the electricity industry. This problem could be overcome by making the objectives of policy clearer to ensure that the industries were not working against each other, but truly for the national interest. Accounting systems can take some of the blame for the present state of affairs, as each industry has its own financial target which is not directly related to the overall aims of energy policy but the short term financial aims imposed directly by the Treasury. The situation is occasionally relieved by special directives, the writing off of capital debt, loans at low interest rates, and special subsidies for projects not in the immediate commercial interest of the industry involved, but all these measures are partial, selective and conducive to short term planning in a field where this is not the best of methods. A national energy corporation would not necessarily solve this problem if the overall objectives of policy were not made clear, for it seems to be the accounting system which is at the root of the problem. There is certainly a real conflict at present between gas and electricity because of the availability of cheap natural gas, and this may induce consumers to make decisions in the short term which will eventually prove expensive when gas increases in price. Consumers can be advised to install twin systems, or easily converted machinery, or be made aware of the short and long term consequences of choice. On the supply side, combined accounting of the gas and electricity industries would solve the problem caused by the need to use gas now but retain the capacity to produce more electricity towards the end of the century. Financial targeting for each industry could also deal with this matter, provided it was not conducted on a simple commercial basis but related to the availability of resources, now and in the future. The imposition of commercial financial targets on an industry which exists to supply energy as its first priority will always make for poor long term policy-making and wasted effort. It is interesting to note that the atomic energy industry is subject to fewer apparent financial pressures although its research costs are high and results will not be forthcoming in the short term. Unlike the gas, electricity and coal industries, it did not begin its life as a commercial venture.

The influences on policy formulation are many and varied, and have been discussed in the previous chapter. The vast number of agencies with an interest in energy policy makes some kind of interpretative model useful in this field, although no single model can entirely explain all events. The differences in time-scale relevant to the Civil Service, to politicians and to the results of policy decisions mean that continuity is ensured by the existence of the Civil Service, with the nationalized industries as sources of pressure. The incremental method of alteration in policy was suitable for energy policy until the era of rapid change arrived in 1973, and the adjustments in policy-making methods since then can be seen as an attempt to cope with large scale relatively rapid developments in a system geared for gentle, almost unnoticed change. Most policy-making models assume that individuals exert little influence, or at least are unable to account for changes caused or initiated by individuals. The formal structural model allows for pressure from sources constitutionally defined as having that function, but does not encompass the differences in approach of the individual office-holders. Tony Benn's years as Secretary of State for Energy have seen the department become one of the most open, with respect to information, in the entire Civil Service, and it is doubtful whether this change would have taken place under any other minister. It is fortunate that energy, with its policy having such wide implications for the future, should have come under the control of a minister with a personal belief in open government.

This vision of open government has resulted in a wide range of advice and alternative policies being propounded, but these have all originated from outside the Department of Energy. The breadth of vision within the department has increased in accordance with popular views on environmental matters, but there still exists a greater consensus of opinion within government than in the outside institutions. In spite of the openness of the department, there is still a reluctance to see suggestions from external sources as being as legitimate as those from within. The energy debate has been so broad in technical terms that most options have been covered, yet policy documents tend to reiterate the same old alternatives. This is not to say that changes are necessary, but rather that the ability to bring forward more options for realistic consideration is missing. This is a serious deficiency, but one which is unlikely to be remedied without a restructuring of the Civil Service, as it is a function of the value systems present in the institution itself. As a short term measure, the introduction of special advisers on the technical side into the department might prove useful. The advisers would perhaps be seconded from the academic or commercial world for a short period, certainly no longer than the maximum term of one government, in order that the departmental staff could be exposed to fresh ideas and methods. The 1970–4 Conservative Government brought in several businessmen to rejuvenate the administration, but this was not a complete success because the intention was to change the system itself rather than the ideas being discussed within the department. Advisers in the Department of Energy (as opposed to the ministerial special advisers), would work directly with the divisional groups in the manner of a short term fellowship at an academic institution. The Official Secrets Act is something of a barrier to wider dissemination of information, as is the commercial secrecy demanded when, for example, BNOC works with the oil companies, but this should not be used as an excuse to prevent the discussion of policy, at least in general terms. Neither the nature of the Official Secrets Act nor the functioning of the Civil Service appear to be likely to change in the near future, so that pleas for change are of less use than suggestions for improvement within the present policy-making system. The Civil Service has proved extremely resistant to change, and a further problem with energy policy is that it suffers from two levels of unaccountability: not only is it impossible to allocate responsibility for policy decisions to particular civil servants now, but it is highly likely that when the effects of the policies are fully felt, towards the end of the century, they will no longer be in the service. The system of policy-making mirrors energy policy itself in its vagueness and uncertainty, and perhaps the process of continual reworking of policy can maintain its robustness; however, the addition of outside opinion, the possibility that new ideas would be more acceptable if they came from people at least partially in the department, would improve the policy-making mechanism.

The essence of energy policy lies in its implications for future lifestyles. One way of broadening the debate, or starting new debates which include this, is to begin in schools where the subject of energy has always been treated partially, within other subject categories. The growing number of courses based on energy at higher education institutions reflects a demand for people with a broad knowledge of the subject, and an increase in teaching of energy studies or related topics in schools would eventually produce greater awareness and knowledge of the implications inherent in apparently straightforward policy decisions. The policy-makers themselves are bound, by the constraints of their institutions, to regard energy policy in a somewhat narrower sense, but this need not be too much of a disadvantage provided the decision environment is not similarly restricted. An addition to the bodies which give an airing to energy matters would be a Select Committee on Energy, once proposed by Tony Benn. If this was given rather more technical and secretarial assistance than the present range of select committees are allowed, it would become a very useful means of investigation. Here again, reform of select committees falls within the general movement to increase Parliament's control of the Civil Service, and a greater flow of information, particularly concerning the nationalized industries, might be the outcome.

The mere fact of the existence of the Windscale inquiry has proved that a variety of points of view can be publicly heard on energy matters. No doubt a number of changes in procedure will be made for any further inquiries, and perhaps a less judicial approach will be considered more suitable for matters which by their nature have no ultimate single answers. However, as a first attempt, it increased popular awareness of energy as a subject worth considering and forced most of the parties involved to think through their positions more carefully. If the original spirit of the inquiry can be maintained, then this need not result in views becoming completely entrenched. Over and above all the energy related considerations lies short term political expediency, and even the best planned policy decisions can be negated by the need to remain in power. Thus apart from the uncertainty of energy matters in the future another reason for the formulation of robust policies is to combat the vagaries of political life. The Department of Energy at present takes the lead in defining the limits of the energy argument, its departmental view holding sway over the disaggregated ideas from outside the government. Energy policy-making certainly requires an institution which provides a long term, consistent view of the world, but it also requires the ability to respond rapidly to change and the willingness to consider all ideas on their merits. The addition of a few more sources of policy options would improve the capacity of the department to think broadly about policy and add to its proven ability in simply overseeing the supply of energy. This, its main objective in the past, is undergoing a process of change, and the continued efficient functioning of the department and thus the whole of the economy depends on its ability to comprehend the state of public opinion in a changing world.

The main thing in life is to leap to every possible conclusion on every possible occasion.   (Vian, 1970, p. 7)

References

ABRC (1974), *Energy Research: The Research Councils' Contribution* (ABRC, London).

Allison, Graham T. (1969), 'Conceptual models and the Cuban missile crisis', *American Political Science Review*, vol. 63, No. 3 (September), pp. 689–718.

—— (1971), *Essence of Decision* (Little, Brown, Boston, Mass.).

Ash, Maurice (1977), 'The meaning of Windscale', *Town and Country Planning*, vol. 45, No. 6 (June), pp. 295–8.

AUEW–TASS (1977), *Workers Power* (AUEW–TASS, Manchester).

Bachrach, Peter and Baratz, Morton S. (1963), 'Decisions and nondecisions: an analytical framework', *American Political Science Review*, vol. 57, pp. 632–42.

Bailey, Joe (1975), *Social Theory for Planning* (Routledge & Kegan Paul, London).

Barber, James (1976), *Who Makes British Foreign Policy?* (Open University Press, Milton Keynes).

Berkovitch, Israel (1977), *Coal on the Switchback* (Allen & Unwin, London).

BGC (1977), *Annual Report and Accounts 1976–77* (HMSO, London).

Blume, Stuart S. (1977), 'Policy as theory: a framework for understanding the contribution of social science to welfare policy', *Acta Sociologica*, vol. 20, No. 3, pp. 247–62.

BP (1978), *Annual Report and Accounts 1977* (BP, London).

Bridges, Lord (1964), *The Treasury* (Allen & Unwin, London).

Brittan, Samuel (1969), *Steering the Economy* (Secker & Warburg, London).

Brown, Michael Barratt, Emerson, Tony and Stoneman, Colin (eds) (1976), *Resources and the Environment: a Socialist Perspective* (Spokesman, Nottingham).

Bruce-Gardyne, Jock and Lawson, Nigel (1976), *The Power Game* (Macmillan, London).

Bugler, Jeremy (1977), 'Atom-Energie über alles', *New Statesman*, vol. 94, No. 2440/2441, 23/30 December, pp. 872–3.

Burn, Duncan (1978), *Nuclear Power and the Energy Crisis* (Macmillan, London).

Butler, David and Sloman, Anne (1975), *British Political Facts 1900–1975*, 4th ed. (Macmillan, London).

Caldwell, Lynton K. (1976), 'Energy and the structure of social institutions', *Human Ecology*, vol. 4, No. 1, pp. 31–45.

Carvel, John (1978), 'Public spending falls short', *Guardian*, 31 January, p. 14.

Chapman, Peter F. (1977), *Proof of Evidence for Windscale Inquiry*, ERG 019 (ERG, Milton Keynes).

—— (1978), 'Energy in the future – the non-debate', *Electrical Review*, vol. 202, No. 12 (31 March) pp. 28–9.

CIS (1972), *The General Electric Company Limited* (CIS, London).

Civil Service Department (1977), *The Civil Service Year Book* (HMSO, London).

Cmd 6762 (1946), *Domestic Fuel Policy* (The Simon Report) (Ministry of Fuel and Power, London).

Cmd 8647 (1952), *Report of the Committee on National Policy for the use of Fuel and Power Resources* (The Ridley Report) (Ministry of Fuel and Power, London).

Cmnd 1337 (1961), *The Financial and Economic Obligations of the Nationalised Industries* (HMSO, London).

Cmnd 2798 (1965), *Fuel Policy* (Ministry of Power, London).

Cmnd 3437 (1967), *Nationalised Industries – a Review of Economic and Financial Objectives* (HMSO, London).

Cmnd 3438 (1967), *Fuel Policy* (Ministry of Power, London).

Cmnd 3638 (1968) Report of the Fulton Committee, *The Civil Service* (HMSO, London).

Cmnd 4027 (1969), *Ministerial Control of the Nationalised Industries* (HMSO, London).

Cmnd 5696 (1974), *United Kingdom Offshore Oil and Gas Policy* (D.En., London).

Cmnd 5731 (1974), Nuclear Power Advisory Board Report, *Choice of Thermal Reactor Systems* (HMSO, London).

Cmnd 6388 (1976), *The Structure of the Electricity Supply Industry in England and Wales* (The Plowden Report) (D.En., London).

Cmnd 6618 (1976), Royal Commission on Environmental Pollution, Sixth Report, *Nuclear Power and the Environment* (The Flowers Report) (HMSO, London).

Cmnd 7049, I and II (1978), *The Government's Expenditure Plans, 1978–79 to 1981–82*, vols I and II (HMSO, London).

Cmnd 7101 (1978), *Energy Policy, a Consultative Document* (HMSO, London).

Cmnd 7131 (1978), *The Nationalised Industries* (HMSO, London).

Cmnd 7134 (1978), *Re-organisation of the Electricity Supply Industry in England and Wales* (D.En., London).

Cmnd 7143 (1978), *The Challenge of North Sea Oil* (HMSO, London).

Cmnd 7236 (1978), *The Development of Alternative Source of Energy* (HMSO, London).

Cook, Charles (1977a), 'Retiring electric chief hits out', *Guardian*, 6 May, p. 14.

—— (1977b), 'GEC wins nuclear power battle', *Guardian*, 25 October, p. 16.

—— (1977c), 'Nuclear debate gets a booster', *Guardian*, 1 November, p. 12.

—— (1977d), 'Why Britain's atom men are splitting', *Guardian*, 7 December, p. 15.

—— (1978a), 'Indignation problem faces the powermen', *Guardian*, 13 February, p. 12.

—— (1978b), 'British gas pricing policy attacked', *Guardian*, 15 February, p. 14.

—— (1978c), 'Electricity Council denies reactor rift', *Guardian*, 5 January, p. 2.

—— (1978d), 'Public rap for MacAlister', *Guardian*, 9 May, p. 20.

CPRS (1976), *The Future of the United Kingdom Power Plant Manufacturing Industry* (HMSO, London).

Crossman, Richard (1975), *The Diaries of a Cabinet Minister*, vol. 1: *1964–66* (Hamilton and Cape, London).

—— (1976), *The Diaries of a Cabinet Minister*, vol. 2: *1966–68* (Hamilton and Cape, London).

—— (1977), *The Diaries of a Cabinet Minister*, vol. 3: *1968–70* (Hamilton and Cape, London).

D.En. (1977), *Coal for the Future* (D.En., London).

D.En. (1974), *Coal Industry Examination, Final Report* (D.En., London).

D.En. (1977), *Development of the Oil and Gas Resources of the United Kingdom 1977* (D.En., London).

D.En. (1978), *Development of the Oil and Gas Resources of the United Kingdom 1978* (D.En., London).

D.En. Fact Sheet 3 (1976), *Gas from the UK Continental Shelf* (D.En., London).

D.En. Fact Sheet 4 (1977), *Coal in the UK* (D.En., London).

D.En. Fact Sheet 5 (1977), *Nuclear Energy in the UK—Organisation* (D.En., London).

D.En. Sunningdale Seminar on Nuclear Policy (1977), *Record of the Meeting 13/14 May 1977* (D.En., London).

D.En. (1977), *United Kingdom and Community Energy Policy* (D.En., London).

D.En. Energy Paper No. 8 (1976), *The Offshore Energy Technology Board: Strategy for Research and Development* (HMSO, London).

D.En. Energy Paper No. 11 (1976), *Energy Research and Development in the United Kingdom* (HMSO, London).

D.En. Energy Paper No. 12 (1976), ACEC Paper 3, *Energy Prospects* (HMSO, London).

D.En. Energy Paper No. 13 (1976), National Energy Conference: vol. 1, *Report of Proceedings*, vol. 2, *Papers submitted* (HMSO, London).

D.En. Energy Paper No. 14 (1976), *Tripartite Energy Consultations* (HMSO, London).

D.En. Energy Paper No. 22 (1977), *Energy Policy Review* (HMSO, London).

D.En. Press Notice, Ref. No. 348, 13 October 1977.

D.En. Press Notice, Ref. No. 427, 12 December 1977.

D.En. Press Notice, Ref. No. 25, 24 January 1978.

D.En. Press Notice, Ref. No. 52, 13 February 1978.

D.En. Press Notice, Ref. No. 105, 4 April 1978.

Donnison, David (1972), 'Ideologies and policies', *Journal of Social Policy*, vol. 1, No. 2, pp. 97–117.

Downs, Anthony (1972), 'Up and down with ecology – the "issue – attention cycle"', *The Public Interest*, Summer, pp. 38–50.

Eglin, Roger (1977), 'Our offshore industry plan works after all', *Sunday Times*, 4 December, p. 63.

Eiloart, Tim (1978), 'Progress chaser', *New Scientist*, vol. 77, No. 1088, 2 February, pp. 292–4.

Electricity Council (1975), *Electricity Supply in Great Britain* (Electricity Council, London).

—— (1977), *Annual Report 1976–77* (Electricity Council, London).

Energy Commission Paper, ENCOM (77) 8 (1977), *Comments by UKOOA on Energy Commission Paper No. 1* (D.En., London).

Energy Commission Paper No. 1 (1977), *Working Document on Energy Policy* (D.En., London).

Energy Commission Paper No. 2 (1977), *Report of the Working Group on Energy Strategy* (D.En., London).

Energy Commission Paper No. 12 (1978), *Energy Research and Development* (D.En., London).

Energy Commission (1978), *Minutes of First Meeting 28 November 1977* (D.En., London).

England, Glyn (1977), 'Energy elegy – replies', *Electronics and Power,* vol. 23, No. 9 (September), pp. 733–5.

ERG 019 (1977), Peter F. Chapman, *Proof of Evidence for Windscale Inquiry* (ERG, Milton Keynes).

ERG 024 (1977), Peter F. Chapman, *Alternative Energy Sources: an Analysis of their Role in Energy Policy* (ERG, Milton Keynes).

Forman, Nigel (1977), *Towards a More Conservative Energy Policy* (Conservative Political Centre, London).

Forman, R. (1977), 'The role of electricity', paper given at the 1977 BAAS meeting, University of Aston in Birmingham.

Friend, J. K. (1977), 'The dynamics of policy change', *Long Range Planning*, vol. 10, No. 1 (February), pp. 40–47.

Grainger, Leslie (1977), 'Coal and nuclear power', *Coal and Energy Quarterly*, No. 12 (Spring), pp. 9–22.

Haines, Joe (1977), *The Politics of Power* (Coronet, Sevenoaks).

HC371-i–iii (Session 1967/68), SCNI, First Report, minutes and appendices, *Ministerial Control of the Nationalised Industries* (HMSO, London).

HC549 (Session 1970/71), Select Committee on Expenditure, Third Report, *Command Papers on Public Expenditure* (HMSO, London).

HC147 (Session 1971/72), Select Committee on Expenditure, Steering Sub-Committee, *Minutes of Evidence* (HMSO, London).

HC117 (Session 1972/73), SCST, *Minutes of Evidence, Nuclear Power Policy* (HMSO, London).

HC122 (Session 1972/73), Committee of Public Accounts, First Report, *North Sea Oil and Gas* (HMSO, London).

HC350 (Session 1972/73), SCST, Second Report, *Nuclear Power Policy* (HMSO, London).

HC145, 73i–vii (Session 1973/74), SCST, First Report, *Report, Evidence and Appendices, The Choice of a Reactor System* (HMSO, London).

HC487 (Session 1974/75), SCST, First Report, *Energy Conservation* (HMSO, London).

HC623 (Session 1975/76), SCST, General Purposes Sub-Committee, Minutes of Evidence, *SGHWR Programme* (HMSO, London).

HC89 (Session 1976/77), SCST, First Report, *The SGHWR Programme* (HMSO, London).

HC481 (Session 1976/77), SSRC, *Report of the Social Science Research Council April 1976– March 1977* (HMSO, London).

HC534-i–iii (Session 1976/77), SCST, Third Report: *Report, Evidence and Appendices, The Development of Alternative Sources of Energy for the United Kingdom* (HMSO, London).

HC564 (Session 1976/77), SCST, Fourth Report, *The Exploitation of Tidal Power in the Severn Estuary* (HMSO, London).

HC567 (Session 1976/77), Natural Environment Research Council, *Report of the Council for the period 1 April 1976– 31 March 1977* (HMSO, London).

HC568 (Session 1976/77), Science Research Council, *Report of the Council for the year 1976– 77* (HMSO, London).

Heclo, H. Hugh (1972), 'Review article: Policy analysis', *British Journal of Political Science*, vol. 2, (January), pp. 83–108.

Heclo, Hugh and Wildavsky, Aaron (1974), *The Private Government of Public Money* (Macmillan, London).

Henderson, P. D. (1977), 'Two British errors: their probable size and some possible lessons', *Oxford Economic Papers*, vol. 29, No. 2 (July), pp. 159–205.

Hetherington, Peter (1977), 'Reactor bill may go to £14m', *Guardian*, 3 December, p. 24.

Hoggart, Simon (1977), 'Literary labours', *Guardian*, 27 October, p. 14.

—— (1978), 'Liberal's veto frustrates Benn', *Guardian*, 24 February, p. 28.

Hutber, F. W. (1974), 'Modelling of energy supply and demand', in *Energy Modelling Workshop Papers* (IPC, Guildford) pp. 4–32.

IIED (1977), Gerald Leach, *Written Evidence to Windscale Inquiry* (IIED, London).

Jackson, Michael P. (1974), *The Price of Coal* (Croom Helm, London).

Jones, G. W. (1978), 'The Prime Minister's men', *New Society*, vol. 43, No. 798, 19 January, pp. 121–3.

Jones, P. M. S. (1978), 'Nuclear energy prospects', *Atom*, No. 256 (February), pp. 26–30.

Kenward, Michael (1977a), 'Benn sacks Marshall in nuclear controversy', *New Scientist*, vol. 74, No. 1058, 30 June, p. 757.

—— (1977b), 'An interrupted interview', *New Scientist*, vol. 76, No. 1079, 24 November, p. 473.

Kenward, Michael (1977c), 'EEC holds public debate on nuclear power, *New Scientist*, vol. 76, No. 1081, 8 December, p. 620.

Kerr, John (1978a), 'Full cost of leak', *Guardian*, 10 February, p. 2.

—— (1978b), 'SNP revives claim for oil revenues', *Guardian*, 7 March, p. 4.

Klein, Rudolf (1974a), 'Policy-making in the National Health Service', *Political Studies*, vol. 22, No. 1, pp. 1–14.

—— (1974b), 'Policy problems and policy perceptions in the National Health Service', *Policy and Politics*, vol. 2, No. 3 (March), pp. 219–36.

Klein, Rudolf and Lewis, Janet (1977), 'Advice and dissent in British Government: the case of the special advisers', *Policy and Politics*, vol. 6, No. 1 (September), pp. 1–25.

Leach, Gerald (1977), *Written Evidence to Windscale Inquiry* (IIED, London).

Lean, Geoffrey (1978), 'Britain's energy needs may fall, says report', *Observer*, 19 February, p. 2.

Lewis, P. O. (1977), 'Future demand for gas and sources of supply', paper given at the 1977 BAAS meeting, University of Aston in Birmingham.

Lindberg, Leon N. (1977), 'Energy policy and the politics of economic development', *Comparative Political Studies*, vol. 10, No. 3 (October), pp. 355–82.

Lindblom, Charles E. (1959), 'The science of "muddling through"', *Public Administration Review*, vol. 19, No. 2, pp. 79–88.

Lovins, Amory B. (1977), *Soft Energy Paths* (Penguin, Harmondsworth).

Lucas, N. J. D. (1977), *Energy and the European Communities* (Europa, London).

McLoughlin, Jane (1978), 'Government tilts cash to windmills in energy study', *Guardian*, 7 June, p. 2.

McMullan, Ann (1977), 'American women back the atom', *Electrical Review*, vol. 201, No. 19, 11 November, pp. 16–17.

Mulkay, Michael (1976), 'The mediating role of the scientific elite', *Social Studies of Science*, vol. 6, Nos 3 and 4 (September), pp. 445–70.

National Coal Board (1950), *Plan for Coal* (NCB, London).

—— (1956), *Investing in Coal* (NCB, London).

—— (1959), *Revised Plan for Coal* (NCB, London).

—— (1974), *Plan for Coal* (NCB, London).

—— (1977), *Report and Accounts 1976/7* (NCB, London).

National Nuclear Corporation Ltd (1977), *The Choice of Thermal Reactor Systems* (NNC, London).

NCAT (1977), *An Alternative Energy Strategy for the United Kingdom* (NCAT, Machynlleth).

NEDO (1976), *A Study of UK Nationalised Industries, Their Role in the Economy and Control in the Future* (HMSO, London).

Norton-Taylor, Richard (1978), 'The doors that open, if you know where to push', *Guardian*, 23 January, p. 11.

Open University (1972), 'Patterns of decision making?', D203 VIII, parts 1–4 (Open University Press, Milton Keynes).

O'Riordan, Timothy (1976), 'Policymaking and environmental management: some thoughts on processes and research issues', *Natural Resources Journal*, vol. 16, No. 1 (January), pp. 55–72.

Page, Bruce (1978), 'The secret constitution', *New Statesman*, vol. 96, No. 2470, 21 July, pp. 72–6.

Palmer, John (1977a), 'EEC energy meeting disappoints Benn', *Guardian*, 14 December, p. 5.

—— (1977b), 'EEC claims a stake in Britain's oil', *Guardian*, 23 December, p. 1.

Powell, Enoch (1976), Speech in discussion, D.En. Energy Paper No. 13, vol. 1, p. 48 (HMSO, London).

Raphael, Adam (1977), 'Benn in nuclear clash', *Observer*, 18 December, p. 1.

—— (1978), 'Benn wins Cabinet nuclear row', *Observer*, 15 January, p. 1.

Report by the Hon. Mr Justice Parker (1978), *The Windscale Inquiry*, vol. 1: *Report and Annexes 3–5* (HMSO, London).

Ritchie, Berry (1978), 'Wass going on?', *Sunday Times*, 19 February, p. 59.

Robens, Lord (1974), 'Towards rational energy policies', *Nature*, vol. 249, 21 June, pp. 698–700.

—— (1977), 'Coal on the Switchback', *Coal and Energy Quarterly*, No. 15 (Winter), pp. 3–9.

Rodgers, Peter (1978), 'Callaghan set to veto Benn and go for US and British reactors', *Sunday Times*, 8 January, p. 55.

Rose, Richard (ed.) (1969), *Policy-making in Britain* (Macmillan, London).

Rush, Howard J., MacKerron, Gordon and Surrey, John (1977),

'The advanced gas-cooled reactor: a case study in reactor choice', *Energy Policy*, vol. 5, No. 2 (June), pp. 95–105.

Ryle, Martin (1977), 'Economics of alternative energy sources', *Nature*, vol. 267, No. 5607, 12 May, pp. 111–17.

Sampson, Anthony (1976), *The Seven Sisters* (Coronet, London).

Schumacher, E. F. (1974), *Small is Beautiful* (Abacus, London).

Self, Peter (1972), *Administrative Theories and Policies* (Allen & Unwin, London).

Sheriff, Peta (1976), 'Career patterns in the higher civil service', *Civil Service Studies*, No. 2 (HMSO, London).

Solesbury, William (1976), 'The environmental agenda: an illustration of how situations may become political issues and issues may demand responses from government: or how they may not', *Public Administration*, vol. 54 (Winter), pp. 379–97.

Spaak, Fernand (1974), 'Energy policy vital to EEC's future', *Coal and Energy Quarterly*, No. 2 (Autumn), pp. 9–15.

SSRC (1977), *Energy Topics in the Social Sciences* (SSRC, London).

Steel, David R. and Stanyer, Jeffrey (1977), 'Administrative developments in 1975 and 1976: a survey', *Public Administration*, vol. 55 (Winter), pp. 385–433.

Sweet, Colin (1978), 'Accountability and the costs of AGRs', *Electrical Review*, vol. 202, No. 6, 10 February, pp. 36–8.

Targett, W. D. (1977), 'Financial objectives: the record of British Gas', *Public Administration*, vol. 55 (Summer), pp. 171–9.

Townsend, Peter (1976), *Sociology and Social Policy* (Penguin, Harmondsworth).

Tucker, Anthony (1975), 'Benn fights to improve energy system', *Guardian*, 15 December, p. 6.

—— (1978), 'Open nuclear debate, says Liberal peer', *Guardian*, 23 January, p. 2.

UKAEA (1977), *Annual Report 1976/77* (UKAEA, London).

Vian, Boris (1970), *Froth on the Daydream* (Penguin, Harmondsworth).

Vig, Norman J. (1968), *Science and Technology in British Politics* (Pergamon, Oxford).

Watt, D. C. (1976), 'Britain and North Sea oil: policies past and present', *Political Quarterly*, vol. 47, No. 4 (October/December), pp. 377–97.

Whale, John (1977), 'Jim promotes his old "batman"', *Sunday Times*, 4 December, p. 4.

—— (1978), 'At war with Whitehall', *Sunday Times*, 22 January, p. 17.

White, David (1977), 'Friends or FOE?', *New Society*, vol. 40, No. 767, 16 June, pp. 553—4.

Williams, Marcia (1975), *Inside Number 10* (New English Library, London).

Wilson, Harold (1974), *The Labour Government 1964—70* (Penguin, Harmondsworth).

Wynne, Brian (1978), 'The politics of nuclear safety', *New Scientist*, vol. 77, No. 1087, 26 January, pp. 208—11.

Young, Hugo (1978), 'The very public plots of Tony Benn', *Sunday Times*, 29 January, p. 32.

Young, Ken (1977), ' "Values" in the policy process', *Policy and Politics*, vol. 5, No. 3 (March), pp. 1—22.

RADIO TRANSCRIPT

Talking Politics, BBC Radio 4, 16 April 1977, Saturday briefing presented by Anthony King.

TELEVISION PROGRAMMES

ITV, 8 November 1977, Royal Institution Conference on Nuclear Power and the Energy Future.

ITV, 23 January 1978, *Personal Report*, Peter Odell.

BBC 2, 21 October 1977, *Newsday*.

PERIODICALS

CSO, *Monthly Digest of Statistics* (HMSO, London).
Guardian
Hansard
Review of Parliament
The Economist
The Times
Who's Who

Index